Praise for Tom Danielson

Praise for *Cycling On Form*

"Through the FORM method, Tom has constructed a model for not only being a better cyclist, but for moving beyond 'the numbers' and toward realizing full potential both on and off the bike." —RICH WILLIAMS, GROUPON CEO

"After training with CINCH for the past three years, I've learned the cycling-specific techniques that make me a better rider and racer; healthier and injury-free; and more effective and positive off the bike. A core concept CINCH has taught me is that life is a process of trying, failing, learning, and growing, in order to move forward to a better version of yourself."

—LILBURN SHAW, 2018 MASTERS ROAD NATIONAL CHAMPION

"Tom is one of those rare individuals who can coach as well as he can compete. He has a compelling teaching style and the CINCH methods found in *Cycling On Form* have helped me to improve cycling skills hugely even with limited personal time."

—GINNA HENDRICKS, CINCH COACHING CLIENT, DENTIST, AND MOM OF THREE

"Tom has taken his pro understanding and created an unmatched coaching system that can transform novice and professionals alike. The CINCH system pulls back the veil on many myths about what it takes to be great in the sport of cycling and creates a pathway for athletes of all abilities to win their rides."

—KRIS HENDRICKS, AGE-GROUP WINNER OF THE 2019 BRECK EPIC MTB STAGE RACE

Praise for *Tom Danielson's Core Advantage*

"A strong midsection makes for a more efficient stroke. Try the 50 exercises in *Tom Danielson's Core Advantage*." —*BICYCLING* MAGAZINE

CYCLING
ON FORM

A PRO METHOD
OF RIDING FASTER
& STRONGER

**TOM DANIELSON AND
& KOURTNEY DANIELSON**

VELO.
press

BOULDER, COLORADO

4745 Walnut Street, Unit A
Boulder, CO 80301-2587 USA

VeloPress is the leading publisher of books on endurance sports and is a division of Pocket Outdoor Media. Focused on cycling, triathlon, running, swimming, and nutrition/diet, VeloPress books help athletes achieve their goals of going faster and farther. Preview books and contact us at velopress.com.

Distributed in the United States and Canada by Ingram Publisher Services

Library of Congress Cataloging-in-Publication Data

Names: Danielson, Tom, 1978- author. | Danielson, Kourtney, author.
Title: Cycling on form: a pro method of riding faster and stronger / Tom
    Danielson and Kourtney Danielson.
Description: Boulder, Colorado: VeloPress, [2020] | Includes index. |
Identifiers: LCCN 2019049569 (print) | LCCN 2019049570 (ebook) | ISBN
    9781948007047 (paperback) | ISBN 9781948006170 (ebook)
Subjects: LCSH: Cycling—Training. | Bicycle racing—Training.
Classification: LCC GV1048.D35 2020 (print) | LCC GV1048 (ebook) | DDC
    796.6—dc23
LC record available at https://lccn.loc.gov/2019049569
LC ebook record available at https://lccn.loc.gov/2019049570

This paper meets the requirements of ANSI/NISO Z39.48-1992 (Permanence of Paper).

Art direction and interior design by Vicki Hopewell
Cover design by Nate Herschleb/Ember Co.
Cover photo by Eric Meyer
Illustrations by Charlie Layton
Photographs pp. 253–254 by Holly Mathews

20   21   22 / 10   9   8   7   6   5   4   3   2   1

To the sport of cycling, for first giving me my freedom, for providing me a place to chase my dreams, and now for giving me the opportunity to help others achieve their own dreams.

CONTENTS

PUTTING IT ALL TOGETHER

INTRODUCTION

The Tour de France is the most celebrated and highly anticipated event in cycling. Even those who have never clipped into a pedal can recognize the yellow jersey of the Tour de France race leader, but few understand the complexities of training and racing at the sport's highest level—and what it truly takes to zip on the *maillot jaune.*

If watching the pros battle for glory in your favorite race makes you want to emulate whatever it is they're doing to go so fast, well, you have come to the right place. If you've picked up this book, you most likely have made some progress in cycling over the years. You've grown stronger, but perhaps now it seems like you have hit a plateau. You want to reach the next level in cycling, but don't know where to start, don't know why you can't improve. Are you too old? Do you have enough time to train? Have you lost the fire within you? Have you already reached your full potential?

What if I told you the answers to all these questions are an emphatic no? That everything you need to get to the next level is already inside you? Put our training system to work and you will experience the physical and personal growth you have been craving from the sport of cycling.

This book is not another silver-bullet training solution built around only one measurement of performance. Nor is it full of a bunch of old-school training methodologies disguised behind new names. This is a plan for proven success developed from real-world lessons learned, practical wisdom, timeless truths, and roll-your-sleeves-up, hands-on experience.

The FORM Performance Method shows cyclists step-by-step how to transform their cycling from the level of an amateur to that of a Tour de France rider, all within the scope of their current fitness, time, and resources. This is your personal guidebook to peak performance on the bike.

What Is FORM?

We often hear the term "form" in pro cycling, but what does it really mean? For us, it means consistently showing up with peak fitness, the right nutrition in your tank, effective execution, and a focused mindset. But it is not just in professional cycling that these four components matter. In fact, to participate in the sport of cycling you must incorporate these four concepts and interconnect them so they work as a whole. Take any one of these four elements away and your entire performance can fall apart. Many training methods focus on the most obvious dimension of cycling: fitness. But merely being strong isn't enough for consistent peak performance. This is why we teach and coach riders to master their Fitness, Execution, Nutrition, and Focus—what we call the Four Pillars—for the most comprehensive approach to cycling training.

Is the FORM System Only Suitable for Traditional Bike Racers?

Absolutely not. All athletes define competition in their own way. For one cyclist, competition might mean winning a masters national road race; another would find it in finishing a local group ride without getting dropped; a different rider would see it as landing in the top five of an age-group category in an epic gravel race. Our system is built for athletes short on time but high on motivation. We want athletes to read this book because they are fired up and ready to go all-in on the path to peak performance.

How Did the FORM System Get Its Start?

If you are like most cyclists, you have probably experienced one, if not all, of these frustrations:

→ Low confidence in your riding, racing, strategy, or overall ability

→ Not feeling strong enough or fast enough or having enough endurance for the level of cycling to which you aspire

→ Feeling you lack control in competitive scenarios, struggle on challenging terrain, and waste energy with your pedaling technique and position on the bike

→ Confusion from contradictory nutrition advice or having tried everything to improve your diet, with no results

Even as a professional racer, I found myself feeling all of these things at one point or another. When I reflect on my racing career, it is evident that physical talent was never in short supply. After I dabbled in motocross at a young age, my parents decided it was too dangerous. A neighbor that I looked up to was a mountain biker, so I asked my parents if we could buy a bike. We did, and what sweet freedom it was! Shortly after, at the age of 15, I entered my first mountain bike race, called Meadow Muffin Madness. I placed second. After that, I won nearly every mountain bike race I entered. I went on to race with some of the cycling world's biggest teams, including Fassa Bortolo, Discovery Channel, and Garmin-Sharp.

I excelled as a climber. My favorite thing to do was test my fitness on different climbs, like Mount Washington, Mount Evans, and the Col de la Madone, and smash records. Most years, my lactate threshold tests showed that I could ride at a very high 7 watts per kilogram. On VO_2max tests, considered the purest measure of a cyclist's performance potential, even in college I would score just above a 90 mL/kg/min. (For comparison, most middle-aged recreational athletes score 40 to 55. Chris Froome scored 84.6 in 2015, a year he won the Tour de France.)

Sports scientists told me that, genetically, I was the most gifted athlete they'd ever seen. That with these numbers I was going to win the Tour de France. After hearing those kinds of predictions, I set out to fulfill them, year in and year out. I felt the pressure, too, and I made it my mission to out-grit, out-work, and out-train my competition.

But I was always chasing the idea of "just getting a little stronger." Every day I would do the math in my head: If I could just increase my power by X watts and lose Y pounds, then I could do Z watts per kilogram at threshold. That would be enough to win. I would train for six hours, come home, eat some vegetables, and think to myself, *I'm one step closer*. Getting stronger dictated every single one of my actions on and off the bike. The sad thing was that even when I did reach these threshold power and weight goals, I still didn't win. This would send me into a downward spiral, feeling worthless and weak.

I did do well in some races; I won some big events and placed eighth in the 2011 Tour de France. But it is clear to me that I did not live up to my real potential. And there is one simple reason why I didn't: I did not have a comprehensive program to prepare myself for performing and succeeding at that level. I didn't have a program that allowed me to be consistently on form—peaking in my Fitness, Execution, Nutrition, and Focus. I can think of countless opportunities that I squandered throughout my career because I was missing one of these components.

Often, I showed up to races insecure and without purpose. I was easily derailed by team politics and unable to mentally pivot when things didn't go as expected. I had a massive fear of failure, so even when I did feel good, I would settle for fourth or fifth place rather than risk it all for the win.

In training, I could hit 6–7 watts per kilogram, but when racing, I would often get to the final climb and be barely able to hold 4 watts per kilogram; I'd get dropped. I was continually feeling confused and defeated. In retrospect, I can see that I hadn't developed those lower power zones. The lesson learned? I needed to train for the demands of my events.

In most races, I didn't have an execution strategy and I would bleed power all over the road. I didn't practice attacking or sprinting while on training rides. And I rarely trained on my time trial bike. My overly restrictive diet, which I thought was the key to my success, was weakening my immune system, compromising my recovery, and drastically reducing my overall performance.

I thought that at the highest level of the sport there would be people to help riders sort through all the intricacies of training. And maybe there were on other teams, but not mine. Sure, there were intelligent directors, scientists, dietitians, and trainers, but they each had their own theories and specialties. Often, it seemed as though they did not communicate with each other. I always felt as though I was being inundated with information, with "go full" as the guiding principle. So that's what I often did.

Only when I met my wife, Kourtney, did I start to put it all together. She asked me hard questions about training and racing—questions that I didn't have the answers to. When something would work, and I would try to change it, she would ask, why change it? We started to talk with the team staff, trying to sort out what made sense and what didn't. We distilled all the information I had learned over the years, trying to pinpoint the absolute best thing gained from each specialist I worked with. We weren't aware of it then, but we were slowly gathering research and information for the future.

I started paying attention to the best guys in the race. I watched Alberto Contador adjust his body position as he wound up for an attack. I would come down to breakfast at the hotel and peek over to see what Alejandro Valverde was eating. I took it a step further and would analyze other riders' power files. In one race early in my career, I had seen Chris Horner's power file. He had finished ahead of me with significantly less power, so the next day I followed him. I took note of the way he finessed his bike in the peloton to gain and carry momentum and to conserve energy. I didn't realize it then, but I was creating the foundation for my most fulfilling job yet.

The Beginnings of My Coaching Program

I've always loved being around people. Toward the end of my career, I found that sharing my passion helped me keep my mojo high in the off-season. So while I was still racing, I created my own cycling camps that I would host out of my property in Tucson, Arizona. In the beginning, it was really pretty simple: I wanted to take people on great rides; eat tasty, nutritious food; and just hang out. My hope was that by the time people left, they felt like part of my community.

Just as I had done in races, I would ride next to these training-camp athletes and study them. For a while, I did not say anything; I just watched these bizarre creatures in their natural habitats. I silently wondered why their seat posts were so high, why they stopped pedaling on every downhill, and why so many suffered from chronic leg cramps. I began talking with them and suggesting minor adjustments to how they rode. Immediately, I could see the difference these seemingly simple changes had made, and by the end of the week, the attendees would look like completely different riders.

People began asking me if I would continue to coach them remotely at home. At first, I said no, explaining that the words "cycling coach" would leave a sour taste in my mouth.

I thought about all the people who call themselves coaches when in reality they had little to no real-world experience and would merely cut and paste recycled workout plans for their clients.

But there was one moment in particular that completely altered my perspective on coaching and training. It was January 2016. I had been training my face off, unknowingly implementing the first version of the Four Pillars I'd developed. I had finally put together a comprehensive program that was sustainable and that truly worked. At 128 pounds, I was the leanest I had ever been. I would look down at my body and see veins everywhere. I practically flew out of bed, I had so much energy. I recovered faster than ever before.

At the end of our cycling camps, we've always had a grand finale kind of event. All week we had worked on different skills, and it was time for the athletes to put it all together. It was an individual time trial up the bottom part of Mount Lemmon, one of my favorite climbs in Tucson. We let the athletes go off in 30-second increments based on their projected times. So the least experienced people started ahead of the more experienced athletes, and everyone had a carrot to chase. I started in the last position, almost 6 minutes back.

It was my turn. I channeled all of my energy and frustrations of the past, and lit it up. I rode at 430 watts for 12 minutes. At the age of 36, it was the fastest I had gone in my entire career, and I did it on a training ride with a group of amateur athletes. When I reached the top, I turned around and rode back up with each rider, cheering for them as they finished.

I'm embarrassed to admit this now, but I was so thrilled with my own stellar performance that I thought everyone else was going to be awe-inspired by it, too. But not one person had noticed. At dinner, everyone was excited that I had supported them through those final seconds and that they were able to dig just a little deeper. They thanked Kourtney and me for the progress they'd made throughout the week. Some riders were emotional with pride, having overcome some of their long-standing barriers to great performance.

For me, it was a defining moment in how I perceived coaching. Throughout my career, I had wanted to inspire people—beating my competition was never my motivation. I thought my racing inspired people, and that seeing me win races or go fast up hills, as I had done that day, would be the source of their inspiration. But when I saw what had excited these riders on the time trial, I realized that I could use my sport, the sport I've devoted my life to, to transform people's lives. That was the kind of impact I had always wanted to have. It was then that I decided to go all-in and deliver a WorldTour-level training system for every athlete, regardless of age, ability, and experience.

And that was where the real work began. It started with just a few athletes: business executives, aspiring pros, mothers, riders young and old . . . from the highly experienced to the novices. It was the ultimate case study. I began manipulating the workouts using lots of different zones, cadences, and body positions.

I rejected the notion of functional threshold power (FTP) and developed my own key performance indicators to measure progress where it actually mattered. People were getting a lot fitter, but I began noticing other issues that were holding them back.

I saw that nutrition was often a huge source of anxiety and confusion, so Kourtney and I started developing a nutrition plan based on what we had learned from racing. Everyone was really strong, but they didn't know what to do with their newfound strength, so I developed execution tactics and strategies. I saw that people's mindsets were holding them back on the bike and in life, in general. Mindset had been my biggest struggle, too, so I developed the mental strategies needed to overcome challenges.

These real-world experiences are what inspired me to create the Four Pillars that became the cornerstone of the FORM Performance Method. I've spent the past three years testing and refining the system. I've added new components and thrown out others. But I've used the same framework in this book to help hundreds of athletes unlock their true potential. Yes, this book will help you get stronger and faster. But the intent is to do so by providing you with a sustainable process for training, competing, and winning in life.

WARM-UP

THE FOUR PILLARS OF COMPLETE CYCLING PERFORMANCE

Take a minute to envision a really great day you've had in the last few months . . . one that was fulfilling, rewarding, and satisfying. Maybe you wrapped up a successful project at work, perhaps even getting a bonus or a promotion. You managed to fit in a nice ride in the morning or at lunch. When you came home, your family was in a great mood and you all enjoyed a meal together, or perhaps you even got out for a date night with your partner.

Whatever made your great day great, it probably was a combination of successes. On their own, these happy moments are fantastic. When they merge on one magical day, things just seem elevated. In cycling, too, that kind of synchronicity can be fleeting. A great ride requires the convergence of variables that are almost as hard to wrangle as unruly kids or a conference room full of colleagues.

Day after day, week after week, month after month, we cyclists chase "form." We put in long winter hours, endure painful intervals on the indoor trainer, and slug it out in early season races with the hope of discovering that mythical Atlantis that is form. However, most riders aren't diving deep enough to get to this perfect moment—but they could. A simple static training plan will tune up your musculature and your aerobic system. But in some way, you know that's not enough.

That is why you're reading this book, after all. I've been in this place before, where I was fixated on watts per kilogram but blind to the bigger picture. It took years of pro cycling for me to realize that I needed more than a brutal training plan to reach peak form.

As a coach, I would ride with clients at my CINCH Cycling Camps, talk to them over dinner, and hear from them on email afterward. I discovered that many of them had the same problems that I did—especially in my early days as a pro rider. They were devoting themselves to their training, and their performance metrics seemed pretty good, but they were still struggling: They were getting dropped on their favorite group rides. Their buddies would thrash them on the big local climb. Or they were stuck in the doldrums, finishing a race midpack every weekend when they wanted to upgrade to the next category.

After years of listening to my clients—cyclists who are probably a lot like you—and finding ways to meet their needs and help them achieve their goals, I developed the Four Pillars of the FORM Performance Method: Fitness, Execution, Nutrition, and Focus.

I have ordered them in this way to progress from the easiest to work on to the hardest. The thing is, you need all four to truly reach your peak form, much like you need all of the different, competing aspects of your day-to-day life to harmonize for a truly great day to happen. So don't pick and choose which pillars you like, or which are easiest to achieve. It is a challenge to perfect all Four Pillars of FORM, but they'll provide you with all of the tools you need to win your ride, whether that's the Wednesday-night hammerfest, the epic gran fondo on your calendar, or your masters state championships.

Pillar I: Fitness

I have never been in a race or group ride that was a steady effort, start to finish. Have you? Unless you're riding with some incredibly disciplined training partners, I doubt it. Instead, we cyclists naturally surge up short hills. We ease up on fast downhills or on particularly twisty corners. We smash it on the final climb to the finish, whether it's for a podium finish or bragging rights at the end of the group ride. That's what makes cycling so fun and dynamic—the ebb and flow, the rhythm of a peloton.

So why, then, is most training focused on steady-state efforts? Why are most training programs predicated on functional threshold power (FTP), a single number . . . a single point along a wide spectrum of efforts? The Fitness pillar of the FORM Method is built around 11 PowerTrain Zones (PTZs), each with a specific purpose to suit the demands of cycling's dynamic nature. In any race or group ride, you could find yourself using all of the zones. They are like keys on the piano. Every ride is a different song; it just depends on how you play those keys, in what order, and for how long. You wouldn't want to play the same note for three hours straight, would you?

These 11 zones are split into three categories: Endurance, Threshold, and Explosive. The majority of your rides will be in the Endurance zones. The pace is slow, and it results in minimal muscle damage. This level of effort primarily relies on fat for fuel, which means it is sustainable for many hours. It may not feel like you're getting faster when you ride in one of the four Endurance PTZs, but they are essential for performance in the long run.

Unlike the Endurance zones, the three Threshold zones should feel like you're really hammering, like you're making gains. These three zones are essential in the crucial moments of a race, whether it's a major climb, a breakaway, or a blistering time trial effort. Your body relies primarily on glycogen to fuel Threshold efforts, and when you hit this intensity, you start to incur moderate to high levels of muscle damage.

Finally, there are the four Explosive zones. Here, you are doing extensive muscle damage, relying on glycogen and ATP for fuel, and essentially throwing down the nastiest effort you can to win the race. These PTZ efforts can be up to 4 minutes in duration or as little as 10 seconds for PTZ 11.

Which of these zones sounds like the most fun to you? The super-fast sprint finish or the slow, boring endurance pace? Yes, it is easy to get caught up by the need for speed and focus your training on only the Threshold and Explosive zones. I see this all the time with my CINCH clients when they get started with our program. But you can't build a house without a rock-solid foundation. You're not going to see the hard work that went into the underground concrete when you walk in the beautiful entryway. As you admire the sleek kitchen or the spacious dining room, you won't be thinking about the engineering that is holding the house up above your head. It's there, though, and you need it!

So, we start with those Endurance zones and gradually develop your foundation. Then, we add on the Threshold and Explosive zones. Each zone has a role to play in both training and racing. As you become more familiar with the FORM Method, you'll be able to use your zones as a blueprint to success. You'll know where you need to do more work to improve. The zones will inform your racing tactics and your nutrition. When you've begun to master these zones, you'll be able to strategically apply them to different scenarios—and sometimes you'll win.

Pillar 2: Execution

The power meter is an awesome invention for the sport of cycling. It has changed the game. However, it has also warped our perception of what it means to have a good ride. We now have unrealistic expectations. I witness this in some of the riders I work with, who come to me perplexed by the numbers they see in their power files. "My numbers are actually pretty good," they argue. "So how come I'm always getting dropped? Do I need to lose weight? My buddy puts out the same normalized power and he ends up in the front group every week."

A power meter has given you a convenient numbers-based assessment of your quality as a rider or your performance in a race. Is your FTP better this month than it was last? Good, you're getting faster! Was that last race a new best average for your normalized power? Impressive, post about it on social media! But the problem is that you might not be using your power output to the fullest potential. In this pillar, I'll show you how to make the most of your power numbers;

it's illustrated by our North Star of Execution—a five-point guide to riding like the pros, even if you aren't able to produce the same wattage as they do. The five points on this star are Power Control, Cadence Control, Body Position, Separation, and Transitional Control.

We'll explain these concepts in depth in Chapter 6, but for now, here's a quick look at what they can do for your riding.

Power Control

When it comes to our power on a bike, we are all too focused on the numbers themselves, not what they can actually do for us in a real-life cycling scenario. Is a soccer player obsessed with the amount of force they can apply to a ball when taking a free kick? Is a football quarterback fixated on the miles per hour of their hardest spiral? Of course not. Those players, and people in practically any other sport, are obsessed with how to control the power they have for maximum advantage.

Cycling is all about building and maintaining momentum. You want to use your power strategically so you can build momentum over the crests of climbs, maintaining it on the downhills and into the flat sections of roads. This is extremely important on rolling terrain like you'd find in New England or the Basque Country.

The system I've developed to help riders like you focus on momentum throws away the old concept of power averages for intervals. You aren't average, are you? Of course not. So, we look at two key power numbers for any given interval: the Power Floor and the Power Ceiling. If you go below the floor, you waste momentum by slowing down, and you're forced to make an effort to return to your targeted PTZ. Even if you're having the best day of your life on a bike, you also do not want to break through the Power Ceiling. Your body can only handle so many spikes through the Power Ceiling. Often, after such an effort, your power will dip below the Power Floor. Ideally, when you stay between the Floor and Ceiling, you're holding your maximum momentum for a given time, without overtaxing your body with the stress of surges to regain momentum.

Cadence Control

I'll continue the sports analogies for the second point on our North Star, Cadence Control. But this one is a little more relatable than a soccer player or a star quarterback. Car racing is different from cycling in a lot of ways, but there's a similarity: Fundamentally, race-car drivers and cyclists are both chasing maximum speed, efficiency, and endurance. Instead of pushing their legs to the limit, the drivers are pushing their engines to the limit. But they can't do it in just one gear on the car. They run through the gears frequently, using each with purpose. They downshift to accelerate at high rpms. Soon, they're out of that gear and up to the next for more top-end speed. If you know how to drive a manual transmission, you've gotten a little taste of this feeling.

Bikes are no different. When you see Chris Froome spinning an insanely fast cadence up Mont Ventoux or L'Alpe d'Huez, don't assume he will ride 120 rpm for all 21 stages of the Tour de France. I guarantee you that he, and most other pro riders, use cadence strategically, and that's what I'm going to show you how to do, too.

Use your cadence correctly and you'll start riding with more torque, meaning you'll translate more of your power into raw speed. Combine this with good Power Control and you'll be maintaining momentum more efficiently. And for that matter, your cadence will help you use your fuel tank more economically and save yourself from excess muscular and cardiovascular stress.

Body Position

Cadence is a commonly misunderstood part of cycling. Just as often as I see someone on a cadence hamster wheel, spinning extremely fast while going extremely slow, I see people who don't have their Body Position correct to perform the basics of Power Control and Cadence Control. This is the third point on our North Star.

As I'll explain in depth in Chapter 6, there are Three Points of Power that affect your Body Position: hands, core, and feet. Each of these points has a role to play and, believe it or not, you actually have to adjust them all simultaneously depending on what sort of effort you're doing, whether you are seated or standing, and what sort of cadence you're riding.

Separation

Once you start focusing on these elements of Execution and improving, you'll be able to more consciously shift gears like that race-car driver to get into the right zone at the right time. This is the fourth point on the North Star, Separation.

When you set out to do intervals, they should never blend together in terms of either cadence or power. There needs to be clean separation of the zone and effort. For example, if your warm-up is too hard, then it becomes more difficult to hit the PTZ you have planned for your intervals. Your power output in the interval ends up too low, and before you know it, everything blends together and your progression stalls.

Instead, if you clearly separate your intervals with both power and cadence, you'll be tapping the intended energy system, resulting in the greatest fitness gains. Once you get comfortable looking at the graphs of your power files, you'll start to see if you were able to get the separation needed, or if everything was blended.

Transitional Control

Finally, Transitional Control is the fifth and most advanced point on the North Star of Execution. This is where many of the fundamentals come together so you can use your legs like a Swiss Army knife, using the right tool for each task. As I've said already, cycling is not a steady-state effort. It ebbs and flows depending on terrain and your competitors, and I intend to help you build an arsenal of options in your legs that will make anyone with a red-handled knife green with envy.

By harmonizing your use of PTZ, Cadence Control, and Body Position, Transitional Control helps you efficiently build and maintain momentum. It gives you the self-awareness to select your most potent weapon, assess your competitors' weaknesses, and hit them with an attack that they won't be able to handle. And if it isn't your day to boss the race and control the tempo, Transitional Control lets you respond to moves that others make. There are plenty of ways to bridge a gap to an attacker or to respond to an acceleration on a climb. Wouldn't you like to have the ability to choose which one will work best for your own abilities and talents?

When I look back at my pro racing career, there are a lot of riders that really impressed me with their execution. I think Chris Horner makes the top of my list, though. As I mentioned earlier, I once compared one of his power files to mine from the same race, when we were riding at similar levels. His numbers were shockingly lower than mine. Now that may seem like a bad thing, but Chris actually finished ahead of me on the stage. How was that possible? His execution was better than mine. Somehow, he'd found little ways to conserve momentum, use his cadence wisely, close down gaps without too much effort, and make the terrain work in his favor. My goal is that, after training with the FORM Method, you'll be the rider turning heads like Chris Horner did.

Pillar 3: Nutrition

It doesn't take long for new cyclists to adopt our sport's most unhealthy tendency, the obsession with weight loss. From the top rungs of the peloton all the way down to the local Category 5 crit, riders never feel like they are skinny enough, even if their performance is visibly suffering. I was one of those people. I was the guy who'd be in the airport on my way to the Tour de France choking down a low-calorie salad when my biggest, most demanding event was just days away.

Our mentality about food needs to change entirely. It is fuel. You need to start viewing your fuel as something you add strategically to boost your performance, not something you take away, chasing a weird European fetish of a stick figure climbing through the Pyrenees. Following our method, you'll fuel yourself based on the 3-Sigma Nutrition System, which is founded on the concepts of Purpose, Composition, and Timing.

When you eat your daily lunch at work, are you thinking about that ride you have planned for 6 p.m.? Or did you consider the morning workout you did before you rushed to the office? You should be. Your body needs that fuel, whether it is to prime for a weeknight throwdown or to recover from the dawn patrol ride. Don't assume your routine sandwich and chips is always the right fuel.

Purpose

Every meal needs to have a purpose. This may be the simplest of the 3-Sigma concepts, but it is critically important, setting you up for success with the other two. Before you grab that sandwich from the refrigerator or go out to lunch, ask yourself why you're eating. Ask what you're hoping to gain from any given meal, both physically and mentally. And then, based on factors like your day's workout plan, ask what macronutrients are required to fuel yourself optimally.

Composition

Your nutritional needs vary wildly depending on what PTZ you'll be training in that day. Our program focuses on macronutrients: fat, carbohydrates, and protein. I'll teach you how to adjust your meals to address the needs of everything from a long, steady endurance ride in PTZ 2 all the way up to a super-intense threshold effort in PTZ 7. Again, not all rides are created equal, so not all fuel will work as effectively when you clip in for the day's workout.

In addition to the three macronutrients, I also focus on anti-inflammatory nutrition. I began incorporating this approach into my diet as a professional rider and it made a huge difference. Every time we do an intense ride, we are inflaming our bodies—legs, lungs, ligaments, and more. To cut down on the toll of hard training, our nutrition system incorporates alkaline foods into the diet that will help your body recover from training.

You may be thinking that our system will set you on a strict, boring diet. But don't worry—you won't have to give up every indulgence that satisfies your cravings. I tell my athletes to stick to the 80:20 rule: 80 percent of the time you eat healthy and stay with the plan; the other 20 percent is your chance to enjoy a post-ride beer or eat a slice of your kid's birthday cake.

Timing

The third key to our nutritional program is the timing of when you fuel. Your body doesn't care when the clock strikes midnight—it doesn't have some internal calorie tally that gets reset every day. While the concept of carbo-loading the night before a big race is a bit antiquated, it hits on a fundamental point related to timing nutrition. You need to plan more than 24 hours in advance when you're fueling for a major event.

Also, you should know that as you become a more fit, more experienced cyclist, your calorie demands will go through the roof. Your tank will empty quicker. The margin for error will become much thinner.

It takes a little time to adapt to the 3-Sigma System and to make a habit of planning your meals and measuring your food. However, I can tell you that you won't want to skimp on this pillar. Toward the end of my career, careful nutrition planning helped me feel better at age 37 than I had my whole life. Imagine what it will do for your riding and overall well-being!

Pillar 4: Focus

What drives you as a competitive cyclist? Why are you here, reading a book about the intricacies of training and nutrition?

Throughout my career, 99 percent of mistakes I made and anxiety I felt occurred because I lost my "why." I wasn't paying attention to my purpose in cycling. I was reading *VeloNews* or *CyclingNews*, just searching for my purpose. Or I was listening to my team director for his take on my purpose. I made a lot of bad decisions because I was too busy looking outward. I needed to be focused inward.

As a new rider becomes acquainted with some of the fundamentals of cycling, they can follow others' lead with good results because they're learning the simple things, the obvious stuff like food or training techniques. But eventually they'll lose their way because they reach the level of why, and the answer to that is unique to each rider. If you're too focused on other riders when the why question comes up, you won't have any substance to support your purpose, and the better rider you are at this point, the harder the fall will be.

In the Focus pillar of the FORM Method, I'll guide you through an arsenal of tools you can use to prepare yourself mentally for any race scenario. The Core Performance Qualities will give you reassurance and motivation. And I'll guide you through a process of developing a focused vision that will help you tap into your purpose and give you perspective on your strengths and weaknesses, leading to an outcome that will be meaningful to you.

I will also introduce you to Performance Chains, which provide a toolkit of different mindsets to focus on so you can use your brain to drive your effort on the bike. At first this concept might seem a little new-agey: We'll use metaphors like switching into a Lightning mindset for a fast attack, using the Fire mindset for a long, hard climb, flowing through the peloton with a Water mindset, or enjoying a recovery ride with a Cloud state of mind. But don't underestimate your mind's power to drive your body.

Don't believe me? Well, turn the page for a story from my pro racing days that illustrates just how important it is to be in the right state of mind when you're in the middle of a key race.

When the Fire Went out on Brasstown Bald

In the 2005 Tour of Georgia, I beat Floyd Landis by lighting up the climb on Brasstown Bald, going hard right from the bottom and beating him by more than a minute.

Fast-forward to 2006: I went into that race hungry and really wanting to win it again. It had become a big race in the US and was a priority for a lot of American sponsors. My Achilles' heel had been my time trial the year before, so I had worked a lot on my time trial to be closer to Floyd.

I did a very good job with the Fire mindset in the time trial. I primed for it; I visualized; I pre-rode the course a lot. I did probably one of my best time trials ever. I finished second in the time trial, beating Dave Zabriskie, and I finished second to Floyd by four seconds.

Going into Brasstown Bald in 2005, I had to make up a minute on Floyd, and this year I only had to make up four seconds. I had the number one on my back. I was very confident because of the time trial. Or at least I thought I was very confident . . .

All day on the Brasstown Bald stage, I was using my Fire mindset quite a bit. I was moving up on climbs at unnecessary times, going back to get water bottles when I could have asked a teammate to do it, being super-intense. I remember jumping into the early breakaways at the beginning of the race as we went over some hard climbs when I didn't need to. It was full Fire mindset.

Finally, when we got to Brasstown Bald I didn't have any mental gasoline left. I got to the base of the climb and my team did a really hard pace like I asked them to. After Yaroslav Popovych, my last guy, pulled off on the finish climb, I tried an attack, but I really wasn't mentally checked in. Because of what happened the year before, I expected that attack to work. It didn't. I didn't use my Explosive zones. I didn't use my Fire mindset. I kind of had a Water mindset, and because my brain wasn't driving the effort, it didn't work.

I didn't drop Floyd. He sensed, I think, that mentally I was fragile and that I wasn't completely committed. So he rode next to me and started up some serious shit talking. He said I sucked, was no good . . . all kinds of other bad things to get into my head. He was unbelievable.

After that, I got into a pattern where I didn't commit to the Fire mindset. I tried to use a little bit of a Lightning mindset to attack, and he would just ride next to me. On each climb he'd knock me down and just say "Oh, that was a shitty attack. Do you think you're going to drop me with that?" I had never experienced anything like that before. I didn't know what to do.

At the end, my teammate Popovych came from behind and just passed us, so he was leading. I think the combination of that and me realizing I'd messed up just got me pissed off. At the very last part of the climb, things came together and I was able to get back to that Fire mindset. I was able to do one big hard effort at the end, caught Popovych, and passed him. But I had waited too long to drop Floyd.

When I crossed the line after winning the stage, Floyd came off his bike and passed out. I saw that and thought, *Holy shit, he was totally on the rivet*. He walked over to me after the race and said, "Hey dude, I totally played you. I was fucked." I had no idea.

Brasstown Bald is a Fire climb, and I didn't have the Fire ready because I'd wasted all that mental energy going into it and maybe some the day before, too. I didn't have it. Even though I won the stage, I didn't win the race overall when I should have. And the fact that Floyd was able to capitalize on that, take advantage of that, really shows how powerful the mental pillar of the FORM Method is.

The year before, I went into Brasstown Bald ready to light the whole climb on Fire. From the bottom I just went—full commitment, full Fire. Levi Leipheimer was with me, and I never even thought twice to question my effort. I knew I had to light the whole climb on Fire, and he was going to burn up eventually, which is exactly what happened.

One of the big mistakes I made in 2006 that shows you how badly I got my mental prep wrong was that I was visualizing my victory salute. Never do that. And if you're in the Fire mindset, you can't even do a victory salute. Everything is on Fire.

02

THE 10 KEYS TO SUCCESS

Cycling has a lot of rules, guidelines, keys . . . many of them unwritten. Blogs, forums, and social media platforms are chock-full of experts telling you what color socks to wear or how your bike should look. Then there are plenty of riders who are quick to yell at anyone in the peloton who isn't quite following their interpretation of rules and etiquette. So I know what you're thinking: *Oh brother, more rules I'm supposed to follow?*

Don't worry. These 10 Keys to Success are far different than any other cycling rules you've read about. These essential elements of cycling are not designed to cage you in but instead set you free to become the best cyclist you can be by eliminating the barriers of progression.

Through my coaching and my own experience, I've identified the most common mindsets, actions, and beliefs that hold people back. The 10 keys are meant to shatter some of cycling's idols, the sport's common beliefs (and rules) that are born out of stuffy tradition and misconceptions about how and why pro riders are so good.

I want these concepts to spark your self-awareness. I want them to help you start focusing on your personal progress, on what's best for you. The majority of riders don't know where to go to get better. They end up focusing on granular things, like FTP, because that's what they've been led to believe is the key to cycling success. I want the 10 Keys to Success to open a door for you so you can see your path to getting better at cycling, to frame your mission in the sport. These 10 truths help keep you on track toward your personal goals.

Depending on where you are in your cycling journey, some keys may resonate with you more than others, and that's perfectly OK. Choose the ones that speak to you, write them down, and refer back to them whenever you need to.

1. You Are Not Your FTP

FTP, or functional threshold power, is one of those terms that cyclists and coaches toss around casually. Simply put, FTP is the maximum number of watts that a rider can sustain for over an hour. While it can be a useful number in terms of measurements, I've banned it from the FORM Performance Method for a few different reasons.

First and foremost, I exclude FTP because people constantly define themselves by their FTP; it becomes their identity. It's not surprising that people latch onto it, considering that so many training software programs, like TrainingPeaks and Zwift, ask you to enter your FTP at the start of your program or ride. These training programs need a baseline to compute your power zones, and FTP has become the standard benchmark for cycling fitness.

Athletes are going to group rides and events with a predetermined marker of how good they think they are. Or worse, they aren't even showing up at all. They did the test and calculated their power-to-weight ratio. They've researched what's considered good and bad FTP. They've put it in their Zwift accounts and training programs. Even if they aren't consciously aware of it, they've tied up their self-worth with this number and it is holding them back.

If they have a low power-to-weight ratio, then they don't try on climbs, they don't jump in breakaways, and they don't push through in the moments when the elastic splits. Instead, when things get hard and the doubt starts creeping in, they think about their shortcomings and use their power-to-weight ratio as an excuse to sit up when it could have been an opportunity for a breakout performance.

Counterintuitively, I find that FTP can also be detrimental for those with high numbers. So many people call me up and use their FTP to explain how good they are. But again, it does not directly translate to efficient, powerful riding. These same athletes with really high FTPs tend to "bleed" or waste power everywhere. They pull for too long and too hard on the front of the peloton. They are constantly wasting energy with super-pulls, moving up in the peloton at the hardest moments, not attacking, just riding hard at the front hoping they will drop everyone off their wheel. But if you waste all your energy, you will not win.

So, whether you have a high FTP or a low FTP, it is more important to figure out the best ways to use it to your advantage. On one hand, it can be helpful for those wanting to self-coach. Spend a couple minutes on Google and you can learn a whole lot about FTP, from how to test it to simple workout plans to increase it. In fact, it's relatively easy to improve. Science says if you simply train just below it, it will go up—which is true.

However, FTP is only a test. In my opinion, this test's result doesn't actually translate to real cycling performance. It provides a benchmark for a steady-state effort. The problem is that cycling is not, in fact, a steady-state sport. Think about it: Any competitive event—group rides, races, or gran fondos—is pretty uncontrolled and rarely steady. Not even time trials are steady-state if you are executing them correctly.

My other criticism of a focus on FTP is that it encourages athletes and coaches to train for the FTP test. They do everything to increase that one specific zone, hoping it will translate to overall increased cycling performance. Athletes are using it to justify their training, and coaches are using it to justify the rate they charge their athletes.

I have seen just how well this logic works in our public schools. Instead of equipping our students with the knowledge to function as adults, we teach them to test well. From age 5 onward, students begin standardized testing, and teachers have to prepare students for the tests to get funding for their class-rooms. I understand that administrators need a benchmark to assess schools, but this should be one small part of evaluating a student's overall academic ability. A high SAT score does not necessarily translate to real-world tasks like balancing a budget, filing taxes, interviewing for jobs, investing your income, or working on a team—skills that you need to be successful in the sport of life. Imagine if we placed less emphasis on standardized testing and more focus on teaching teenagers these valuable life skills before they graduated from high school.

The same thing happens in cycling. Instead of looking at cycling fitness as a whole, people tend to oversimplify and focus on one small part of it. And what happens when you pour all of your attention into one measurement? The rest goes mostly ignored and you're left with a high score with no real-world ability to apply it.

Instead of using FTP in this book, I'm offering a better solution. We are going to identify the type of rider you are by looking at natural strengths and weaknesses. We'll consider your mindset and tendencies as we build a cycling program based on who you are as a rider. And in the process, I'll help you realize that how well you'll do in the actual sport of cycling is not defined by the number you can hold in a 20-minute test.

2. You Have to Go Low Before You Can Go High

If I were to ask a cyclist how they plan to get from where they are now to where they want to be, fitnesswise, chances are their answer would be something along the lines of "More power, more volume, more hard work."

It's not a surprise—many of us go to group rides and feel pinned from the start. We sign up for races only to get shot out the back. So people think to themselves, *I'm getting dropped at my current level, so I need to train above that.* But this doesn't work; it has the opposite effect, actually.

The key to improving your upper zones is to focus on your lower zones first. You need to develop your muscular strength and cardiovascular efficiency. To build each of these things, you need to work on them separately. When you train at a low intensity, you're teaching the muscle fibers to fire in a specific way—and training the hands, core, and legs to support these neuromuscular connections. By wiring your brain and body in this way, they unconsciously know exactly what to do when it's go time.

I want you to envision your cycling fitness like a ladder. Each rung represents a specific fitness zone. Each of those levels corresponds to different fuel systems, which use different ratios of fat to sugar. In order to build a tall ladder with many rungs, you need to build the lower rungs so you have somewhere to step when installing the higher rungs. The same applies to fitness zones. You need the well-built lower zones to stand on so you can efficiently ride in the top-end zones with the correct fuel systems.

Most people do the opposite because we are naturally attracted to the top part of the ladder. But without any foundation, the top part of your fitness zone ends up being only as high as you can reach from where you are currently standing. If you try to build out your top levels while you are still standing on the ground, there won't be any space between your low zones and high zones, limiting most of your options as a cyclist.

I've seen it time and time again. You go riding with a friend who is better than you are. So you think to yourself, *I'm at my limit, so it's these power numbers I need to train above.* But the place where you are flooded with lactate is not ground zero. That's not your starting point. Training this way often leads to injuries, burnout, and a lot of pain for not much gain.

I will teach you how to build the low zones first. There are four Endurance zones, and each burns different amounts of fat. These zones are essential for endurance, but they are also critical to establishing the foundation for the higher-end work. Develop them first, and then you can start climbing up those rungs until you've built a really tall ladder—a dynamic cycling engine.

3. Planning for Your Workout Is Part of Your Workout

Whether you have a coach or you self-train, planning for your workout is as important as your performance in the workout. This includes getting ready for the ride, mapping the route, prepping your equipment, fueling properly, and more. I think many of us don't realize that planning is part of our training. But the planning process affects the quality of the session in a critical way, so be sure to give planning the consideration it deserves.

The first step is to place all your workouts in a calendar where you can look at your obligations and commitments. At a minimum, you should be looking at your workout the day before. Ideally, you plan ahead a week in advance. Treat your workouts like a doctor's appointment or work meeting and schedule them in ahead of time. You wouldn't casually blow off a business lunch with your boss, would you? Keep this commitment with yourself so you can show up in an even bigger way in other aspects of your life. I promise you, if you try to "get it in when you can," you will not have the consistency needed to attain the next level.

The next step is to plan your nutrition. This may sound like a no-brainer, but it is one of the most common things that derails progression. The quickest way to turn a sturdy V10 engine into a scrawny V2 engine is to starve it of fuel. The same applies to your body, so you must make sure you are fueling yourself with the correct macronutrient ratios before and after workouts.

I categorize workouts based upon the fuel zones they use so riders can gauge how much fuel they should have in the tank to get the job done. When you are looking over your workout the day before, think about what fuel systems you are going to be using and make sure you have the right food at the right time.

Finally, my biggest planning recommendation is scheduling your workouts in the "lowest-friction" part of your day. Take a look at your schedule and ask yourself, what time of day offers the least amount of resistance? What hours of the day can I usually get away? This is your window of least friction. Try to schedule your workouts during that time frame.

Plan for rest days as well. Schedule them on the highest-friction days. Ask yourself, which days of the week feel like an all-out sprint? Is there a day you like to use for catching up? Make those days your rest days. A lot of the athletes I work with prefer to set Monday or Friday as rest days for this reason. They can use Monday to get back in the groove and Friday to wrap everything up and be ready to do some longer rides on the weekend. Your situation might be completely different. The time right after work might be the best for you, or during your lunch break, or in between classes if you are in school.

Throughout my coaching, I've seen time and time again that the busiest people are often the most consistent. They know if they miss their window their workout will not happen, so they make it a priority every day; they schedule it in. Training at the same time on the same days conditions your mind and body to know when it's go time. Your cycling training should enhance your life and not become another chore on your to-do list. Realize that with the correct planning, cycling will make you more equipped in life.

To get you started on planning, work through the following steps. This process will help you manage time beyond your workouts, too.

1. Look at your schedule, identifying all commitments in each day.
2. Identify high- and low-friction times and days of the week.
3. Schedule workouts during the lowest-friction times.
4. Schedule rest days on high-friction days.
5. Rock it out; stick to the schedule.
6. Repeat.

4. Group Rides Do Not Count as Training

This might be a shock, but group rides do not translate to better cycling.

In the majority of group rides, the strongest person dictates the pace. If you are not the strongest, you are essentially participating in someone else's workout.

Chances are that workout is above your ceiling, and this kind of intensity is costly both in physical energy and mental stress. Riding above your zones for long periods, reacting to hard efforts, and expending emotional energy can put you in such a deficit that it compromises your training for the next week. As I've explained before, riding hard does not mean you are working in the areas necessary for actual improvement. And the zones used in a group ride are not necessarily the same zones that you would use in a competitive event or ride.

The short duration of typical group rides, combined with predetermined stops where the ride regroups, attract a type of cyclist that I've dubbed the "kamikaze." Like kamikaze airplane pilots, these are the heroes of the group. They look amazing. They are usually pretty strong. But most importantly, a kamikaze is willing to take themselves down in order to blow up the group. What's their favorite tactic? The super-pull of mass destruction! You know what this looks like: When you are riding along in the peloton and suddenly the pace becomes incessantly hard, you look up to see who the heck is on the front. That's a kamikaze taking a pull. If it were a race or a longer ride, these types of efforts would not be sustainable. But because of the way so many group rides are structured, kamikazes can detonate themselves and blow up the group with little consequence.

What upsets me about this style of riding is that so many athletes lose their self-esteem from being shelled out of the group in these scenarios. In reality, super-pulls and "Ninja Star Pace Lines," where the focus is getting rid of people from the group rather than going faster as a group, is really just lousy cycling. I've been on these rides and have seen that after the leaders sit up, the pace slows down dramatically once 80 percent of the group is dropped.

Whether you make the headlines as the strongest kamikaze or you're just trying to avoid getting shot down, these rides do nothing to help you improve in the right areas.

Consider a typical weekly schedule of a successful group-ride kamikaze:

Sat.	Sun.	Mon.	Tues.	Wed.	Thurs.	Fri.
Ridiculously hard group ride	Totally beat, in a body bag; easy ride	Still wrecked; no ride	Easing back in; easy ride	Motivated; good training day	Rest day to be ready for the group ride	Opener ride to get ready for the group ride

Does that pattern seem familiar? If you look closely, this group-ride champion only gets one day of training a week that actually makes them better. Don't fall into the trap of thinking you are improving by following this pattern.

Now, group rides do have a place and a purpose. In fact, I host one weekly with the local clients in our coaching group. The simple fact is that not all group rides are created equal. A proper group ride's purpose should fall into one of two categories: It should be either therapeutic in some way or allow you to practice execution and skills.

In the therapy category, group rides can be a lot of fun, especially if they are organized correctly. If you find yourself out there doing what you love with your friends, then that's therapy. If it's increasing your overall mojo and you feel better after it's over then, yes, by all means, keep attending. We all know that cycling is an individual sport, but it should be practiced as part of a group and the social aspect is a big part of it. Group rides are a great way to socialize and connect with people who are on the same wavelength.

The other reason (and my personal favorite) to attend a group ride is that it can be a great place to practice Execution techniques; we'll dive deeper into Execution in Chapter 6. We all know riding in the peloton is entirely different from training alone. Group rides can be a fantastic opportunity to work on real-life scenarios. Use the ride to practice maintaining your zones in the group, positioning in the peloton, and conserving energy. Try out different strategies and tactics to figure out what works before your next race or event. Work on the execution of techniques like attacking, changing cadence, decelerating, and adjusting your body position.

A Better Group Ride

Take a moment to evaluate the group rides you join. Do they fit the profile of being good for either practice or therapy? If your group ride does not provide either of those, it's time to look for a new one.

If you want to take it a step further, start your own group ride and designate yourself as the leader. Every group ride should have a leader who assigns the rules and routes and maintains order. I'm the leader of my group ride with my CINCH clients. It's my responsibility to make sure everyone has the skills they need to ride safely in the group. I don't randomly show up to other people's group rides expecting everyone to know my rules and do things my way. That's why I host my own ride; even with my experience as a pro, I don't want to participate in what I mentioned earlier.

The CINCH group has ridden this way for so long that we are now a well-oiled machine. We operate as a team similar to what you would see in a WorldTour race. Most importantly, athletes know what to expect when they show up to the CINCH group ride. In case you want to try this on your group ride, I'll outline how I host mine.

First, we have "social time," about a 30- to 45-minute warm-up at a relaxed pace. People can chat and ride two by two; riders pull for a few minutes, then drift to the back of the group. The next stage is when the real fun begins—and it's the part that gets me really excited. I create a specific race scenario and assign roles to each of the riders. One scenario might be putting the weaker riders in a breakaway group and giving them three minutes while the group chases behind. We might have a specific rider who we'll protect, maybe save for the final climb, and we can only use designated domestique riders to bring back the gap. And when the breakaway is caught, the strongest riders don't attack.

Creating race scenarios makes it possible to structure your group rides in such a way that everyone can participate and get a lot out of the ride. Get creative with different teams and different types of riders. Find ways to handicap the stronger riders so they have to out-strategize people rather than just outride everyone. Give opportunities to the less-experienced riders to be protected in the group or in breakaways with a head start so they can learn from the more experienced riders. This is how the sport of cycling should be played!

Most importantly, participate in a way that's conducive to the type of rider *you* are, even though you might be riding among many different rider types. If you are newer to cycling, something you could work on is as simple as grabbing a bar out of your pocket and eating it while riding. Or you could work on remembering to drink during fast-paced moments in the ride. A more advanced concept that you could work on would be practicing mentally checking in when it's go time and detaching when it's over. Create an intention before the group ride and focus on executing on that intention rather than just reacting to other people.

5. Averages Make You Average

Stop focusing on averages. Whether that's average power, average cadence, average speed, average weekly distance, or average TSS (Training Stress Score). These metrics are best used to merely describe your training, not guide it. You use them to execute an intended exercise or activity. Or you can use them to define a planned workout or event.

When you focus on the averages of these metrics, well, you tend to game the system by riding above your intentions to improve the average score. When you focus on averages, you stop focusing on the things that matter. As a coach, when I design an interval or workout, I am putting specific concepts into the workout. There are certain zones I want you to work on and specific neuromuscular connections you need to make. If you are focused just on the average, you might as well throw all the things that make an interval an interval out the window.

For example, a simple interval might be 10 minutes at your medium or Zone 3 power, which, let's say, is 200 watts. I want you to do it with a cadence of 100 rpm. In this interval, I'm asking you to maintain this low power, at a high cadence, without spiking the power. It's a specific zone. In this case, it's the highest amount of power output you can use while burning fat as fuel. When I give you that interval, I'm working on the low-end zone and Cadence Control, creating neuromuscular pathways that will help resolve any inefficiencies in your pedal stroke. You might finish the interval with an average power of 200 watts, but when your power graph looks like an EKG, spiking and dropping, and you merely *averaged* 200 watts, did you ace the interval?

Simply put: No, you didn't. I'll look at that graph and point out that you did time at 150 watts and 250 watts. These are entirely different zones that require different muscle recruitment, fuel sources, and neuromuscular connections. While the average of 200 watts might be spot-on, you did not control the power, so you did not complete the task.

Averages often encourage athletes to do too much work by accumulating fatigue. They even have a measure for this: TSS. Training Stress Score is a composite number that averages the duration and intensity of a workout to arrive at an estimate of the overall training load and physiological stress created by that particular ride.

I have a term for the athlete who loves to game the metric averages, TSS among them: the fatigue millionaire. Yes, the fatigue millionaire loves to go around and knock out the big averages in watts, speed, weekly distance, and my favorite, TSS (pure fatigue). They collect this fatigue in their fatigue bank account and then wait for the right time to cash it all in: "Yes, sir, I have an important race coming up, and I'd like to cash in all my fatigue now for race-winning fitness." Sound ridiculous? Well, it is! Unfortunately, this is how most people believe training is done, and it just doesn't work. When you become a fatigue millionaire, there's no direction. Sure, maybe you're growing in your ability to overtrain. But you aren't becoming more efficient; you are just putting your body under stress and will have to pay the bill later in the form of injuries or burnout.

What's the worst offender of averages? Average speed. I hear it all the time: "Yeah, that was a pretty good ride . . . I averaged 21 mph." Or athletes use it to describe themselves: "I average about 17 miles per hour." I have no problem with people looking at averages post-ride or post-race, but only for fun. Looking at the averages during the ride typically encourages athletes to go to hard between intervals. There should be a clear separation between intervals. I often see athletes blending it all together to increase their average speed. If you're worried about this, you most likely aren't getting the quality and intensity in the top-end intervals you should be getting. Step away from averages and step into a calculated and cutthroat approach to maximizing time and energy investments on the bike.

6. Progress Is Not Pass/Fail

There is no pass/fail in cycling—progress always happens, and you can view it as either growth or practice.

Have you ever stopped a ride in the middle of a workout, telling yourself you're just having a bad day? Have you ever found yourself dropping out of a race when things don't go right, blaming it on a lousy month leading into it? Or maybe you've been in a mental funk and blamed it on a loss of motivation because your year "hasn't gone right"?

If you said yes to any of these, listen up. Stop wasting your time trying to categorize your experiences, efforts, days, and years as good or bad. You are just finding excuses to justify what you already know. Things don't always work out; life happens; we fall short. Our realities do not always meet our expectations. It is part of the human experience. The act of labeling every occurrence does not help you progress; instead, it forces you to stay stagnant and lose momentum. But so many people do it. Most athletes go into events and rides and score their performances on whether they met or exceeded their expectations. Did I measure up to my expectations? Did I measure up to the expectations of others?

Once in a blue moon, when all the stars align, we are absolutely ecstatic because we had a good race and we met or exceeded that expectation. But more often than not, we are left feeling like we failed because we did not meet whatever arbitrary metric we assigned to that particular event. That could be a number on the results sheet or a certain PR time. Chances are, even if you didn't receive that external validation of a spot on the podium, you still experienced progress in your event.

From now on, I want you to reframe your experiences. Experiences, events, and the days that go as planned (those you'd call "good") should be reframed as *practice*. You just practiced what you were already capable of doing. You are refining the process using the ability, skill, and direction that you already have.

If everything went right, you were in the correct position, you nailed the nutrition, and you had the expertise for the job. It was a great day of practice. It is nice when it comes together. It's your moment to enjoy.

In contrast, experiences, events, and days that do not live up to our expectations should be reframed as *growth*. Growth only occurs in moments where we fall short; we pivot and have to adapt. When things don't go as planned, there's no reason to get down. You just found the barrier to your next breakthrough.

To progress in life, you need continuous practice and growth. Progress is a constant balance between these two. With this new mindset, there's no reason to beat ourselves up when we fall short. Know that you are getting stronger. You are becoming better. And you are finding new opportunities to grow—whether it's in your Fitness, Execution, Nutrition, or Focus. So let's change our mindset and own all our experiences. We are either practicing or growing.

7. You Create Motivation; You Don't Find It

Motivation is your responsibility. Motivation is within your own power to create. No one can give it to you. Now, another person can guide you in helping you create your own, but that's all they can do. As a coach, I often hear athletes say, "I'm not motivated" or "I'm running low on motivation." It makes it sound like you're a victim of low motivation, as if you were just walking down the street and low motivation fell out of the sky and hit you on the head. And now you need a doctor to help you get your motivation back.

Life gets hard sometimes, but in my experience, low motivation almost always stems from a lack of vision. If you are continually looking every which way, wondering what you should do with yourself, you are not focusing on what you want to do or what needs to happen over the long haul. To get motivated, you need something to inspire you. The only way to identify what will inspire you is to perform the introspective work to get to know yourself inside out. Learn what aspects of the sport you feel passionate about and map out a plan for a cause greater than yourself. That is your vision. Commit 100 percent to the process of achieving that vision.

Instead of viewing motivation as something you need to learn or find, work on becoming more of yourself. From a bird's-eye view, imagine yourself in 20 years if everything were to go right in your life. What is that outcome? What does the ideal version of you look like, act like, and feel like? Write it down! That's your motivation.

Motivations tend to fall into one of two categories: Intrinsic motivation comes from within ourselves, and extrinsic motivation stems from outside sources. So many of us use "carrots" to keep us motivated. But what happens when that event passes by or we receive that reward? We often find ourselves out of motivation. Leaning on incentives to stay motivated might come from how we were raised. As children, we are told to do X and receive a reward. Disobey and we'd get punished. But think about what you've accomplished, what you are really proud of in your life. Chances are that the motivation to do those things came from a fire within. External motivation doesn't lead to long-term achievement. That kind of real progress appears only when intrinsic motivation is involved because your passion is in the driver's seat. If you're counting on external factors like race wins and other people to keep you motivated, you may feel like you are on a roller coaster. Your motivation will be more steady if you shift your motivation to values that align with your character.

Lastly, be sure to maintain and nourish your motivation over time. Build your vision into your daily life to keep that motivation fresh and prominent in your life. Review it daily, post it prominently, write about it, check in with a coach daily, or do whatever it takes to keep you focused on your vision and, in turn, forever motivated.

8. Consistency Is King

Have you ever wondered how some cyclists are endlessly progressing while others seem to work just as hard but achieve very little? The answer lies in their consistency. There's no substitute for putting in the work every single day. There's no gene that you are born with that makes someone consistent or not. No matter how many highs and lows anyone has, it is the daily grind that counts. You must develop a training process that you can realistically perform every single day in order to stay on the path to your highest priorities and goals. Much of consistency depends on your ability to hold yourself accountable for your daily choices. You and you alone are responsible for what you do and what you don't do.

To be consistent, you need to be able to focus on the present moment while maintaining a long-term view of what you want to become. Even though the concept of staying consistent seems pretty straightforward, most people struggle with its execution. I get it. It's hard to remain consistent in a world that blasts so many distractions at us. We are constantly being pulled in different directions, and it can be challenging to maintain the discipline to stick with something in the short-term in hopes of yielding long-term results. But I believe there is a solution to all of these forces that derail consistency.

The only way to maintain consistency is to be 100 percent confident you are taking the right steps and the right path, and to do so with constant feedback. Feedback takes the guesswork out of progress. Without proper performance feedback, athletes are forced to make guesses about their results. With the technology available to us today and the key performance indicators I will teach you about later, you won't have to worry or wonder if you are improving or not.

Your daily process should consist of two components: adaptation and evolution. Through the repetition of training, we are building the pathways and neuro-muscular developments so our bodies can adapt. It's about mindfully repeating the same actions over and over again, tracking feedback from these actions, then adjusting and evolving as needed to improve continuously.

The best way to learn is to study daily and in small increments. Your cycling training should also become more advanced as you advance through the sport. This is about gaining ever greater insights and knowledge about what it is you are doing, and afterward making the important modifications to these actions to help improve your outcomes and performance over the long haul. We want to focus on increasing your effectiveness and efficiency at each step of your journey.

From now on, don't stress about the big rides for the show. Keep it simple. Develop a daily process you can execute five to seven days a week. That is where you will find progress. Consistency is what breeds change to experience this shift; you must stay vigilant and focused on putting in the daily work and making adjustments as needed and not just maintaining the status quo. Use the adaptation and evolution in your daily process and own your consistency.

9. Chasing after Someone Else's Level Pulls You Further Away from Improving Your Own

Do you know people who are better than you? Do you base your objectives on what those other people are doing? How often do you set your sights on peers, friends, or rivals? Almost all of us are guilty of doing this. But looking at other people for direction takes you in the *wrong* direction. When you try to become another person, you become much worse at being yourself.

One of the biggest mistakes riders make is participating in rides and events with people who are much better than they are. Their thinking is that if they ride with people who are faster or stronger, they'll be forced to match their might. Sure, it's an easy way to push yourself hard, but you are pushing yourself in the wrong direction. You might say, "But I feel a lot of pain when I go hard on these rides chasing the better riders, and pain equates to gain, right?" Sorry, that's not how it works.

If you ride beyond your abilities to try to keep up with someone else, you are not creating your own zones. You have no footing. You are building a roof with no foundation to stand on. And you certainly aren't focused on the type of rider you are.

Each cyclist has a unique Rider Type (we'll help you find yours in Chapter 3). Your Rider Type is a product—and representation—of your natural-born mental and physical capabilities. These are your own God-given talents and gifts. But your unique capabilities need to be cultivated, and it's your responsibility to hone them. When you chase better riders around, you go above and beyond your own

Rider Type zones and abilities. Because your intensity level is so high, your focus is compromised and you are unable to execute a proper riding technique. Additionally, in these rides you are also using much of your valuable energy stores so that you are left with little fuel and mental strength, often compromising your training in the days ahead.

Instead of looking at other people and trying to emulate them, you should understand who you are, what you want to do, and where your current level is. Specifically work your way, your pace. Keep your perspective, desired outcome, and your dreams in focus. Spend your precious time and energy identifying and developing your personal Rider Type, and then become the best version of yourself.

10. There's Nothing Good Back There

Never sit up. Never give up. It sounds simple, right? It's not. The premise is that when you feel like you can't do it anymore, that's when you don't back down. This is your moment! It's when the selection in the race is going to happen. It's when you have primed yourself to have a mental, physical, and emotional breakthrough. You must give it your all because nothing good will come from giving up. "Back there" is where your past regrets, old versions of yourself, bad habits, and toxic patterns exist. But many of us never get that breakthrough because we make the mistake of thinking, *I can't do this forever*, so we sit up.

Let's say you've signed up for a 100-mile race. The start gun goes off, the pace is hard, but you're protected in the peloton. Twenty miles into the race you start up a medium-length climb. Riders start attacking right at the bottom of the climb. The pace is getting harder; your breathing is through the roof. You feel a burning sensation as the lactate fills your legs. You start thinking to yourself, *I'm only 20 miles in, I can't do this for 80 more miles*. The negotiations start, and all you can focus on is the pain. Then you hit the "screw-it" switch, swing off, and sit up. You've pulled the parachute cord, and in the process you've given up on whatever it is you wanted to accomplish when you pinned that number on in the first place. Even worse, you have to ride another 80 miles by yourself.

You're upset because you're no longer in the place you think you should be. To top it off, your legs still hurt. The negative self-talk starts: "You're not good enough." "You don't work hard enough." "Your job is too stressful." "Your family isn't supportive enough." "Your bike isn't good enough." "You're too heavy." You're frustrated, and it's going to take you longer to get to the finish. Not only is it going to take you longer, but it's going to be harder than when you were in the group.

You find a couple of folks to ride with, but they aren't as strong as you are and aren't much help. It then hits you that if you had just held on a little bit longer, the group probably would've slowed down after the selection happened.

It's never better behind. I know that when you're suffering it feels like sitting up will bring you relief. But it won't. You need to hang on. This is the time when you need to break through. Embrace it. Fight for it. Because on the other side of that movement is the outcome you wanted when you signed up for the race in the first place.

03

WHAT'S YOUR RIDER TYPE?

I will never forget the day I figured out what kind of rider I was. I had been racing mountain bikes for a couple of years and had done pretty well. I trained a lot with my friend Neil. I looked up to Neil because he was older and stronger than me. We would ride, rain or shine, usually on the trails near our houses. To get to the trailhead, we had to ride up a long road climb (long by Connecticut standards is around six minutes). But every day on our way to the trailhead I would get excited and gun it up this climb. One day I did my thing and looked back; Neil was pretty far behind. As he caught up, I could hear him breathing hard.

He looked me straight in the eyes and said, "Dude, you are a climber." With my limited experience only in mountain biking, I stared blankly and asked him, "What's a climber?" He said, "You know, a skinny guy that goes up hills fast." He then pointed to my legs and told me they were long and skinny—good for climbing. Then pointed to my barrel chest and said that it was also good for climbing. I stood there dumbfounded and thought to myself, *You mean this strange body of mine has a name and a purpose?*

My mind was blown and my world changed forever. More specifically, my perspective of myself within the sport changed. Before coming to this realization,

I had turned myself inside out during training and even more so in racing, trying to be the absolute best at every aspect of mountain biking. If the racecourse was flat and I was beaten, I would assume I had a bad day. If someone was faster than I was on a downhill section, I would beat myself up for not being good enough and resolved to train even harder. Mentally, I was completely worn down, and physically I was spreading myself too thin in my quest to be the best at every dimension of the sport.

But when the way I viewed myself changed, a whole new world opened up to me. Instead of trying to go fast during the entire race, I changed my pacing strategy so I could go bananas on the hills. Before the races, I would pick out all the climbs and plan my moves. If some guys were faster than me on the downhill, I knew I had to go that much faster on the climbs to beat them. I had a solution to my problems, whereas before I thought the answer was that I just wasn't good enough.

As I progressed, I started targeting races with big climbs. I even chose the college I went to (Fort Lewis College, in Durango, Colorado) because of my Rider Type. Knowing the kind of rider I was naturally gave me a direction to go in. Most importantly, it gave me confidence; no longer was I ashamed of my skinny frame because I knew it was my weapon. From that moment on I owned my cycling: I was a climber, and that was special.

Your Spot on the Team

From years of analysis as a professional athlete and coach, I've concluded that there are essentially four types of riders in the peloton. Some Rider Types present an obvious contrast, such as the difference between a climber and a sprinter. Some may share specific attributes but have subtle differences that completely change their approach to training and winning races. The FORM Performance Method is in fact made up of two components: the Four Pillars (Fitness, Execution, Nutrition, and Focus) and your FORM Rider Type, which is determined by your genetic, physical, energy system, and mental characteristics. The two go hand in hand and they build off of each other.

The easiest way to explain the Rider Type is to consider this: If I were a team director and I wanted to sign you onto my Tour de France team, what position would you fill? Different types of riders specialize in different races and individual stages, and they vary widely in shape, size, and abilities, as well as in personalities. But all play a valuable role in a Tour de France team. Each team in the race will have identified its targets and will create a group to help achieve these goals, which are usually focused around their team leader—the rider they feel is most capable of winning the competition they are targeting (such as general classification, points, or King of the Mountains). The supporting riders are chosen to help the team leader achieve the team's goals, and they will each have a specific role within the group.

Team Sky (now Ineos) offers a good example. For much of the 2010s, this team has been committed to retaining the yellow jersey on the shoulders of one of its riders. This requires a massive team effort, as they show up with a team of both pure climbers to assist in the mountains and steadier, more classics-type riders that can set the tempo on the front and control the race. The riders are chosen for their specific traits—types—and not all of them share the same type. Each is a tool to be used very intentionally.

Meanwhile, Peter Sagan and his sprint rivals will be eyeing the green jersey competition. Even with Sagan's exceptional prowess, he can't do it alone. He needs a team of strong classics-type lead-out men who will stay with him and ensure he is always sheltered, help him get over the mountains, and make sure that they're up at the front for the final sprint. His team will help him with positioning so he is able to get in the breakaways on the mountain days and win the intermediate sprint points. He will also use his teammates to bring back breakaways so the stage ends in a field sprint that he feels he can win.

At the other end of the spectrum, the Pro Continental teams in the race will most likely focus on individual stages, as opposed to the overall competitions, and will aim to establish themselves in as many breaks as possible to get TV time for their sponsors. So they bring riders capable of getting into these kinds of breaks, or of supporting the teammate that does get into the break.

Professionals don't go to a race like the Tour de France wondering what role they have or with anything less than an outline of their strategy. Likewise, you shouldn't go to an amateur race without knowing precisely what you are trying to accomplish and, more importantly, how you are going to do it.

Make no mistake: Even though only one rider stands on the top step of the podium, it takes a team of people to get him there. While teams can be a game changer in amateur races, most racers don't know how to use teammates effectively. The good news is that you don't need a team of riders to win races. You just need to learn how to compete in accordance with your Rider Type.

Stick to Your Type, but Adapt to Win

So, if you are built like one of the domestique roles I described, are you always relegated to working positions? Hardly. There are countless ways to win a race. With so many types of races these days, such as hill climbs, gravel grinders, endurance time trials, stage races, and criteriums, there's something for every kind of rider to love. You don't even need to be of a certain Rider Type to be successful in events that are conducive to that type. When I was racing, I witnessed firsthand a great example of this truth at the 2009 Tour de Suisse, won by Fabian Cancellara. In case you haven't heard of him, Cancellara is a gold-medal-winning Olympic time trialist, a one-day classics specialist, and a stellar domestique for his teammates who have general classification aspirations.

The Tour de Suisse is a nine-day stage race that ends two weeks before the Tour de France starts and, along with the Critérium du Dauphiné, is seen as an ideal race for riders to test their form before the July showdown. Cancellara was born in Switzerland, so this race obviously meant a lot to him, but it's a mountainous race with many strong climbers at their peak fitness, so, not being a natural climber, he had to be calculated in his approach to this race.

Day one of the race was the prologue, a very short, intense time trial effort. He won it outright by 19 seconds. It was impressive that he put that amount of time on the second-place finisher in such a short distance, but it was not entirely outside of his wheelhouse of specialties. Cancellara is a 6′1,″ 180-pound ball of muscle, so he's much more suited to time trial efforts than to floating up mountains.

What impressed me was the way he rode the climbs. He had his team drill it on the flatter parts of the race, making it hard for a break to get away. Even when he was isolated with just climbers, he would accelerate on the troughs of the climbs, forcing us all to accelerate hard to keep up so we were gassed for the steep sections. He made it all but impossible to attack. When he did get disconnected on the climbs, instead of panicking or trying to go with the climber's attacks and then subsequently blowing up, he just let them go up the road and brought them back steadily in a way that suited his Rider Type.

Cancellara did lose some time to the GC riders over the next few stages, and was third going into the last stage, a time trial. But then he absolutely demolished the TT, winning by 1:27 and taking the overall! It was clearly an impressive feat, considering the type of rider he is . . . and he accomplished it by staying to true to his Rider Type.

Find Your Rider Type

Discovering my Rider Type was such a game changer for me. And through my coaching, I've seen it transform hundreds of athletes. Now I want to do the same for you. Identifying the type of rider you are is the next crucial step in taking your cycling to a higher level.

Throughout the book we will be referring back to these Rider Types, as they have a fundamental role in your fitness, performance, execution, and the plays you need to master. Rider Type even influences the kind of food you eat. We don't want to train a generic, "does-it-all" kind of rider; there is no such thing. That's why we train to your specific Rider Type—you're much more likely to develop if you train this way.

Take the quiz and discover your Rider Type. I've purposely presented the questionnaire before explaining the Rider Types in detail because I didn't want them to sway your answers. After finding your Rider Type, read the complete

What Is Your Rider Type?

Read each question and select the answer that best describes you.

1. **Which occupation best suits your strengths?**
   - Ⓐ Mechanical engineer
   - Ⓑ Hollywood actor
   - Ⓒ Artist or creative
   - Ⓓ Fighter pilot

2. **Choose the physical makeup that best describes your own.**
   - Ⓐ Taller, athletic build, well-defined muscles, long femurs, high overall strength, gains muscle easily, sensitive to weight gain
   - Ⓑ Shorter, muscular, small frame and bone structure, moderate muscle mass, moderate weight, smaller shoulders, low and stable center of gravity
   - Ⓒ Small and thin, small frame and bone structure, lean, minimal muscle mass, less muscle definition, lightweight, small shoulders, fast metabolism
   - Ⓓ Moderate height, athletic build, high muscular definition, very high overall strength, gains muscle easily, sensitive to weight gain

3. **Choose the set of strengths that best defines you as a rider.**
   - Ⓐ Excels in longer, sustained TT-like efforts; powerful; favors in-the-saddle riding to develop power; prefers steadier riding overall; moderate explosive ability; prefers steady, shallow climbs
   - Ⓑ Excels on short, explosive climbs; able to sustain high, explosive speed for longer, 2- to 4-minute efforts; strong at producing power both in and out of the saddle; prefers non-steady riding; high explosive ability; can sprint well; strong in short time trials
   - Ⓒ Excels on moderate to steep long climbs; strong in sustained threshold zone riding; favors out-of-the-saddle riding to develop power; able to change the rhythm and remain strong
   - Ⓓ Excels in sprints; powerful; strong at producing power both in and out of the saddle; prefers non-steady riding; explosive ability; does well in both short, explosive

efforts and short, explosive climbs; strong in very short, prologue-like time trials

4. **Choose the set of mental strengths that best describes your own.**
   - Ⓐ Calculated, numbers oriented, gritty, determined, resilient, long attention span, often introverted
   - Ⓑ Adventurous, adaptable, unpredictable, positive, intense short focus, often extroverted
   - Ⓒ Creative, high pain tolerance, emotional, long attention span, often introverted
   - Ⓓ Clever, aggressive, impulsive, resilient, intense short focus, often extroverted

5. **Choose the set of ideal events for you.**
   - Ⓐ Events with challenging terrain, tough conditions, longer time trials, endurance focus
   - Ⓑ Events with short, punchy climbs, short time trials, shorter races, explosive uphills
   - Ⓒ Events with long climbs, hilly terrain, steep gradients
   - Ⓓ Events with flat and more rolling terrain, criteriums, less selective, favorable to a larger group to arrive at the finish together

6. **Choose the race strategy that you'd consider ideal in a competition against riders similar in ability to you.**
   - Ⓐ A long, hard race of attrition breaks the group down to a select few. You attack the small group you are with and win solo on flat/rolling terrain.
   - Ⓑ A hilly race with aggressive riding reduces the peloton to a small group. You win solo or in a sprint of a small group on top of a short, punchy climb.
   - Ⓒ A mountainous race; you find yourself with a group of strong riders on the long final climb. You repeatedly attack in the most difficult place and solo away from everyone.
   - Ⓓ A flat to rolling race where the peloton or a smaller group stays together. You stay with the group and win the sprint in the end.

7. **Choose the professional cyclist that you feel is the most similar to you in riding style, personality, and physical characteristics.**
   - Ⓐ Fabian Cancellara or Chloé Dygert
   - Ⓑ Julian Alaphilippe or Marianne Vos
   - Ⓒ Alberto Contador or Katie Hall
   - Ⓓ Tom Boonen or Kirsten Wild

RESULTS

Mostly As ➡ **CLASSICS TT RIDER**
Mostly Bs ➡ **PUNCHEUR**

Mostly Cs ➡ **CLIMBER**
Mostly Ds ➡ **CLASSICS SPRINTER**

descriptions to better understand the strengths of your type—but also of the other types. It helps to know your competitors, what makes others tick. Also, few riders are purely one type. You'll likely see some of your characteristics appearing in other types.

Rider Types Explained

Puncheur

The puncheur is an explosive athlete who uses their power in short bursts on climbs 2 to 8 minutes in length. They are the most feared riders on these short climbs due to their ability to drop both the sprinters and the mountain climbers with incredible bursts of power uphill. They thrive on rides with rolling to shark-tooth profiles, but are able to hold their own on flat, high-speed routes because of their strength. Puncheurs can also use their short but explosive power bursts to do well in short TTs or long, hard field sprints. These riders are quite well built, as far as cyclists go, with broader shoulders and bigger legs; they tend to seem the most balanced physically. Their attacking style of riding often comes into play near the end of long stages as the day's break is being reeled in, or in stages that end in a short, steep climb.

Puncheurs are the Hollywood actors of the group. They are all about the show. That's not necessarily a negative thing. They just love a platform to showcase their abilities. They are great storytellers and don't subscribe to what everyone else is doing. They love the thrill of putting it all on the line. But at the end of the day, they are in it for the experience and notoriety. They don't stress too much about the end result. But they are confident in their abilities and perform with panache. Puncheurs are highly aware of their strengths and don't fall into the trap of comparing themselves to other Rider Types. They will try for the win and if it doesn't happen, they chill out and wait for the next chance. Even if they are dropped, you won't see them pouting or throwing their bike into the bushes. They are out there having a party, whether it's off the front or in the grupetto. But they aren't willing to take on a role that's not the leading role. You won't see a puncheur racing for 18th place. They want to be the star of the show, and if they don't get the opportunity, they accept it and look for another role. But they aren't going to become an extra in someone else's film.

The Makings of a Puncheur

Pro Rider Examples
Alejandro Valverde, Philippe
    Gilbert, Coryn Rivera

Physique
Shorter, solid frame
Muscular
Ideal center of gravity

Physical Strengths
Explosive speed for longer efforts
Strong at producing power both
    in and out of the saddle
Prefers variable-pace riding
Can do short, explosive efforts
    and is a good sprinter
Strong on short climbs
Strong in very short time trials

Physical Weaknesses
Sustained efforts on the flats
Crosswinds
Multiday stage races or hard efforts
Long time trials
Endurance and recovery are not
    as good as that of the climbers
    or GC riders

Mental Strengths
Aggressive
Determined
Resilient
Strong mental endurance
Intense short-term focus

Mental Weaknesses
Often too focused on other riders
Struggles with intense focus for
    long periods of time
Uncomfortable with physical
    pressure on long climbs

Ideal Races/Events
Endurance events with short,
    punchy climbs
Short time trials
Criteriums
Shorter road races with explosive
    uphill finishes

Ideal Race-Winning Strategy
Explosive, surging race that comes
down to a small group in the finish.
Ideally the finish is an uphill in
which the puncheur wins the sprint
from the small group.

Climber

The climber is the most romantic rider in cycling's culture. Climbers use their unique style and body dynamics to ascend roads that most others fear. These featherweight riders seem almost as if they are dancing up the big climbs. They thrive on longer, mountainous ascents where the speed drops and drafting benefits are limited. Pacing and clearing lactate are vital. Due to their low weight, climbers are able to put in repeated accelerations to drop heavier rivals. Their high endurance levels enable them to recover quickly.

The climber is an artist, highly creative and usually the most introverted of the types. They have all the talent in the world. Whether that talent translates into any real results is up to the individual. Some use their talents to become extremely successful, while others never sell a single piece of work. Climbers are just fine riding alone and prefer to ride hills at their pace, their way. Each has a unique style. Preferring to plan their moves and react to terrain rather than other people, they race against the course and are not interested in other people's opinions. They have a quiet confidence. Climbers express themselves through their bike, painting pictures on the climbs with their signature styles. In fact, you'll rarely see two climbers with identical riding styles. Sometimes you will see climbers converting into a general classification rider, becoming the leader of their team. These types of climbers resemble more of a musical artist rather than a painter—they're more like a lead singer in a rock band: Think Axl Rose, Mick Jagger, and John Lennon. These riders like to put on a show. They are most comfortable when they are center stage with their bandmates surrounding them, putting on the performance of a lifetime. But there's a lot of pressure that comes from being "the guy." When things don't go their way, they can become emotional. They animate the race with their colorful personalities and flair. A lot of times you will see them hiring their friends as teammates or a family member on the team staff. Their entourage helps them feel supported, which is key to their success and sometimes failings. Climbers are arguably some of the most successful riders in the sport, but without a team of trustworthy people around they are predisposed to self-destruction.

The Makings of a Climber

Pro Rider Examples
Egan Bernal, Alberto Contador,
    Katie Hall, Marco Pantani

Physique
Smaller stature
Lean
Lightweight

Physical Strengths
Strong power-threshold zones
Strong endurance
Favors out of-the-saddle riding
    to develop power
Prefers explosive riding
Can change rhythm quickly
Strong on all types of climbs
Strong multiday recovery

Physical Weaknesses
All time trials
Flat roads
Crosswinds
Rough road
Sprint finishes

Mental Strengths
High pain tolerance
Aggressive
Determined
Intense short and long focus
Strong mental endurance

Mental Weaknesses
Executes on impulse and emotion
Often overly driven on emotion

Ideal Races/Events
Mountaintop finish during
    stage races
Mountainous one-day events
Hill climbs

Ideal Race-Winning Strategy
Attack! Climbers embrace pain and
love to attack. They are the first to
attack in the most difficult spot on
a climb and then solo away. If that
doesn't work, they attack, follow,
attack . . . until the elastic snaps.

Classics Time Trial Rider

The classics time trial rider is an endurance-centric athlete who matches this ability with unmatched short, explosive power, creating a unique ability to time trial. They are the hard men and women of cycling who embrace difficult terrain, harsh conditions, and adventure. They can ride solo off the front of a group, climb medium-length hills well, time trial strongly, and ride at a high level in the peloton. This rider is like an engineer who is methodical in their approach to almost everything in life. They love to analyze data and solve complicated problems and are rarely seen of out of control. They approach situations with logic rather than emotion. They rarely go into competitions without a solid plan that they've forged through research and experience. They have a very specific way of doing things, which lends itself to a certain degree of stubbornness. If this develops, they can get in their own way. Whether it's at a spring classic or a gravel event, these athletes are gritty and are not shaken easily.

The Makings of a Classics TT Rider

Pro Rider Examples
Fabian Cancellara, Bradley Wiggins, Chloé Dygert, Thomas De Gendt

Physique
Taller
Muscular
Long femurs

Physical Strengths
Strong endurance
Powerful
Favors in-the-saddle riding to develop power
Prefers steadier riding overall
Explosive ability
Can do both short, explosive efforts and longer, sustained TT-like efforts
Steady shallow climbing

Physical Weaknesses
Long, sustained climbs
Long climbs with terrain changes
Multiday stage races or hard efforts

Mental Strengths
Gritty
Determined
Resilient
Strong mental endurance
Intense short focus

Mental Weaknesses
Often too focused on other riders
Struggles with intense focus for long periods of time
Uncomfortable with physical pressure on climbs

Ideal Races/Events
Rolling endurance events
Events with rough terrain or difficult weather conditions like rain, wind, cold, or mud
Short and long time trials
Endurance time trials

Ideal Race-Winning Strategy
In a hard, long race of attrition, break the group down to a select few. Win with a strong solo attack or ride away from the other riders.

Classics Sprinter

The classics sprinter is an endurance-centric athlete who converts unmatched short, explosive power into a potent sprint. They are also hardmen and -women of cycling who embrace difficult terrain, harsh conditions, and adventure. They can make the key selections on short climbs, crosswinds, or rough terrain, and can ride at a high level in the peloton. Then, this rider closes the deal by beating everyone in a finish-line sprint. The career most similar to the sprinter is a fighter pilot. We've all seen the film *Top Gun*, right? To be a fast jet pilot, you must be confident and quick, and able to do what's needed, even when the going gets tough. If you're a fighter pilot, you have to be ready to fight and stay calm amongst the chaos. You have to have the right height-to-weight ratio to fit in the cockpit—and be ready to jump out in emergencies. Fighter jets can go more than twice the speed of sound, or 25 miles in a minute. Only the best pilots in the world can fly a plane that fast: You have to be able to think and act very quickly. You must be comfortable flying in the pack but also flying solo.

Classics sprinters frequently have to put out giant efforts at big speeds in a very chaotic and dangerous environment. They hide in the peloton, conserving energy and waiting until it's their turn to launch. They rely heavily on their teammates, but ultimately it's up to them to get the job done. They cover moves, following the train to outsprint the less-explosive riders at the end of a grueling race. They do not give up easily and might try lots of different approaches until they get the result they want. They have a keen ability to read the race and react accordingly. Their downfall is that they are often overconfident in their own abilities, so they don't always do the necessary positioning to set themselves up for the win. They aren't afraid of situations others would deem dangerous, so they are predisposed to taking risks unnecessarily, leading to crashes. Classics sprinters are ready to risk it all in the name of glory.

The Makings of a Classics Sprinter

Pro Rider Examples
Tom Boonen, Peter Sagan, Kirsten
  Wild, Greg Van Avermaet

Physique
Shorter, more solid rider
Muscular
Ideal center of gravity

Physical Strengths
Strong endurance
Powerful
Strong at producing power both
  in and out of the saddle
Prefers non-steady riding
Explosive ability
Can do short, explosive efforts
  and is a good sprinter
Good on short, explosive climbs
Strong in super-short time trials

Physical Weaknesses
Long, sustained climbs
Long climbs with terrain changes
Multiday stage races or hard efforts
Long time trials

Mental Strengths
Gritty
Aggressive
Determined
Resilient
Strong mental endurance
Intense short focus

Mental Weaknesses
Often too focused on other riders
Struggles with intense focus for
  long periods of time
Uncomfortable with physical
  pressure on climbs

Ideal Races/Events
Endurance events on rolling terrain
Events with rough terrain or
  difficult weather conditions like
  rain, wind, cold, or mud
Gravel races
Short time trials
Criteriums
Shorter road races

Ideal Race-Winning Strategy
Explosive, surging race that comes
down to a small group in the finish,
from which this sprinter will win
the sprint.

THE FOUR
PILLARS

04

FITNESS: THE FORM PERFORMANCE ENGINE

I n one of my first winter training camps as a pro rider, I was introduced to the mythical concept of "zone 2." We were out on a ride in Europe. You see photos of these camps on bike websites, with riders in their new kits, bundled up to stay warm, putting in the hours ahead of something like Paris–Nice or Milan–San Remo.

On one of these rides, we turned up a fairly long climb, and before I knew it, we were going Mach 10. As far as I knew, this was supposed to be an easy base ride—zone 2, right? Well, one of my teammates came up next to me riding like it was a mountaintop finish in the Tour de France. I looked over at him and asked, "What are you doing?" He said, "It's a zone 2 ride."

I was confused. Afterward, he explained that he was staying well below his 410-watt threshold, riding a steady 400 watts on the climb. As far as he was concerned, everything under threshold was zone 2.

Eventually, zone 2 became a running joke on our team and with other friends in the peloton. But we never seemed to do much to change the way we thought of these power zones. We didn't talk to our coaches about tweaking our training to focus on what's actually going on in races and how we should prepare for it. We just stuck to the cookie-cutter formula.

As I began coaching riders through CINCH, I started to consider what zones we actually needed to be focusing on as riders and racers.

It became clear to me that there are 11 actions in cycling—real-world cycling at the races, gran fondos, and group rides you love to ride and in which you'd love to do better. I have also seen that in all cycling events, whether it is the Tour de France or your local throwdown, the pace is constantly changing. The riders who succeed are those who can shift gears throughout their 11 zones to handle the terrain, the race dynamics and, most important, to play the pacing game to their strengths.

The FORM Method is built to train you for the dynamics of a race with its changes in pace and unexpected bursts. You need to refine all of these zones if you want to have the full arsenal of weapons at your fingertips when the race action heats up or the gran fondo gets moving.

The key to cycling is efficiency. The simple mechanics of the bike take you and create a super-efficient, low-energy form of transportation. In racing, we are constantly looking for ways to take this and make the ultimate efficiency sport. When we talk about efficiency, we're looking at economy. How do we get the most out of our energy—that is, how do we get more mileage with less exertion? When you use the PowerTrain Zones (PTZs) correctly, you will maximize your economy.

Underlying Principles of the PowerTrain Zones

Before we dive into the specifics of the 11 PTZs, let's talk about three key variables that will help define the zones, beyond your raw power measurements.

The first variable to note for any given PTZ is fuel type. Fundamentally, your body relies on either fat or glycogen to power any kind of effort, cycling or otherwise. The lower four, the Endurance Zones, burn primarily fat. Once we arrive at the three Threshold zones and the four Explosive zones, your body switches over to glycogen. Think of it like a hybrid car. When you're driving slowly around

FIGURE 4.1. Muscle Strain/RPE scale

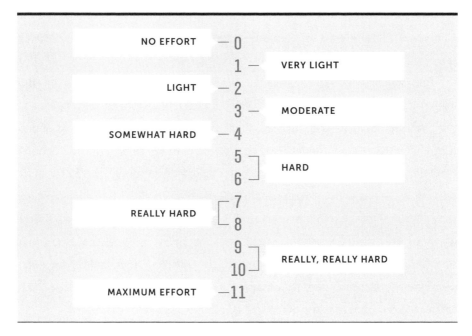

How hard are you going? It takes practice, but using RPE to monitor your effort will develop your sensitivity to the PowerTrain Zones.

town, picking up the kids at soccer or getting groceries, it uses electric, which is more efficient. Then, when you are up to highway speeds, running late for work, the combustion engine kicks in for speed and performance. Maybe this isn't a perfect analogy, but the point is that we are all running hybrid engines. Refer to Chapter 5 for more on fueling the PTZs and how nutrition relates to performance.

The second component of PTZs is the muscle strain you create during an effort. Each PTZ has a corresponding RPE or sensation of muscle strain. When you start to train with PTZs, you should monitor these sensations in your body (Figure 4.1). Ask yourself, what does the effort feel like to you? Are you smashing the pedals like Mark Cavendish, or are you gently spinning like you would on a bike path on a Sunday afternoon? It can be quantified, albeit somewhat subjectively, using the Rating of Perceived Exertion (RPE). I've modified the traditional 10-point scale to contain 11 points, to better align with the 11 PTZs (I'll explain more in Chapter 11). RPE is used to label the intensity of your effort, and it works well once you get used to discerning the nuances of your exertion.

The third and final variable is lactate buildup. This is the by-product of intense exercise. Your muscles can buffer it to a point, meaning your body can process and remove it, but eventually it will accumulate too rapidly and result in a loss of performance. PTZs 1 to 4 produce little to no lactate. In the three Threshold zones, you'll be producing lactate, but you're able to buffer it (although at PTZ 7, you're right at the limit of what you can handle). PTZs 8 to 11 aren't sustainable for longer than a few minutes, partly due to muscle strain and partly due to lactate buildup.

So let's dive into the specifics of the PowerTrain Zones. I realize that 11 zones may feel overwhelming at first, but once you spend a few weeks riding the workouts based on the PTZs, you'll quickly learn the language. At the end of the chapter, we'll help you calculate your own PTZs following a field test.

Endurance

Let's begin with the four Endurance zones, as this is where all cyclists should begin regardless of their level of experience or fitness. To return to our house analogy, this is the foundation upon which we will build your cycling house. Do you want it to be a studio apartment or a 20,000-square-foot mansion? The bigger your Endurance base—your foundation—the more potential you have to develop your cycling form.

All four of the Endurance zones are fat-burning zones. The muscular strain you'll experience in these PTZs ranges from 1 to 4, so not very much. If you are out on a ride and planning to only do PTZ 2, don't let your friends goad you into sprinting for a town line. Don't be tempted to chase a short Strava KOM. Save those high-muscular-strain, glycogen-depleting efforts for another day. In addition to building your aerobic base, Endurance zones are used for rest intervals between hard efforts, such as Threshold or Explosive intervals.

PTZ 1: Base

Imagine a friend of yours who doesn't ride. You're trying to get them hooked on cycling, but you know they'll be turned off if you drop them on the first hill and leave them for dead on the side of the road. That gentle pace you should use to take them on their first 10-mile loop is PTZ 1. Muscle strain is 1 out of a possible 11. This feels like there is little tension on your muscles. Spin gently, use as few calories of fuel as possible. Don't drop your buddy!

PTZ 2: Low Medium

I imagine PTZ 2 as my winter pace. It is ideal for those rare days in February when the weather breaks, you get a stretch of sunny weather and dry roads, and you head out on that first four-hour ride of the year. You can't smash a fast group ride at this point, but you're not going to go as slow as PTZ 1 unless you've been off the bike for an extended period. Sometimes this is referred to as a tempo pace, but that's a pretty vague term. This zone feels comfortable, with just a little bit of tension on the muscles, no burn in the muscles, just like slowly walking up the stairs. Muscle strain is a 2, and you're still using only fat as fuel.

PTZ 3: Medium

Now we are starting to ratchet up the speed in the Endurance PTZs. Imagine a brisk paceline that is trying to fend off a chasing peloton. Or you could be out on a solo ride shorter than three hours, still focusing on burning fat but riding at a muscle strain level of 3. This feels like a small increase in muscle tension from PTZ 2, no burn, but with an increased respiration rate. This feels just like doing an uphill hike—you'll be tired when you get home but not destroyed.

PTZ 4: High Medium

This is the end of our fat-burning zones and the type of effort you'd use in a breakaway move that is two hours or shorter. Again, we move one notch higher on the muscle strain scale to level 4. This zone has a higher muscle tension, where you feel a stronger muscular effort, but no burn in the legs. Your respiration rate is higher, but very controlled. This should feel just like doing continuous step-ups in the gym. You could use PTZ 4 on a steady climb. Unless you're an absolute beast, you won't break any KOMs, but you'll get to the top fairly quickly, and you won't dip into your glycogen stores. Sometimes, when pro riders drop back from the peloton on the final climb of an epic mountain stage, they'll ride to the finish around PTZ 4 so they do less damage to their muscles and avoid tapping their glycogen stores. You can deploy it strategically in that way, or you can use it if you're totally cracked and can't manage a threshold effort.

Threshold

When most people imagine race pace, they are thinking of the Threshold zones. This is hard riding. You are pushing close to the effort you can physically sustain for more than an hour or two, depending on how fit or experienced you are. If you are trying to get a PR on the longest climb in your area, racing the local weeknight time trial series, or off the front of a road race in a breakaway, you're usually in one of these three Threshold zones.

It is important to train for this level of effort, but too often I see riders who exclusively ride in their Threshold zones. Perhaps they just think that if they aren't suffering, they aren't making fitness gains. Whatever their reasoning, you cannot train exclusively in these zones. For one, the muscular fatigue and damage is too great for most riders to handle. People who ride this way end up overtrained and burned out. The second reason to avoid overdoing Threshold work has to do with your body's fueling system. In PTZs 5 through 7, your body shifts its fuel source to glycogen. This fuel tank isn't unlimited, which is why you cannot ride indefinitely at Threshold pace. If you are constantly forcing your body to tap glycogen stores and not training it to burn fat, your performance at lower PTZs will suffer. Your hybrid car will lose its electric power supply, and then you're left with an inefficient gas-only vehicle.

PTZ 5: Low Threshold

Every zone is important, but Low Threshold is the gold standard of our FORM Method. It is what we do differently than other training programs because it is fueled by a mixture of fat and glycogen. At this pace, you can produce high levels of lactate, but you can continue to clear it as you make efforts above threshold, like when you cover attacks or push up short hills. There is a fine line between where you produce as much lactate as you can clear and where you can't; this zone rides that line perfectly for up to an hour at a time. A mountain bike race is a great example of where this zone can shine, allowing you to attack small hills and technical sections while recovering between each key section. The Low Threshold has a muscular strain score of 5. You should feel a deep muscular effort where you feel some burning sensation. Respiration rate now is higher, but it can be controlled with a focus on the exhale of the breath.

PTZ 6: Threshold

This zone is a step above Low Threshold, slightly higher in its muscle strain at a 6 out of 11, and also not suitable for efforts that are quite as long as Low Threshold. This zone feels equal in muscular load and burn, and it's where most athletes end up by default when they do intense, longer efforts like climbs at or just above 20 minutes in length. Respiration rate is quick, but it can be controlled with mindful focus on the exhales. You feel muscular pressure while a cardiovascular pressure keeps your effort in check if you want to keep going. You can use this zone on extended climbs or time trials, but your ability to clear lactate will be compromised given the elevated pace. In general, you'll be able to handle fewer surges and accelerations. This and all of the remaining PowerTrain Zones will rely on glycogen for fuel.

PTZ 7: High Threshold

Here we reach the limit of what your body can handle in terms of sustained effort. Sure, you can buffer lactate at this intensity, but if you're already at this zone, don't think you'll be able to go with the climbers when they attack the group on the steepest pitches of the race's key climb. Or, if you choose to settle into this blistering pace in a time trial effort, beware the leg-sapping rollers or head-winds that could push you into the red. You're already revving close to your maximum. This zone has a muscular strain score of 7 and the sensation is a euphoric burn. This PTZ feels better physically than PTZs 5 and 6 as the burn overcomes the deep muscular pain that both prior PTZs have. Respiration rate is high, feeling controlled when you begin the effort, but gradually losing control of the breath consistency as the effort progresses.

Explosive

The most exciting highlights you'll see on a replay of a Tour de France stage or any other major pro bike race come to you courtesy of the Explosive PTZs. These zones are where champions are made or, more often than not, the group ride is won.

Throughout the course of a race or competitive ride, you should be constantly changing gears in terms of your PTZs. You ease into the Endurance zones to recover. You use the Threshold zones for hard, sustained efforts. The Explosive zones are special because you have a very limited number of matches to burn—you can only redline your engine into these zones a few times before you are unable to recover from the efforts.

So use these zones wisely. And, as you'll see when we explain workouts in detail, use these zones in combination with other PTZs to train your body to shift into high gear, recover, and then do it again. Usually, it isn't the first or second attack that sticks—it's the third or fourth. It's our goal to train you to last until that crucial moment and then be able to make the move.

PTZ 8: Nuclear

Similar to PTZ 5, which combines elements of Endurance and Threshold, the Nuclear zone is a crossroads between the Threshold zones, where we rely on the cardiovascular system, and the Explosive zones, which are all about the muscular system. A Nuclear effort usually lasts 2 to 4 minutes. That will feel like an eternity as we hit an 8 out of 11 on the scale of muscular strain. It feels like an explosive muscular effort that is cardiovascularly conservative at first, but toward the end of your effort you reach maximum cardiovascular output, forcing your muscular effort to back off. This ends up being a lung-searing effort as you cross into the final time in this zone. But this effort is actually repeatable. It's a critical tool to bridge gaps or put your rivals into the box on climbs.

PTZ 9: Long Surge

Remember how I was saying that the Low Threshold zone is a critical pace to maintain so that you can handle repeated bursts of speed but still clear lactate? Well, the Long Surge is the PTZ that you've been waiting for. You're cruising in the bunch, steady at PTZ 5, and then out of nowhere, someone attacks. You know you can close the gap in about a minute, and you know that if you return to Low Threshold, you can recover. So you engage the Long Surge and chase down the break . . . or you make a break of your own and it sticks. This PTZ has a muscular strain score of 9. This zone feels very similar to the Nuclear effort, meaning it starts out muscular and at the end is met with intense, lung-searing discomfort. But there is a subtle difference: The Long Surge is disruptive. Nuclear is primarily used in a controlled fashion in order to make it to the end of an effort or a 2- to 4-minute push. In contrast, the Long Surge is part of an explosive, but repeatable, effort to disrupt another's pace or rhythm. When you are using the Long Surge PTZ, you are usually accelerating to it for approximately one minute, and then going back to a lower PTZ. Riding in this zone feels aggressive and disruptive.

PTZ 10: Short Surge

Like a Long Surge, the Short Surge is a tool to cover attacks or gain separation from your rivals at a crucial moment in the race. However, this PTZ is far more explosive and intense. It is repeatable, but not for many times before you're cooked.

It will also take longer to recover from this effort, which is nearly an all-out sprint. The Short Surge PTZ has a muscular strain score of 10 and feels deeply muscular, similar to a sprint. However, it is a slightly different sensation from a sprint. Since the objective of this zone is to provide you with a platform to launch an effective yet repeatable attack or surge, the effort must feel just like that to avoid going too hard. So the feel is an easier muscular sprint in which you are holding back for the first 15 seconds, but the last 15 seconds will feel like an all-out effort.

PTZ 11: Maximum Explosive Strength

Finally, we have the pure all-out sprint. This is not a repeatable effort; this is when you're charging to the finish of the race, emptying everything in your tank to win the day. In training, this effort is almost more of a benchmark for CINCH athletes. It helps us gauge the development of their top-end power, almost like you'd do with a maximum-weight strength rep in the gym. The MES sprint has a muscular strain score of 11. This zone and effort feel exactly like the name implies: your maximum, all-out effort.

The PowerTrain Zones in Action

Now that I've laid out the 11 PTZs, I can imagine what you're thinking: *This seems complicated.* You'll have to work to memorize them all, or maybe you'll tape a long sheet of paper to your bike's top tube to keep track of the difference between PTZs 6 and 7 or 3 and 4. I get it. I have worked with many coaches over the years and it can be hard to adjust to a new system. But here is your motivation to stick to the 11 zones of the FORM Method: This is way more than a training framework. This is a way for you to harness the natural engine that is your body to achieve maximum efficiency, like I mentioned earlier in this chapter.

Whenever I watch a pro bike race, I can pick apart the details of what is happening in the bunch. I can see who is working hard, who is sitting in, what strategies they're playing to have their best chance of winning. So, let me describe a race where all 11 of the PTZs are used, each with a specific purpose.

Let's tune in to stage 19 of the 2018 Tour de France, the final mountain stage of the race through the Pyrenees. This 200-kilometer route takes on some of the region's epic climbs. It starts with the Col d'Aspin and the Col du Tourmalet, followed by the Col des Borderes, the Col du Soulor, and the Col d'Aubisque before plummeting to the finish.

As is the case in almost every major race, the first hour is a wild ride. Guys are attacking left and right to try to make it into the breakaway, or simply surviving, praying they don't get dropped with the Paris finish only days away.

I can promise you that the start out of Lourdes is raging fast as they fly up the valley to the day's first climb. Riders are spiking into PTZs 8, 9, and even 10 to close gaps or attack off the front of the bunch. If they use their zones well—and I bet most of them can—they hit the accelerator on one of these attacks, and then if they get caught or find their way into a breakaway, they settle back to Low Threshold zone (PTZ 5). If you think your weekly interval workout is painful, just imagine these repeated accelerations in the peloton, just an hour into what would turn out to be a six-hour day for most of the guys in the bunch.

You can bet that once the breakaway finally sticks, most of the riders' glycogen stores are pretty tapped out from the repeated efforts. Fortunately, as things relax in the peloton, they are able to settle into one of the fat-burning zones, probably High Medium (PTZ 4). This gives them a chance to refuel, taking on more glycogen, which they're sure to need later in the day.

Up the road, a pretty large breakaway group is clicking along, gradually extending their lead. At this point, you might wonder how those guys pace themselves with more than 150 kilometers still to race, not to mention the four categorized climbs at the end. This is where strategic use of PTZs shines, especially the four Endurance zones.

Riders in a breakaway like this are in a tug-of-war between two different needs. They need to preserve their energy for a six-hour day of racing, ideally enough that they can be racing for the win by the end of the day. But they also need to keep extending their gap on the peloton, or else their breakaway will be caught and all the effort in the Explosive zones during the first hour of racing will be wasted.

So, they use their zones strategically on the undulating terrain through the valley leading up to the Col d'Aspin. When they have an opportunity to gain momentum, they push into the High Medium (PTZ 4) zone. They can't hold that effort for more than a couple hours, so it has to be spent at the right times. When they are carrying momentum, they can shift into an easier zone, possibly Medium (PTZ 3) or even Low Medium (PTZ 2), if they get to a fast downhill or a section of tailwind. As the paceline rotates, everyone gets a little break after their turn when they can drop down to PTZ 1 to recover as much as possible and use as few calories as they can.

On the Aspin, the day's first climb, they probably could hit it at Threshold (PTZ 6), maybe even High Threshold (PTZ 7). It's only about a 12-kilometer climb, so it shouldn't take these pros more than 40 minutes or so. Instead, with so much racing left, they play it safe and ride a steady Low Threshold (PTZ 5) so they can effectively clear lactate and continue burning some of their fat stores along with some glycogen.

The breakaway doesn't last over the climbs, so let's focus on the action in the group of GC riders, which eventually catches all the escapees. The top GC teams light things up on the Tourmalet, a long, steady climb that's much more of a highway than most of the climbs in the Pyrenees. Each team puts a key climbing domestique on the front to set the tempo. If they want to save this domestique for the climbs to come, he'll ride a steady Low Threshold, able to respond to accelerations but ride within himself, clearing lactate as he goes. Or, if the domestique only needs to rip the peloton apart on the Tourmalet, he might go as high as PTZ 6 or 7.

After they top out on the Tourmalet, almost 7,000 feet above sea level, the peloton has a long, steady descent and then rolling valley roads before the final climbs. Here, they are recovering in the Endurance zones as much as possible. They're also taking on as much fuel as they can to replenish their glycogen stores for the final Threshold and Explosive efforts in the last 50 kilometers of racing.

This is where we get into the most interesting aspects of strategy as it relates to the use of PTZs. The best riders know how their strengths match up to those of their competitors, and they try to position themselves to take maximum advantage.

On that stair-stepping climb up Borderes, Soulor, and Aubisque, a rider could take the scorched-earth approach. He could be confident that his High Medium zone is better than anyone else's. So, he would take them to the limit, using his teammates' and attacks of his own to make sure everyone's glycogen stores are empty by the key points of the climb. Then, he would settle into PTZ 4 and feel confident that no one else can maintain the pace. This might be the type of strategy a rider like Tom Dumoulin would use, given his massive engine.

But no one decides to go all-in with that kind of strategy in stage 19 of this Tour de France. Instead, the key riders decide to launch attacks as they get closer and closer to the final mountaintop finish of the 21-day race.

Many of the attacks, like those by Primož Roglič, Dan Martin, or Mikel Landa, fall into the categories of Nuclear (PTZ 8) or Long Surge (PTZ 9) efforts. They're designed to create separation. And they do that, at least for a little bit. They're also meant to drop riders from the bunch, to whittle things down. They also manage to do that, dropping a couple of race leader Geraint Thomas's key Sky teammates, Michał Kwiatkowski and Egan Bernal.

The small group of GC superstars keeps reeling in the attackers. Nothing sticks on the cloudy slopes of the Aubisque—that is until Roglič hits them with one final attack. With the summit only about 750 meters away, he rides away with a Short Surge (PTZ 10) effort that can't be matched by any of the other riders.

From there, he flies down the 10-kilometer descent, extending his lead while also settling down to the Endurance zones for a final breather. When he gets to the flat valley roads, he rides a High Threshold (PTZ 7) time trial all the way to victory at the finish.

Behind, Thomas surprises the group by sprinting to second place, reminding us all that he used to race on the velodrome, with a Maximum Explosive Strength (PTZ 11) burst of speed.

The race is still not over for the majority of the peloton, though. The riders in the grupetto, some of them sprinters who are dreaming of a chance to win stage 21 on the Champs-Élysées, have to finish. And they have to do it within a specified time cut or they're out of the race. So, like the riders racing for the win, they use their zones strategically, gaining momentum whenever they can and conserving momentum and fuel as the opportunities come up.

All of these little details are what makes cycling such a complex sport. It is the kind of sport that can crush you in nearly every scenario you face. The key is seeing success in each of them.

Each PTZ Is a Tool in Your Kit

In all honesty, you won't likely get selected to race the Tour de France every July, but I'm giving you the tools to ride like those pros. That means looking at the 11 PowerTrain Zones and viewing them as a Swiss Army knife. All the tools are right there, and they are your way to unlock your potential. The zones are your tools to give yourself a chance to ride to your full potential, no matter what scenario you're in.

Developing these zones will take time, though. This is particularly obvious when it comes to fuel usage: Your body will need to get accustomed to shifting between fat and glycogen for fuel. The body is naturally inclined to use glycogen as fuel. That is the path of least resistance, and if you've conditioned your body to expect Threshold efforts and frequent high-sugar fuels, like energy gels, that's all it will know how to do. Even though the math says you have fat-burning zones, if you don't teach your body how to burn fat in those zones, it's not going to do it.

The workouts in the FORM Method are designed to teach your body to go back and forth between sugar and fat fuels by switching zones during the workout. This is one of the keys to successfully employing the PTZ system. We are training your body to pivot, to change gears depending on your needs in a given race scenario.

This process will take some time, but trust me: The end result will give you the power to control your efforts in any race or ride, and to push yourself beyond what you thought was possible.

I learned this the hard way in Europe as a pro rider. I was relying on conventional training methods, based on FTP. I fully believed that if I did 400 watts at threshold, then I could ride 300 watts and above and I'd be OK. I assumed I would not be using glycogen, not doing damage to my muscles. It was zone 2, right? But I wasn't training correctly or using my zones correctly.

I will help you create these zones and understand what they do, but you have to put in the time to train them to work the right way.

Find Your PowerTrain Zones

I have created a testing protocol to find a baseline around which you'll build the different PTZs. You may already work with power zones that differ from the Power-Train Zones, and that's OK. We are programming you with the ability to succeed in all competitive and terrain scenarios. The baseline number established from the 12-minute effort described on the next page will serve as the input number for the calculation of all of the zones.

To perform this test and calculate your PTZs, you'll need a power meter. But if you don't have a power meter there's another way to set your baseline: use RPE instead. See "Using RPE in Lieu of Power Meters" on pp. 196–198 to learn how the RPE scale corresponds to the PTZs.

Please don't stress about the test. If your number is higher or lower than you thought it would be, it doesn't make a difference. Today you are taking a big step in becoming the best cyclist you can be. Now get out there and crush it!

Set Your PowerTrain Zones

Part of the purpose of this exercise is to see what your natural tendencies are in relation to your Rider Type, so I am giving you limited instructions. Just try to evenly distribute the power throughout the duration of the 12 minutes. Don't worry about finding the perfect road for this test; a few slight downhills or corners are just fine. If the road is representative of what you'll ordinarily be training on, then it is great for your PTZ test.

TOTAL RIDE TIME: 1 hour

15 min. warm-up

Medium Effort: 10 min. (RPE 3) 90 rpm

10 min. easy

All-Out Effort: 12 min. at the highest power you can hold for this duration

15 min. cooldown

How to Analyze the Data

1. Look at the trend of the 12-minute effort. Is it linear, does it build, or does it decline? The trend most likely represents the Rider Type physical characteristics as well as the Rider Type mental tendencies that you have.
2. Look at the period of time between 8 and 12 minutes. The average power in these 4 minutes will be set as your High Threshold zone. If you started slow and then smashed the last 4 minutes, retake the test and try to distribute your effort more evenly.
3. To find your PTZs, multiply your High Threshold number by the factor below.

FACTOR	YOUR PTZ
0.59	1 (BASE)
0.62	2 (LOW MEDIUM)
0.67	3 (MEDIUM)
0.7	4 (HIGH MEDIUM)
0.8	5 (LOW THRESHOLD)
0.95	6 (THRESHOLD)
1.0	7 (HIGH THRESHOLD)
1.05	8 (NUCLEAR)
1.07	9 (LONG SURGE)
1.25	10 (SHORT SURGE)
1.51	11 (MAXIMUM EXPLOSIVE STRENGTH)

RPE = Rating of perceived exertion

RPM = Revolutions per minute/cadence

05

HIGH-PERFORMANCE NUTRITION

When we first get into cycling, we don't care much about nutrition. Riding isn't about diets or weighing your food—it is about getting out with friends, hopping in a local group ride or race, or just watching the Tour de France and getting pumped to get on the bike. It used to be so simple—we ride, we have fun, and then we do it again the next day.

The concept of nutrition doesn't come into play until we become more serious about our riding. Maybe that's why nutrition is one of the most challenging aspects of competitive cycling. A lot of riders don't think about it until they decide it's the path to better results, faster times up the local climb, or even a pro contract. Then, it becomes an obsession as riders try to fine-tune their diets to lose weight. From what I've seen, there is a lot of confusion out there about what works and what doesn't. And above all, there's a general misconception that diet is an "easy button" to make a good cyclist a great one.

A lot of that confusion and struggle comes from a culture that cycling has created for decades. Cycling convention teaches us from a young age that we can simply cut back on food, little by little, to achieve increasingly better performance. The temptation is irresistible: With a bit more willpower, I can eat a little less, weigh a little less, and climb a little better. But that's not the right way, not the healthy way, to riding your best. The FORM Method's approach to nutrition is quite simple. You just assess the nutritional needs of your rides and you meet those needs to fuel properly and recover well.

Instead of starting with nutrition and treating it like a volume dial that can be adjusted infinitely without changing the music that's playing, we should start with the music itself: our riding, training, and racing. How much volume do we need for things to be just right? Are we going to rock out today? Well, crank it up: Eat more carbohydrates to fuel a big, hard ride. Is it more of a mellow evening when we play something relaxed? It should probably be soft and low—fewer calories to match a recovery-day spin.

Our 3-Sigma Nutrition System demystifies nutrition and breaks it down into three simple criteria to help you plan the fundamentals of your diet: Purpose, Composition, and Timing.

Purpose

We've all found ourselves at an awkward party at some point in our lives. Unless you're an immensely outgoing person, uninhibited and happy to break the ice, you've probably gravitated toward the food. It's so much easier to just stand there and pick at the cheese plate or to try all of the different dips than it is to talk to strangers or coworkers you barely know. Admit it, though: This is just mindless eating. When we talk about the Purpose sigma of the 3-Sigma System, this is about as far off the rails as you can get.

Don't feel bad if you've done this before. Food almost always makes us feel more comfortable. It helps pass the time as we snack on gas station junk food during road trips. And it can break up the day, giving us a 60-minute escape from work stress in the form of a turkey sandwich and a bag of chips. Plus, for many people, eating is subliminally tied to time spent with friends and family, like Thanksgiving Day or Super Bowl parties. What's more, over the course of many years, our eating habits are reinforced by daily practice. This means we

A Hard Lesson Learned in Fueling Consistently

Let me tell you a story that really drives home the fact that nutrition is all about your body's fueling and performance on the bike. In 2009, our Garmin-Slipstream team was using the Giro d'Italia as a prep race—it wasn't a priority for our team back then. I came into it unfit, not on point, not mentally in race mode.

I was trying to use this tough, sketchy 21-day race to get fit for races later in the season. That was the root of my problems on stage 10, midway through the race.

A lot of times if you're not highly confident or focused, you're perhaps more relaxed about preparation. You don't pay as much attention to stage profiles. I was just in Italy to adapt, to take whatever was thrown at me.

This particular stage was a medium mountain stage, typical for the Giro. The stage profile looked like a flat line all day with a few little rollers you could jump your BMX bike off of. There was a smooth climb toward end, then an uphill finish, which I always like.

I wasn't a factor in the mountains up to this point in the Giro. When I'd ordinarily be on the attack, I went into those stages focused on building fitness, sitting up on the climbs, riding with the group to stay in my zones to train. On the rest day (a day with no racing to help the racers recover in a Grand Tour), before the 10th stage to Pinerolo, I didn't eat very much as I was tired and had lost my appetite. The next morning, I felt rejuvenated and got my hunger back, so I ate a good breakfast before the stage.

As soon as the gun went off, everyone was on the attack. I remember coming up this little climb in the beginning—there was a big attack, splitting the peloton into pieces and forming a breakaway. I had good legs, so I followed the move. It had Damiano Cunego, Michele Scarponi . . . heavy hitters who were slightly down on GC at that point. My teammate Bradley Wiggins went in this move, too.

As we went over the top, the break was established. Did I plan to get into a breakaway that day? No. But there were so many badasses in that move that I couldn't ➡

just sit up and say, "I'm not ready for this break." We started cruising along and I was excited that I was in it. *Finally*, I thought to myself, *I'm part of this race after just sitting in the group for days*.

It didn't take long for my excitement to change to worry. There were some really strong guys in this move, along with all of those Italian stars, plus some crazy-fast Colombian climbers from the Selle Italia team. As we were riding, we started to come across mountains that were not really on the profile. I kept thinking that we must have already made it to the final climb—there's no way these climbs could be the flat roads shown on the profile! It got so bad that I ended up going back to the car, asking where we were on the route. To my dismay, it turned out that we weren't even halfway through the stage!

We got a little bit past halfway and all these guys started attacking each other on a new, very hard, and, of course, unlisted climb. It was just insane. They were lighting it up, and I was starting to run out of fuel. I couldn't ride in the zones I needed to use for these nasty attacks.

Before I knew it, I had to sit up and I was dropped out of the break. It ended up being the stage-winning breakaway and those guys knew it. At that point, we had a 20-minute gap on the peloton. I was in the middle of nowhere dropping back, embarrassed, and what's worse, I was coming unglued. My legs were cooked. I was bonking. I felt cramps in my hamstrings and my quads; even my arms started to fatigue. It was surreal; I was all alone for the next hour or so, just on a bike ride on closed roads through the heart of Italy.

Finally, the peloton caught me, and I couldn't even stay with them. I went straight through the group and out the back. Then I started to realize how big this problem had become. I had a big code-red bonk, I was falling apart, and there were still two big climbs to go in the finale of the stage.

Races like the Giro have a time cut: Every rider has to get across the finish line by a certain time after the winner; the length of time is a set percentage of the stage winner's finishing time. Don't make it and your stage race is over. Well, when the break has 20 minutes' lead, and you're dropped from the peloton, suddenly you're in time-cut country!

I had to turn myself inside out to chase the time cut. I was doing 200 watts, and it felt like 400 watts because I only had my medium and low zones. I was so bonked that I could only use fat for fuel. I had to chase to get to the grupetto, and I finally caught them. The sprinters were talking and joking—and I was thinking, *This is not right . . . I should not be here, not be so weak*.

In total Giro fashion, the last downhill off that climb into the final finish was all dirt. I was trying to get down this hill with all the kamikaze sprinters, and the downhills are where they make up their time on the peloton. They race down these hills faster than the peloton. I was trying to keep up, all the while so bonked I was seeing four of everything and purple giraffes.

Thankfully, I made it to the finish, but it was a very humbling experience and a huge lesson about the importance of fueling properly with the right nutrition.

are up against well-established, powerful forces when we want to change our eating habits.

First, we need to identify a Purpose that each meal must serve. When you sit down to breakfast before work or head out to grab lunch at the burrito joint next door or cook up your dinner, I want you to ask yourself one simple question: Why am I eating now?

Why Are You Eating?

This question addresses our struggles with eating on autopilot. There are a variety of reasons to eat. The most obvious would be that you're hungry. That's fine, but what is making you feel that way, and how does it relate to everything else going on in your life, both on and off the bike?

Some meals should prime you for an important ride coming up that day. If you're headed out on a hard lunch ride or a throwdown at the weeknight crit series, your nutrition should reflect that to fuel your performance. Lots of athletes find that riding before work in the morning is an ideal time for a productive workout. If you take that approach, the "why" of your lunch should be geared toward recovery.

And believe it or not, even some "unhealthy" meals can serve a purpose, too. Overall, I want you to give your nutrition the same focus and commitment as a 100-mile training ride, but there is a therapeutic purpose to relaxing a little bit. If you're catching up with a few old friends, how much harm would a beer and a burger do? That's still a purpose. I just want you to make sure you are getting the desired outcome of the food you consume. If you always start with the "why" of a meal, the rest will follow.

It is pretty straightforward to understand the general relationships between the food you eat and the physical effect it has on your body, but getting more specific, like calculating just how much of a food you should eat, is unfamiliar to a lot of people. That is why we developed a macronutrient calculator (see Table 5.1, p. 86) that helps you calculate your macro-nutritional needs based on your workout plan and your body weight.

When you're eating to fuel your next workout or a race, the food you should eat will generally emphasize carbohydrates with a fair share of protein. Fat is important, but you won't need to go out of your way to consume it. (You'll see more on that in a moment.)

Midride nutrition should be primarily carbohydrates, which are easy to digest and process to fuel your muscles during the ride.

And afterward, for recovery, we again combine carbohydrates and protein. There will be a higher proportion of protein in the mix to aid muscle repair and recovery. Carbs are crucial now to replenish muscle glycogen.

Composition

Throughout all my years as a pro cyclist I tried many diets, always searching for the perfect way to lose weight. One thing was the same for all of them: When October came around, I gave up whatever I was doing during racing season, and I went crazy. I drank tons of beer, ate ice cream, and simply let myself go, bingeing on all the foods I denied myself—and gained a bunch of weight. Lots of my teammates were like this, too.

The world beyond pro cycling has this same problem. I bet you have a few friends who are always trying trendy diets only to give up after a few months. Whether you're a cyclist or an average person hoping to lose weight, diets always seem too complicated. I think that's why, for a lot of us, diets are never permanent. So, with the 3-Sigma System, I've broken down nutrition into the simplest terms: macronutrients. We've also made it a sustainable program that is doable for anyone long-term.

What Are You Eating?

The composition of our diet is essential to meeting these needs and therefore it's important to understand the two different types of nutrients it can be split into: macronutrients (carbohydrates, proteins, and fats) and micronutrients (vitamins and minerals).

The three macronutrients all have their own specific roles and functions in the body and supply us with calories, or energy. As athletes, we need these nutrients in relatively large amounts for our bodies to grow, develop, repair, and function at a high level. Each macronutrient is almost always found in every item of food, whether that's an energy bar or a raw vegetable; the only difference is how the macronutrients are balanced. For example, the nutritional composition of an avocado is generally made up of 75 percent (good) fats, 20 percent carbohydrates, and 5 percent protein, and therefore it's clearly a fat-based food. On the other hand, a banana consists of 95 percent carbohydrates and only small amounts of protein and fats. We'll teach you to consider the macro balance in your foods and develop meals according to how much of each macronutrient is needed based upon the purpose of that meal. The trick is to understand how each macronutrient plays a different role in the body and tailor your diet accordingly.

In case you sold your biology textbooks at your last garage sale, I'm going to start with a very fundamental explanation of how carbohydrates, protein, and fats work in your diet.

Carbohydrates

For cyclists or any athlete, carbohydrates are critical. They are easily digested, can efficiently fuel activity, and if they aren't used immediately, the body stores them as glycogen. Glycogen is your fuel tank that you tap into on practically every ride. If you've made the mistake of skipping dinner the night before a big ride, you probably felt what it's like to have a low or empty fuel tank. Carbohydrates can also be stored as fat in your body, if your glycogen-carrying capacity is maxed out. When we talk about your Endurance PTZs using fat as a fuel, this is the fat we're talking about, not the dietary fats in an ice cream cone or a hunk of cheese.

We touched on this in Chapter 1, but I want to reiterate that the intensity of exercise affects the proportion of macronutrients you would need in your fueling. Research suggests that when you're training at 50 percent of maximal aerobic capacity, 45 to 55 percent of energy comes from fat. This drops to about 10 to

30 percent when you're training at 75 percent of maximum and zero when you've gone cross-eyed through all-out exertion. As intensity increases, a greater proportion of energy comes via glucose. Viewing macronutrient use from this lens, it's clear why carbohydrates are king in the peloton.

As you can probably tell from all of the different food products advertised on TV or in the supermarket, there are many kinds of carbohydrates. Some are simple; some are complex. In general, complex carbohydrates, with three or more kinds of sugars, are better for athletes like us because they provide sustained energy. Legumes, starchy vegetables, beans, and many fruits are sources of complex carbohydrates. Plus, they provide the added health bonus of vitamins and minerals. Simple carbohydrates, those with two or fewer types of sugar, can produce the sugar rush and then the crash that you get when you eat a cookie or a candy bar. If you see an ingredient on a food label ending in -ose, like sucrose or fructose, chances are it is a simple sugar.

Some carbohydrates are refined; others are unrefined. Whenever possible, try to avoid refined carbohydrates. A big culprit here is anything made from processed, enriched flour: pasta, bagels, packaged cereals, and other bread products. Refined carbohydrates cause inflammation, which is the immune system's response to a stimulus that it thinks may be harmful. In the short-term, excess inflammation can lead to delayed-onset muscle soreness and a compromised recovery. In the long-term, it can lead to a host of chronic diseases. In contrast, unrefined carbohydrates from food like fruits, vegetables, beans, legumes, and unrefined, non-flour whole grains are anti-inflammatory. Anti-inflammatory foods like these specifically reduce the inflammatory response of your immune system. These foods are also sources of nutrients like antioxidants and phytonutrients, which help round out your diet.

Protein

As I mentioned in Chapter 1, my diet and eating habits were not the right fit for my nutritional needs as a professional cyclist. One of the greatest deficiencies I struggled with was protein. Protein isn't a significant fuel source during exercise unless your body runs low on glycogen, which could happen during a prolonged interval workout. Typically, protein makes up only about 2 percent of the fuel your body uses during a workout, but when glycogen is depleted, protein utilization can rise to as high as 10 percent. Unfortunately, a portion of that protein comes from muscle tissue—and muscle degradation is definitely not what you want during training. This is referred to as "going catabolic." Catabolism occurs when the muscles are broken down, destroyed, and "eaten" to produce the necessary energy to perform—not ideal for an athlete aiming to build strength and muscular output. That's why it's essential to keep your muscle- and liver-glycogen stores topped off with carbohydrates during prolonged exercise.

Protein is a crucial source of amino acids, which are often called the building blocks of life. And there is only one way your body can get almost half of the types of amino acids it needs (those called "essential"): by digesting protein-rich food. Once we've accessed these amino acids by breaking down proteins, our body can use them to repair muscles, and sometimes even as an energy source. It is very difficult to get an adequate amount of amino acids through a plant-based diet alone, although it does work for some people.

So shouldn't we be eating as much protein as possible? Lately, some of the trends in nutrition seem to be pointing people in that direction, with high-protein recovery drinks or diets that go light on the carbohydrates and heavy on protein-rich meats. However, there is a limit to how much protein your body can absorb at one sitting. Also, although you need those essential amino acids, which your body cannot produce on its own, you don't need to consume them at every meal.

Our bodies can't function without protein, but when it comes to your diet as a cyclist, focus on getting a variety of different protein sources throughout the day. You can always count on eggs, organic chicken, collagen powder, or fish for your lean proteins. But we also recommend plant-based proteins like quinoa, hemp, chickpeas, and pea protein powder. These are high in antioxidants, fiber, vitamins, and minerals, so plant-based proteins are an incredible anti-inflammatory option for you.

Fat

As I mentioned earlier, there is a difference between dietary fat and the fat in your body that serves as fuel for lower-intensity efforts. If you eat one pound of fat, it isn't going to translate into one pound of fat storage in your body to use during the next endurance ride. Your body doesn't process it as efficiently as it converts carbohydrates into fat storage. That doesn't mean you should cut out fat from your diet entirely, though. In fact, fat is an energy-rich macronutrient that also helps you feel satiated and full after a meal.

In our method, you don't have to go out of your way to eat foods that are rich in fat. In terms of overall share of your calories consumed, fat will be a good deal smaller than carbohydrates and protein. Usually, fat is found in the oils we use to cook or prepare our meals, or it's found in foods like meat or eggs. Even a lean meat like chicken has a little bit of fat in it.

Be sure to avoid unhealthy sources of fat and instead focus on polyunsaturated and monounsaturated fats, like those found in nuts, fish, olives, avocados, or other minimally processed foods. Also, note that even though fat is rich in calories, it is much slower to digest and process than carbohydrates. This is why our pre-ride fueling plan doesn't incorporate much fat at all.

Anti-Inflammatory Foods

Beyond the three key macronutrients, foods that reduce inflammation are also a key component of your diet. When I was racing, I trained four to six hours a day. I was in amazing shape, but off the bike I felt sluggish and it seemed like my recovery after workouts and races was slower than it should have been. Eventually, I learned how the body finds a balance between alkalinity and acidity, and how intense training can cause an immune system response that further contributes to inflammation.

Let's go back to high school to look at the concept of pH, which reflects the acidity or alkalinity of a substance. Pure water is 7 on the pH scale, which goes from 0 to 14. On the acidic side of the scale, lemon juice or vinegar is a 2. Baking soda and milk of magnesia are alkaline solutions, at 9 and 10 on the pH scale, respectively. The average human body finds a good pH balance at around 7.35.

As you'd expect, maintaining your body's pH balance is ideal for long-term health and performance on the bike. Unfortunately, several factors work against us, pushing our body into a state of low-grade acidosis, when our body's cells are inflamed by the constantly acidic environment. This can be caused by stress and hard training. It can also be caused by an overly acidic and inflammatory diet. The good news is that your body can usually return to a pH balance. The bad news is that this balancing act can stress your body and deplete your immune system.

In the long-term, studies have shown that acidosis can lead to problems that are more serious than poor performance on the bike. That long-term inflammation can result in kidney stones, loss of bone mass, reduction in human growth hormone, premature aging, and an increase in body fat.

One nutrient that influences inflammation—and one you can control—is a much-discussed pair of fatty acids: omega-6 and omega-3. Omega-6 fatty acids come from many oils and meats and are pro-inflammatory; omega-3 fatty acids, found in seafood and walnuts and flaxseed, are anti-inflammatory. Both are vital to human function, but the modern Western diet has our bodies consuming 20 times more omega-6 fatty acids than omega-3s (most experts recommend a ratio of 4 omega-3s to 1 omega-6). Why is this?

As a society we consume more grains and oils than ever before, and our livestock has done the same. Cows, chickens, and farm-raised fish are fed not their natural diet but one full of grains and oils. This means that the meat products you eat are lower in omega-3s and high in omega-6s.

Your body can't produce omega-3s and omega-6s on its own; you get them from food. That's why super-low-fat diets are bad for you—they systematically deprive you of the fats your body needs to function at its best. Omega-3s and omega-6s exist in a ratio to one another. There's a cap on the total amount of the two that the body can use, so they end up competing for space. You need both, but because of their opposite effects on inflammation, it's optimal to maximize omega-3s and minimize omega-6s.

The best choices for omega-3 essential fatty acids are cold-water high-fat fish, especially wild Alaskan salmon, sardines, anchovies, mackerel, shad, herring, and trout. Flaxseed oil, flaxseeds, flaxseed meal, hempseed oil, hempseeds, walnuts, pumpkin seeds, Brazil nuts, and sesame seeds are also good options. Avocados, too. Certain dark-green leafy vegetables, including kale, spinach, purslane, mustard greens, and collards offer omega-3s as well.

So, the anti-inflammatory diet is good for both your near-term goals as a cyclist as well as your lifelong health and well-being. To help your body find balance, the 3-Sigma System incorporates alkaline-forming foods that help buffer the inflammatory effects of acids.

Each of our diet's macronutrients can help provide anti-inflammatory nutrients. With carbohydrates, look for unrefined, whole carbohydrates like those found in vegetables, beans, legumes, and grains that are naturally gluten free. While some protein sources, like red meat and pork, can be acid forming, fish is often a great source of buffering alkalinity due to omega-3 fatty acids. Salmon, sardines, herring, mackerel, and anchovies are especially rich in omega-3s. The third and final macronutrient, fat, is key to how our bodies regulate inflammation. Again, the key is to eat whole, unprocessed, natural sources of fat, not artificial or heavily processed foods.

Timing

We have talked about the "why" of your nutrition, the Purpose; we went back to high school to figure out the "what" of this food; and finally, the third piece of the 3-Sigma Nutrition System answers the question of "when." Timing is key to fueling your performance on the bike, and it ties together all of the other details of the first two elements.

With the right timing, you can gain muscle, lose fat, and be properly fueled for any type of ride. If you eat the wrong macronutrients at the wrong time, well, it can be crippling, as I've experienced over years of trial and error with my own diet.

Let's begin with the ride you'd do on any given day and work backward from there. As I've already explained, carbohydrates are a key fuel for most rides, and timing their consumption is key for both the ride itself and what happens in your metabolism later in the day. Plan to consume the majority of your carbohydrates in the three hours leading up to your ride and the three hours after. The three hours before serve to prime your body for the activity. In the immediate time frame before, during, and after your ride, carbohydrates that are quickly assimilated are best—choose starchy foods that you can quickly digest. As you get further away from your workout, in terms of timing, complex carbohydrates that are more slowly absorbed are best to keep your blood sugar steady, avoiding the crash that comes after a sweet treat.

One of the keys to timing carbohydrate consumption, regardless of any other fitness or nutrition objective you might have, is the glycogen window. This window opens up right after your ride, and ideally you should consume carbohydrates within the first 45 minutes of that two-hour window. This gives your body a chance to replenish the glycogen stores that were depleted during exercise.

Some post-ride recovery drinks go heavy on protein, but we recommend avoiding significant protein consumption immediately before and after your ride for a couple reasons. Conventional wisdom says you need to repair your muscles immediately after a hard workout, right? And earlier in this chapter, I was explaining how protein's amino acids are the building blocks that repair your shredded legs after a big day of riding. However, immediately after a ride, the first priority is consuming and absorbing those carbohydrates to replenish your glycogen stores. If you consume too much protein in that time frame, it can interfere with carbohydrate absorption.

The second key to proper recovery is electrolyte intake: Be sure to tailor your hydration to the temperature and workload. Hot day? Coconut water and watermelon juice are refreshing anti-inflammatory options to replenish lost electrolytes. But most days, cold water with lemon and a little Himalayan sea salt will suffice.

Timing your protein intake is important because it takes longer to digest than carbohydrates—a lot longer. Eat a burger for dinner, and you're probably still processing that protein the next morning. You don't want to eat a protein-rich meal only a couple hours before a big ride because it won't be converted into usable fuel in time. In fact, most of the time when your body is tapping its protein reserves to repair damaged muscles, it's using the protein consumed the day before, which has finally reached the point in your digestive process when the amino acids can be utilized by your body's cells.

Like protein, it also takes your body a long time to digest and process fat for energy. By this point you should realize that you don't need to go out of your way to consume fatty foods, but you should avoid them prior to a big ride or workout because the fat will not be ready for use as an energy source.

Post-ride, fat should be consumed after your carbohydrates and protein. I remember walking onto the team bus feeling wrecked after a hard day in a stage race. The soigneurs would have some sort of rice mixture waiting for us. Every day it was different: Mexican, Asian, anything. We would all load up with a big bowl of rice with a little chicken and an electrolyte drink, and we'd go to town. Then, if we had room in our stomachs, we would have a protein shake. Carbohydrates were the first priority, then hydration, and then protein. At dinner we would have a more balanced meal, such as an easily digestible protein—often some fish, more carbs, like risotto or pasta, vegetables for nutrients, and some fat in the dressing and sauces.

It is also best to distribute your protein consumption steadily throughout the day because your body can only use 25 to 35 grams of protein per day for muscle synthesis. Avoid eating it all at once, in part because of the fact that it demands time and energy to digest. So sprinkle protein in throughout your meals. You could have an egg with breakfast, some beans in your burrito at lunch, and a lean piece of meat for dinner. During a hard training block you can even top off your protein stores before bed with a low-carb, high-quality protein shake.

Fat and protein are not the primary macronutrients for fueling your rides, workouts, and races. However, they are the keys to teaching your body to shift gears nutritionally and burn slow and steady with your fat stores. Instead of spiking your metabolism every hour with small carbohydrate-heavy snacks, nutrition outside of the time frame before and after riding should focus on protein and fat. Lean proteins, dark leafy greens, and healthy fats are ideal for the times outside of your carbohydrate window. These types of food will increase your satiation, so you won't feel as hungry. Focusing on proteins and fats will also encourage your body to tap into its energy stores, burning fat instead of carbohydrates.

This isn't to say that your meals cannot have any carbohydrates outside of the window around your ride. Just make sure you're focusing on healthy, fibrous foods that provide complex carbohydrates to keep your energy levels steady.

The 80:20 Rule

At this point, your head might be spinning as you imagine the ridiculous grocery list you'll need to make to stick to the 3-Sigma Nutrition System. Over the years, I've devoted myself to many restrictive diets, so I know that feeling of intimidation you might have. Don't worry. The 3-Sigma System isn't as difficult as it seems at first.

The simplest way to start eating well is to start cutting out processed foods that aren't a good return on your investment. If you are consuming calories, make sure they are high quality. Look for ingredients you can pronounce, ingredients that you can imagine growing in your home garden or buying at a farmers market. High-fructose corn syrup or palm oil? I don't think so.

Then, as you gradually shift toward this healthier way of eating, begin integrating alkaline foods into your diet to reduce your body's inflammation. I noticed a huge improvement in my post-race recovery, sleep quality, and overall energy levels as I shifted into an anti-inflammatory diet. I bet you will, too, which will make the effort much more rewarding.

Sure, the reward of better health and better performance on the bike is great, but that isn't all we have to live for. Even pro athletes can relax and indulge once in a while. You should, too, and that's what the 80:20 rule is about. I tell my CINCH athletes that they should make it a goal to eat healthy foods 80 percent of the time—sticking to the correct blend of macronutrients, eating healthy, natural, minimally processed ingredients, mixing in anti-inflammatory food to buffer acidosis. Then, the other 20 percent of the time, you get the nutritional equivalent of recess. Go out and enjoy yourself, whether that means beers with your friends, ice cream with your kids, or some nachos at a football game.

Similar to how we need regular rest days to recover from the stress of training, we occasionally need refreshing breaks from our nutrition program. I've found that restrictive diets that cut out whole food groups or deny you particular foods are not sustainable. I want you to make healthy nutrition a lifelong habit and the best way to keep it going year after year is moderation.

Be Realistic with Your Nutrition

Nutrition is a complex topic: There are tons of fad diets, everyone seems to have a different opinion, and the science is hard to understand. So I'm going to make this as simple as possible: Your nutrition needs to fuel your performance. This is what 3-Sigma is all about. Your Purpose, Composition, and Timing are all geared toward what will happen when you get on the bike and roll out. Your body has specific needs to perform at its best, and those needs always come first.

The biggest mistake that cyclists make (myself included), is to prioritize weight loss over performance. A lot of people think that quick weight loss is the path to better performance, but that's never the case.

Your ideal performance weight is your real weight. People try to game the system like I did, losing weight and trying to keep power, focusing on weight loss rather than changing their body and fueling system. But if you're doing the work, your body always follows. And you cannot do the work right without the proper fueling.

WHY
are you
eating?

WHAT
are you
eating?

WHEN
are you
eating?

You're never going to see someone who is overweight or unhealthy if they are doing the work that's intended and fueling right.

When I coach people, I ask who they want to become. I hear a lot of similar answers—they want to upgrade to the next racing category, tackle a huge gran fondo, or even just finish the weekly group ride without getting dropped. Many of them think the path to these goals is weight loss, when, really, it is the other way around. If they do the training necessary to achieve their goals, and they fuel to support that performance, the weight loss will follow. True weight loss that is sustainable occurs over time. The best approach is to take it day by day rather than thinking of it as a weight-loss block where you need to lose as much as weight as possible in a short period of time.

Use the 3-Sigma approach to assess your energy needs for the day with the right nutrition, and your body will morph into what it needs to be in order to become that person. Everyone, from the best cyclist in the world to a beginner who just signed up for their first race, has an ideal body weight, and this system will lead you to yours.

Recipes for Your Body, Your Training

Not every rider is built the same—nor is every workout. But it's easy to determine how much of each macronutrient you need because the recommended quantity of fuel is proportionate to an athlete's body weight. The level of effort will also influence how much fuel you need: Workouts in higher PTZs will burn more carbs than a low PTZ Endurance or recovery ride. And the macronutrient composition of recovery meals will also reflect the different intensities of the workout you've completed. Adjust your fueling and the serving size of any meal you make by plugging your body weight into the calculations provided in the following chart. Know your body weight and which PTZs are targeted on a given day, and you'll identify how much protein and carbohydrates are recommended before, during, and after your ride.

TABLE 5.1. Macronutrient Calculator

		Calculation		Example Rider (160 lb.)	
	WORKOUT CATEGORY (PTZ FOCUS)	CARB INTAKE (G)	PROTEIN INTAKE (G)	CARB INTAKE (G)	PROTEIN INTAKE (G)
Pre-Ride	Mix of all 3	BW	BW ÷ 8	160	20
	Explosive	BW ÷ 2	BW ÷ 7	80	23
	Threshold	BW ÷ 3	BW ÷ 6	53	27
	Endurance	BW ÷ 4	BW ÷ 5	40	32
During Ride (per hour)		30–40	5–10		
Post-Ride	Mix of all 3	BW	BW ÷ 4	160	40
	Explosive	BW ÷ 1.8	BW ÷ 5	89	32
	Threshold	BW ÷ 2.7	BW ÷ 6	59	27
	Endurance	BW ÷ 3.6	BW ÷ 7	44	23

Measure your body weight (BW) in pounds, then use that number to calculate the amounts of protein and carbohydrates (in grams) for your planned workout.

How do you adjust a meal to fit these recommendations? If you're using one of the recipes included here as examples, eat more or less than one serving to consume the amount of carbohydrates and protein you found in the chart. For example, one serving of Performance Pancakes offers 60 grams of carbohydrates, but if the 160-pound rider in the example column is planning to do an endurance ride, requiring 40 grams of carbs, they could eat about two-thirds of the pancake.

PRE-RIDE   PERFORMANCE PANCAKES   SERVING: 1

Pancakes are a great pre-ride option, and this is a healthier, more athlete-friendly version.

1	large ripe banana
2	large eggs
½	cup rolled oats
¼	tsp cinnamon
	Dash of almond milk

Eat at least 90 minutes before you ride

1. Put the banana in a bowl and mash with a fork.
2. Add the eggs and mix until well combined.
3. Pour oats into a blender and chop until fine.
4. Add the oats and cinnamon to the banana mixture and stir well. Add almond milk if the batter is too thick.
5. Heat a skillet over medium heat with a dash of vegetable oil.
6. Pour ¼ cup of the mixture into the skillet, cook on one side for about 90 seconds, then turn and cook on the other side for about 1 minute (or until golden brown on both sides).
7. Add syrup and seasonal fruit and enjoy. (Note that additional sugars in the syrup will raise the carbohydrate count of these pancakes.)

CALORIES	CARBOHYDRATES	PROTEIN	FAT
422	60 g	19 g	13 g

MIDRIDE ▶ TOP-SECRET BROWNIES

SERVINGS: 8

On-the-bike rocket fuel. We like these brownies during a ride because their sugars are absorbed quickly and the coconut oil is an excellent natural source of medium-chain triglycerides (MCTs), which, for a fat, are quickly absorbed by the body for use as energy and also assist in fat burning.

½ cup coconut oil, melted
½ cup organic cane sugar
¼ cup maple syrup (or agave nectar)
1 tsp vanilla extract
2 large eggs
¾ tsp baking powder
¼ tsp sea salt
½ cup unsweetened cocoa powder
¾ cup gluten-free flour, such as rice and potato flour blends
¼ cup almond meal

During a ride lasting at least 60 minutes

1. Preheat oven to 350 degrees Fahrenheit (175°C) and lightly grease an 8 × 8-inch (or similar size) baking dish with a little coconut oil, then line with parchment paper.
2. Combine melted coconut oil, cane sugar, maple syrup, and vanilla extract in a large mixing bowl. Whisk until sugar dissolves.
3. Add eggs and whisk to combine. Whisk in baking powder, sea salt, and cocoa powder.
4. Using a rubber spatula, fold in gluten-free flour and almond meal until just mixed.
5. Pour the batter into the prepared baking dish and spread into an even layer.
6. Bake for 17–22 minutes, or until the edges appear dry and slightly fluffy, and the center is no longer wet or sticky.
7. Remove from the oven and let cool in the pan for 10–15 minutes. Use the parchment paper to gently lift the brownie square out of the pan and use a sharp knife to cut into 8 pieces.
8. Store completely cooled brownies in an airtight container at room temperature up to a few days. Will keep in the freezer for up to 1 month.

CALORIES	CARBOHYDRATES	PROTEIN	FAT
226	28 g	4 g	12 g

POST-RIDE   PINEAPPLE FRIED RICE

An excellent recovery option to replenish your glycogen stores with the anti-inflammatory properties of pineapple and turmeric.

Within 90 minutes post-ride or the night before an intense ride

3	**Tbsp coconut oil**
3	**large eggs, whisked**
1	**cup diced yellow onions (about ½ large onion)**
1	**tsp salt**
1	**large red pepper, diced**
1	**large carrot, peeled and diced**
½	**cup (70 g) frozen peas**
1	**tsp turmeric**
1½	**tsp ground coriander**
3	**cups cooked jasmine rice (white or brown)**
3	**Tbsp Braggs Aminos or soy sauce**
1½	**Tbsp brown sugar**
1½	**cups diced pineapple**
2	**scallions, thinly sliced**
3	**Tbsp chopped basil**

1. This stir-fry works best with leftover rice, but if you don't have any just cook 2 cups of dry jasmine rice before you start the recipe.
2. Heat ½ tablespoon of oil in a wok or large sauté pan over medium-high heat. When the pan is hot, add the whisked eggs and scramble with a spatula. Transfer eggs to a plate and set aside.
3. Heat remaining oil over medium-high heat. Add the yellow onions and a little salt and cook until the onions start to soften.
4. Add the red pepper, carrots, and peas and cook for another 2 minutes. Add the turmeric and coriander and stir until the vegetables are coated with the spices.
5. Add the rice and mix well with the vegetables; stir the rice for 1–2 minutes.
6. Mix the soy sauce with the brown sugar in a small bowl and stir into the rice.
7. Add the eggs, pineapple, and sliced scallions to the rice and stir to distribute. Turn off the heat and mix in the chopped basil. Serve immediately.

CALORIES	CARBOHYDRATES	PROTEIN	FAT
446	**75 g**	**11 g**	**11 g**

06

THE FIVE-POINT APPROACH TO CREATING FASTER POWER

Here's a riddle. There are two riders, Jim and Matt. They weigh the same. They can produce the same wattage for given power zones. They're both motivated cyclists who love riding and racing. Matt is one of the best masters racers around, and he's got a national championship title in his age group to prove it. He regularly dices it up with the local pros on the group rides. When Matt shows up for a state championship road race or crit, you better believe he's one of the top favorites that everyone is watching. On the other hand, despite his best efforts, Jim often gets dropped on the weekly group rides. In races, he is no better. At his best, he can hang in with the peloton, basically along for the ride.

So, what is the difference between these two riders?

Believe it or not, I have been faced with this exact dilemma in my experience as a cycling coach. In my first few years running CINCH, I was very focused on power. I was trying to help my athletes raise their zones. The common coaching wisdom was simple: Raise your zones and your threshold, and everything will be good.

But then I came upon Jim and Matt. These riders seemed like they should be almost exact clones of each other, but they weren't—not by a long shot.

This was the start of my two-year investigation into what really made someone fast . . . not what made them produce awesome power numbers. I spent hours staring at power files. I combed through the data produced by riders like Jim and Matt. I compared it with their race results, their feedback on how they felt, and how a race unfolded. I compared this training data with their ride metrics like speed and the elevation profile. I rode next to them and studied their pedaling techniques, cadence, and body position.

I also looked at my experiences in pro racing. I watched race video of top performers like Alberto Contador or Alejandro Valverde, too. Looking at them, I realized these guys don't have more power than everyone else. It's what they do with that power—how they use their technique on the bike and execution. That's what helps them produce more speed. That's what makes them great.

What I learned from my investigation would change how I coach athletes forever. Simply put: Power does not equal performance. It is the delivery of the power that truly makes the performance.

I found that there were five key areas that cyclists, experienced and novices alike, need to work on in order to deliver faster power: Power Control, Cadence Control, Body Position, Separation, and Transitional Control. But the discovery of these areas was just the beginning!

No one teaches cyclists these five points of the North Star of Execution to make the most of their wattage. Information and a training system on these areas did not exist. So how did top WorldTour riders like Valverde and top masters racers like Matt develop these skills? They developed their tools through years and years of racing and competing against top-level athletes in top-level events. So how was I going to help older riders like Jim, who have jobs, families, and limited time, create the skills to make this "faster power"?

Through this analysis I had an epiphany. I realized that my cyclists, and thousands of others like them (even some pro riders), needed a guiding light to direct their training and improve their use of the power they had. They needed a compass to point them to the path of least resistance. Up until then, they were just trying to develop the biggest wattage club possible, so they could smash everyone with it. This compass would become the FORM North Star of Execution.

This star has five points: Power Control, Cadence Control, Body Position, Separation, and Transitional Control. Each has a key purpose to help you improve your technique and execution, to become more like my athlete Matt. While all Four Pillars are critical to your success, it is the Execution pillar that most often gets people excited. This one is a quick game changer as it provides fast and noticeable improvement in areas where cycling progression usually stalls out.

Power Control

In every race, there is the person who averages the most watts and hits the highest numbers, and then there is the person who wins. They are rarely the same rider. Even though our power meter-obsessed sport has gotten to the point where it feels like the only thing that matters is normalized power or FTP, that isn't always what wins races. Cycling is still a game like any other sport.

Take tennis, for example. The announcers might touch on the fact that Serena Williams can serve a ball at over 100 miles per hour, but that's not the key talking point after the match. Instead, they discuss how brilliantly she placed her shots throughout the court, how she responded to her rival's shots, how she used her powerful swing at just the right moment to hit the winning shot.

I want you to stop judging your cycling by the numbers on your power meter and start judging it based on speed—not your miles per hour, but your quickness. While it may be difficult to quantify, this form of speed is what wins races. The first step to build this speed is training and riding enough to establish a foundation of power that you can produce. The crucial next step I'll teach you is how to use that power in the most efficient way possible to maximize speed and momentum. That's what Power Control is all about.

You'll use the terrain to gain momentum when it suits the PTZ you intend to use. As things progress, you'll find opportunities to maintain that momentum without going above or below that PTZ.

I know I just told you not to fixate on your power meter's numbers, but we aren't going to throw out those expensive components. Instead, similar to your own power as a cyclist, we'll use those tools carefully to chase the elusive momentum that will help you win. There are two key Power Control concepts: Power Floors and Power Ceilings.

Power Floors

In my years of coaching athletes, I've discovered that focusing on power averages leads to average cyclists. You don't want to be average, right?

Here's what happens. People are given an average wattage number to hit in their workout and then they game the system. It's only natural. They are told to ride 220 watts and at the halfway point of their 20-minute interval, they realize they've been doing 190 watts. So, they spike it to 250 for the rest of the lap and *voilà*! It was a 220-watt effort, right? Actually, half of the interval was below their zone, and half was above it. I doubt that's what their coach wanted them to do.

So, we start with the Power Floor for any given effort. This is the minimum wattage that you should not go below after you hit the lap button to start your interval. If you go below it, you bleed precious momentum. To build back up to the correct PTZ, you will have to push harder than necessary, wasting energy. It is more efficient to stay above that floor.

Power Ceilings

As I just hinted at, cyclists love to chase those average power stats, even if it means riding above the zone they were supposed to be in all along. But wait—if you're strong enough to push a little harder during an interval, that's OK, right? Sorry, no. It might feel good at the time, or you might have the confidence to bust through that Power Ceiling, but I promise you that you'll regret it later.

When you spike through that Power Ceiling, you're almost always going to drop through the Power Floor right after. You max out your body's physical capabilities with that spike, so it needs to recover by going below the floor. When that happens, you lose that precious momentum. This is one of the most inefficient ways to ride, regardless of what your power averages tell you.

Power spikes can also impact your body's perception of the interval's intensity. While your average might be right in your PTZ, the constant stress of going over the Power Ceiling leads it to think you are at an effort level beyond the zone. If you avoid the spikes, you'll be putting less stress on your body.

Top cyclists have such great Power Control that their Power Floors and Power Ceilings are very close to each other. They can precisely stay in that PTZ for long periods of time, riding efficiently, maintaining momentum, and putting as little stress as possible on their bodies.

Cadence Control

Around the world, cyclists who watched Lance Armstrong win the 1999 Tour de France were stunned. I know I was. And one of the things that stood out the most was his pedaling style, his high cadence. It didn't take long for cyclists everywhere to start mimicking his form, riding at 100 rpm or more, spinning as fast as they could, thinking it would help them ride like the Tour champion.

While they were right to consider changing their cadence to go faster and ride more efficiently, they were thinking of this critical variable in the wrong way. Cadence is not a black or white, wrong or right, fast or slow choice. Never think you can set cadence like a thermostat and leave it alone for the rest of the ride.

Instead, cadence should change dynamically, based on the terrain, race dynamics, and your own needs as a rider, no matter what wattage you are producing. If you've ever paid attention to your car's rpms while driving, then you already understand the basics of how cadence works for cyclists, because it is essentially the same. Higher rpms help you accelerate quickly from a stoplight. Lower rpms give you better gas economy at highway speeds. You wouldn't try to drive in third gear at 70 mph on the highway, right?

For the foundation of the Cadence Control point on the North Star, there are two key concepts that tie in directly with our comparison with a car engine. Both concepts relate to momentum, which, as I've mentioned, is the key to riding fast and riding well. To gain momentum, focus on high cadence, usually 90–100 rpm, combined with high power. To maintain speed, switch to low cadence, around 70–80 rpm, with low power.

If you can develop your Cadence Control and start using it strategically, it translates into a number of cycling's key performance components.

Cadence Control can help you develop more torque when you need it. Simply pedaling a steady wattage won't necessarily translate into speed. People who ride like that often are caught on the cadence hamster wheel, spinning fast but going nowhere. When you time your cadence to deliver power at key moments to gain momentum or sustain it, that's what produces torque.

Like I hinted at with the car analogy, carefully using your cadence can reduce stress on your own human engine. Low cadence is generally more stressful on your muscles. High cadence tends to tax your cardiovascular system. So, by using Cadence Control strategically, you can maximize your body's efficiency.

Have you ever tried to pedal at a high cadence and found yourself bouncing in the saddle? Believe it or not, that uncomfortable feeling wasn't only because your muscles weren't accustomed to spinning at 120 rpm. In fact, there are tons of connections between your mind and muscles, known as neuromuscular connections. Chances are, those lines of communication were old or broken because you rarely engage all of your different leg and core muscles to spin at such a rate of speed. We'll teach you to use high-cadence drills strategically to keep those neuromuscular connections active (you'll see them in the Appendix as efforts with cadences higher than 90 rpm).

You'll be glad you have those connections when you have to call on your legs to do a burst of speed. That's when Cadence Control really shines. You need to gain momentum fast, so you switch into high-cadence, high-power mode to deliver as much circular force as possible to the pedals. Then, if you've mastered Cadence Control, you'll shift into low cadence and lower power to maintain that momentum with less exertion when the terrain or race dynamics allow.

One of the most fun ways to use Cadence Control in real life is what we call "surfing the terrain." Simply by adjusting your cadence, you can smooth out a road that has repeated small hills. You change your cadence strategically to absorb the bumps in the elevation profile. When you roll over the crest of one of these small hills, you can quickly pick up momentum by applying a burst of high cadence. Then, you settle into a low cadence to sustain the momentum into the next little hill.

In that same way, you can smooth out the ups and downs of the pace in a peloton. It can be frustrating to always feel like you're on the back foot as one rider after the next drops the hammer on the front of the group. And you can waste a lot of energy by closing gaps or responding to attacks. Fortunately, once you refine your Cadence Control, these situations become far less taxing. When you're cruising in the draft, you use low cadence to maintain momentum, and whenever the pace picks up, you can hit the high cadence to close the gap. As you ease into the draft again, you move back to low cadence.

When you start to do training rides and workouts with the FORM Method, your cadence is just as important to monitor as your power. Every workout should have a specific objective with your cadence, and sticking to that will help you become an expert at Cadence Control.

Body Position

Even if you aren't analyzing power and cadence data for hours (like I was), you can tell the difference between a rider like Matt, who is using Execution to get the most out of his available power, and a rider like Jim, who is missing out on a ton of speed and momentum. If you have watched enough bike racing and know what to look for, you'll see it in their body positions.

I've seen that the riders who were unable to perform well despite having a lot of power to work with were falling short in three key scenarios. The first was when a rider needed to maintain high speed and high cadence on a fast, flat section of road or a downhill. They simply couldn't stay above their Power Floor. The second area where I realized my athletes were falling short due to body position was on climbs where they needed to hold high power and high cadence while standing. The third and final area was sprinting while seated. Most cyclists can fake their way through a standing sprint, but without proper body position, riders fell apart when I asked them to produce high wattage while seated. In these moments, body position can easily give you an extra 20 or 30 watts to work with.

In all of these situations, body position was being hindered by three areas, or Three Points of Power: hands, core, and feet. How do you hold the handlebars? Are your arms stiff and straight, perhaps how Frankenstein's monster might ride a bike? You need to reanimate the arms—get them bent and responsive instead. Straight-armed cyclists rest with the bars in the palms of their hands. With straight arms, it's impossible to pull on the bars to generate power, move the bike freely beneath you, or rock it back and forth while climbing or sprinting. As you'll learn in the eight body position diagrams that follow, you should be resting on the heels of your hands, and this will free up your elbows to move and flex.

The biggest problem I see with the second Point of Power, the core, is that riders do not have enough core strength, or they are not engaging it to drive their pedal stroke. I am a huge proponent of off-the-bike strength work to improve your core, so stay tuned for specific workouts later on. When it comes to body position, one of the biggest mistakes people make is they let their pelvis sit straight up on the bike, like they're in a chair at their desk in the office. They end up unable to use the upstroke of their pedal stroke, cutting off the glutes, hip flexors, and hamstrings from contributing to their power.

Instead, you should be tilting your hips forward and engaging your core muscles. This gives you more power on the downstroke and frees up the rest of your leg muscles to contribute on the pedal upstroke.

The third and final Point of Power is your feet. It might be easy to overlook the feet because, after all, they're just connecting your legs to the pedals. Your quads are where all the power comes from, right? Although your feet and ankles aren't necessarily generating the power you need to ride fast, they guide your legs through the entire pedal stroke. Usually, I see two extremes with athletes' feet, and both hold them back. On one hand, riders who had once been told to "scrape the mud" off their shoes at the bottom of the pedal stroke greatly exaggerate the motion of dropping their heels. They end up not actually engaging their upstroke. On the other hand, some riders keep a perfectly flat foot through the whole pedal stroke. When I see this, I just imagine them on the elliptical machine in their local health club. Instead of pushing their power into the pedals, they're just supporting their own body weight. In this position, they cannot engage their hip flexors and hamstrings to pull up. They end up wasting half of the pedal stroke this way.

As you might expect, I advocate finding the happy medium between an over-exaggerated heel drop and a flat foot. It is a little hard to learn at first, and it can depend on ankle flexibility and cleat placement, but the heel is the key. Looking at the pedal stroke like a dial on a clock, your heel should be down from one o'clock to five o'clock. Then, it snaps up at the bottom of the stroke and stays up over the top of the clock before dropping to start the cycle again. Your foot is never really flat when you pedal like this. It won't come naturally, and you'll need to practice it, but when you begin engaging all of the other muscles in your legs—hamstrings, glutes, hip flexors, and calves—you'll see the difference.

Now, let's go over the eight body positions in visual form to help you see how the Three Points of Power come together to help you take the power you have and convert it into the speed and momentum you need. We'll identify several aspects of your position on the bike: forward or backward, lower or higher, hand orientation, pedal-foot interaction, and muscle engagement. We also identify what scenario each position should be used in. For example, on a climb, your position should differ when you are accelerating versus just maintaining momentum. (Correctly altering the angle your body weight enters the pedal stroke exponentially increases torque, leverage, and subsequently speed.) The position adjustments need to correlate with fluctuations in the terrain and the desired outcome.

You may notice that there are a lot of similarities in the positions—specifically as they relate to standing versus sitting. But when you look close enough, each one contains subtle differences. It's these nuances that make the big difference.

SEATED POWER FLATS

This is the body position used to produce the most power possible in the saddle, on flat roads. It's intended to generate power efficiently over long periods of time. This position normally follows an acceleration and is used to maintain momentum and speed.

Center of Gravity
In this position, focus on your belly button, as the center of your core will stabilize the power generated from your legs. Understand that your legs and upper body will be moving independently while you ride, but your core will not. This will stabilize your bike by keeping it moving forward in a straight line and enhance torque delivery.

Optimal Cadence
75 to 85 rpm

HANDS: The handgrip should be relaxed and equal on both hands. Hold onto the bars by using your thumbs to wrap around the hoods. Your grip is concentrated on the thumb so much so that the palm of your hand should barely be touching the hood. Move your elbows slightly up and out to allow your forearms to relax.

CORE: The core is fully engaged and locked with your pelvis in a neutral position. Shift the body back slightly on the seat and engage the neutral pelvis by pushing down on the seat with your sit bones. Hold this position by pedaling with a focus on the upstroke, paying attention to your hamstrings, glutes, and calves.

FEET: Focus on the heel. Use it to pull and push the ball of your foot against the pedal. Guide your heel in the direction it needs to go during the pedal stroke to turn the cranks. This means focusing on dropping the heel and pushing with it on the downstroke starting at the one o'clock position, and pulling with it on the upstroke starting at the seven o'clock position.

STANDING POWER FLATS

This position is used to produce the most power possible out of the saddle, on flat roads. When performing a standing body position, it is imperative to add your body weight into the pedal stroke rather than hold yourself up with your arms. Putting your weight into each pedal stroke will increase the torque delivered to the cranks. Doing so allows for more speed out of the same power output, with less overall effort.

Center of Gravity
People often do this incorrectly, so pay close attention. Your center of gravity should be established up over the bike and slightly forward. Your body should be more forward than what feels natural, with your chin directly over the front hub. This creates the perfect angle to drop your body weight with each downstroke. Use your triceps to control your center of gravity.

Optimal Cadence
65 to 75 rpm

HANDS: Hands are located on the hoods, primarily using the thumb to make a firm grip; distribute weight equally on both hands. Opposite of the thumb, use the heel of the hand to bear the majority of your body weight—not the center of your hand. Doing so will help you lock in and engage the core.

CORE: The core is engaged by slightly bringing the elbow in on each upstroke toward the knee that is lifting up. On the upstroke, focus on pulling the knees up using obliques and hip flexors.

FEET: Your body weight should be supported directly on the balls of your feet for the entirety of the pedal stroke. For the downstroke, drive your pedal stroke down on the ball of your foot with your heel up and your toe pointed down. On the upstroke, curl the bottom of the stroke with your toes, and then pull your heels up, focusing on your hamstrings, calves, and glutes. When you perfectly nail both the down- and the upstroke, it should feel like you are dancing on your pedals.

SEATED ACCELERATION FLATS

This is the body position used to produce the most powerful acceleration in the saddle on flat roads. Other scenarios include raising the speed when pulling on the front, closing a gap in the peloton, or raising your speed in a solo effort like a breakaway or a time trial.

Center of Gravity

Lower your center of gravity by bending the elbows and setting your forearms parallel to the ground. The chest is down and close to the top tube to become more aerodynamic.

Optimal Cadence

90 to 100 rpm

HANDS: Handgrip should be firm and equal on both hands with the end of the thumb resting on the top of the hoods. Opposite of the thumb, use the heel of the hand to bear the majority of your body weight, not the center of your hand. Forearms should be parallel to the top tube while your elbows are bent and drawn in toward your body.

CORE: Shift your body forward on the seat while you rotate the pelvis forward. Make sure to flex and engage the core while concentrating on using your hamstrings, glutes, and calves on the upstroke.

FEET: Practice nimbly pulling the pedals with the balls of your feet for the entire pedal stroke. For the downstroke, drive your pedal downward on the ball of your foot with your heel up and toe down. On the upstroke curl the bottom of the pedal stroke with your toes, and then drag your heels up with your hamstrings, calves, and glutes.

STANDING ACCELERATION FLATS

This is the body position used to produce the most powerful acceleration out of the saddle on flat roads. This is done by adding your body weight into the pedal stroke and increasing the torque delivered to the cranks by improving the angle in which the force is going into the cranks. The result is a much faster acceleration with the same power output, with less overall effort.

Center of Gravity
Your center of gravity should be low and over the bike, moved forward so that your chin is in front of the front hub. This provides the perfect angle while being aerodynamic to drop your body weight into each downstroke. Your triceps control your center of gravity in this position.

Optimal Cadence
85 to 90 rpm

HANDS: The hands are located on the hoods; the end of the thumb sits on the top of the hood. Opposite of the thumb, use the heel of the hand to bear the majority of your body weight, not the center of your hand. This is done to lock in the core.

CORE: The core is engaged by aggressively bringing the elbow in toward the bottom of the rib cage on each upstroke toward the knee that is coming up. On the upstroke, focus on pulling knees up using your stomach muscles and hip flexors.

FEET: Your body weight is supported directly on the balls of your feet for the entire pedal stroke. For the downstroke, drive down on the ball of your foot with your heel up and toes down. On the upstroke, curl the bottom of the pedal stroke with your toes, and then pull your heels up with your hamstrings, calves, and glutes. When executing both the down- and the upstroke with perfection, it should feel like you are dancing on the pedals with the balls of your feet.

SEATED POWER CLIMBS

This body position is intended to produce the most power possible in the saddle, on climbs. This position enables you to generate power efficiently on climbs over longer periods of time while staying in the saddle, and usually follows an acceleration or a terrain change to maintain momentum and speed.

Center of Gravity
Focus on positioning yourself more on the front of your saddle with your upper body forward over the front of the stem. Elbows are slightly bent to keep the chest open for breathing.

Optimal Cadence
75 to 80 rpm

HANDS: Handgrip should be relaxed and equal on both hands. Hold onto the bars by using your thumbs to wrap around the hoods. Your grip is focused on the thumb so that the palm of your hand should be hardly touching the hood. Move your elbows slightly up and out to enable your forearms to relax.

CORE: The core is fully engaged and locked while your pelvis is slightly tilted forward. Shift your body forward on the seat and engage the core with a focus on your hip flexors, pulling up during the upstroke. This should result in finding a rhythmic rocking motion side to side with your upstroke. Embrace it, as this serves as your guide to keeping momentum.

FEET: Focus on the heel and use it to pull and push the ball of your foot against the pedal. Guide your heel in the direction it needs to go during the pedal stroke to turn the cranks: concentrate on dropping the heel and pushing with it on the downstroke starting at the one o'clock position and pulling with it on the upstroke starting at the seven o'clock position.

STANDING POWER CLIMBS

This position is used to produce the most power possible out of the saddle on climbs. The purpose of this standing position is to increase torque delivery by adjusting your body weight and the angle of your body over the bike. This can be used for holding your speed and momentum on the climb as the terrain changes or holding your speed in a solo effort like an uphill effort or a time trial or solo move.

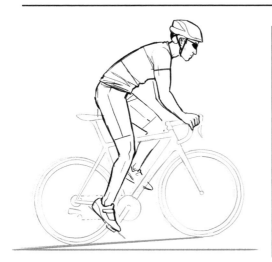

Center of Gravity
Your center of gravity should be lower and more forward on the bike, with the chest over where the stem and handlebar meet. This allows for the perfect angle to drop your body weight into each downstroke. Your triceps control your center of gravity in this position.

Optimal Cadence
70 to 75 rpm

HANDS: Hands are located on the hoods, primarily using the thumb to make the grip firm and equal on both hands. Opposite of the thumb, use the heel of the hand to bear the majority of your body weight, not the center of your hand. This is done to lock the core. Elbows are more bent than the Standing Power Flats position because the chest is lower and more forward.

CORE: The core is engaged by slightly bringing the elbow in on each upstroke toward the knee that is rising up. On the upstroke, focus on pulling knees up using your stomach and hip flexors. Sway the bike more than the Standing Power Flats to really get the connection of the elbow, core, and upstroke together.

FEET: Your body weight is supported directly on the balls of your feet. During the downstroke, drive your pedal down on the ball of your foot with your heel up and toe down. On the upstroke, curl the bottom of the pedal stroke with your toes, then pull your heels up with your hamstrings, calves, and glutes. When you do this with perfection, it should feel like you are dancing on your pedals with the balls of your feet.

SEATED ACCELERATION CLIMBS

This body position is used to produce the most powerful acceleration possible in the saddle on climbs. It can be used to attack, close a gap to another rider, or raise your speed in a solo effort.

Center of Gravity
Drop your center of gravity low by bending the elbows and making your forearms flat, parallel to the top tube. Keep your chest down and close to the stem.

Optimal Cadence
95 to 100 rpm

HANDS: Your handgrip should be firm and equal on both hands with the end of the thumb resting on the top of the hoods. Opposite of the thumb, use the heel of the hand to hold the majority of your body weight, not the center of your hand. Make sure your forearms are parallel to the top tube and your elbows are bent and angled in toward your body.

CORE: Shift your body forward to the front of the seat while you rotate your pelvis forward. Fully engage the core and focus on using your hamstrings, glutes, and calves on the upstroke. Aim to have your chin directly above the stem-handlebar junction. Keep your chest low and far over the front of the bike for a very aerodynamic position.

FEET: Focus on nimbly pulling the pedals with the balls of your feet for all of the pedal stroke. For the downstroke, drive your pedal down on the ball of your foot with your heel up and toes down. On the upstroke, curl the bottom of the pedal stroke with your toes, and then pull your heels up with your hamstrings, calves, and glutes.

STANDING ACCELERATION CLIMBS

This position will produce the most powerful acceleration possible out of the saddle on climbs. Use it to increase your speed on the climbs. This position can be used for attacking on climbs, increasing your speed in switchbacks, surfing the terrain, and a final finish line effort on an uphill TT. This is accomplished by adding your body weight to the pedal stroke, which increases the torque delivered to the cranks by improving the angle at which force is applied. The result is a much faster pickup with the same power output and less overall effort.

Center of Gravity

Your center of gravity should be low and over the bike. Move forward so that your chest is in front of the handlebar-stem junction. This gives you the perfect angle while being aerodynamic to drop your body weight into each downstroke. Your triceps control your center of gravity.

Optimal Cadence

80 to 85 rpm

HANDS: Hands are located on the hoods using the thumb to wrap around the top of the hood to make a firm grip. Opposite of the thumb, use the heel of the hand to bear the majority of your body weight, not the center of your hand. This is done to lock the core. Elbows are bent and brought in toward the core to bring the chest low.

CORE: Core is engaged by aggressively bringing the elbow in toward the bottom of the rib cage on each upstroke toward the knee that is coming up. On the upstroke, focus on pulling knees up using the stomach muscles and hip flexors.

FEET: Your body weight is supported directly on the balls of your feet for all of the pedal stroke. For the downstroke, drive your pedal down with your heel up and toe down. On the upstroke, curl the bottom of the pedal stroke with your toes, and then pull your heels up with your hamstrings, calves, and glutes. When you do both the down- and the upstroke with perfection, it should feel like you are dancing on your pedals.

We recommend understanding the basics of each position to ensure overall proper bike form and then memorizing the details of each. Practicing intervals with these concepts will train your brain and body to automatically perform the most effective body position in any scenario.

Separation

The simplest way to describe Separation is that you are disconnecting your effort from whatever is happening on any given day of riding. Is there a big climb with steep pitches? That's fine. You have your Power Floor and Power Ceiling, and that's where you'll be if anyone needs you. Is the peloton surging and bunching up during the nervous early miles of a race? No problem. You have your plan and you'll use the other five points on the North Star of Execution to build and maintain your momentum to stay in the bunch—and, more importantly, stay in the PTZs you intend to use. Separation allows you to cover the same ground with higher efficiency, save your matches, and train most effectively.

When you look at the power data from a race or group ride, it will be more difficult to see how well you were executing the concept of Separation. Unexpected things happen when you're in a peloton, so your numbers are bound to fluctuate. When you look at workout data, on the other hand, you'll learn quickly how to tell the difference between good use of Separation and when your intervals are blending in with your warm-up, rest, and cooldown phases.

Clear Separation of PTZ and Effort

The first of the three types of Separation applies to your PTZ and your effort. The biggest mistake that new riders make is they get excited to go out and hammer their intervals and end up going too hard in the warm-up and during the rests between efforts. This kills your progression because you end up wasting the energy you need to put in your best effort during the hardest parts of your workout. There needs to be clear, clean separation between the different zones you use in any given workout.

FIGURE 6.9. Separation of the PTZs

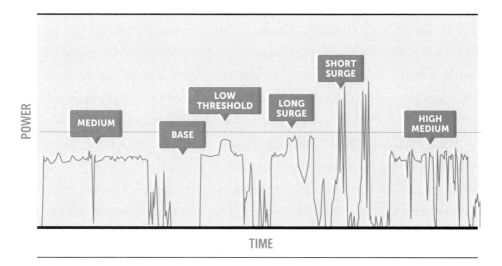

Separation means staying true to your PTZs. If you're supposed to ride in a Medium PTZ, then stay at that zone for the full effort. If a Base PTZ is next, be sure to stay low.

Not only will Separation help you be at your best for the most important parts of your workout, it will also reinforce your body's use of specific fueling sources. As you'll remember, one of the keys to the FORM Method is developing the ability to shift through your PTZs so that you can strategically use your fuel sources. If you can be precise with your Separation, you can be precise with your body's fuel consumption, improving your endurance and saving yourself for the most important moments of a race or ride.

If you have ever done a structured workout and then looked at your power graph, you should have an idea of what Separation of PTZ and effort looks like. You can tell when your intervals begin and when they end based on spikes in power. That's just the beginning. I want you to scrutinize those graphs to see that you are staying within your Power Floors and Ceilings for each effort and rest. Those intervals should look square, not rounded or curved.

Clear Separation of Cadence

As I mentioned earlier in this chapter, people have a bad tendency to set it and forget it when it comes to pedaling cadence. This is extremely limiting. If you only pedal at low cadence, then you're likely going to tax your muscular system too much. Pedal only at a high cadence and you'll rely heavily on your cardiovascular system. And in both cases, depending on the terrain, race dynamics, and speed, you'll be missing out on the torque you need to build and maintain momentum.

Using the FORM Method, you will get to a point where you select the cadence you want to use at any given point. That decision is completely separate from the steepness of a climb or what the competition is doing. Instead of a one-size-fits-all approach to cadence, you'll selectively use high cadence for acceleration bursts to attack or cover attacks on climbs. In a different scenario, during a time trial, you'll use that same separation to shift into a faster cadence to gain momentum at the top of a rolling hill and low cadence to cruise through a fast downhill with a tailwind.

So, when you look at your workout graph, you should be able to tell immediately what cadence you were switching to during a given interval. Riders who aren't experienced will have a cadence graph like a heart-rate EKG because it will always be dictated by the terrain or the race dynamics.

I always give my CINCH athletes a specific cadence to work on, depending on whether they're doing longer climbing intervals or short bursts, or all-day endurance rides. No matter what the effort, you should be able to feel the difference when you're on the bike after you get used to this system.

Clear Separation of Momentum

This third and final type of Separation is where the magic happens. Separation of momentum is where abstract concepts related to power and cadence translate into real results on the road. If you've ever imagined launching a solo attack to win your local race or time trialing faster than you've ever gone before, separation of momentum turns dreams into reality.

FIGURE 6.10. Separation of Momentum

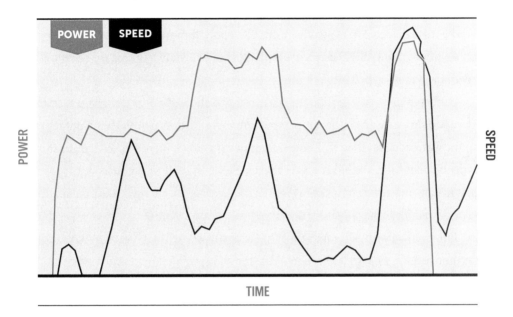

Pairing your power output with cadence and terrain will help you carry speed with less effort—you'll become a much more efficient rider.

It is a complex concept, but essentially, you will strategically use your skills of power separation and cadence separation to generate momentum at the most opportune points of a course.

When you look at a graph that combines power, cadence, speed, and terrain, you'll learn to see those key moments when you build momentum over the crest of a hill, applying your power consistently with higher cadence to produce more torque. This brings you up to speed. Then, if the terrain levels out, you should see a drop in cadence with more consistent power to keep that momentum.

This is how the best cyclists in the world win races, but up until now, the concept was rarely talked about or examined. Remember those rides where you felt powerless to control your effort, lost in the washing machine of the peloton? Imagine what Separation can do for you.

Transitional Control

During the majority of my career as a pro cyclist, my coaches gave me interval workouts that focused on steady efforts. I'd shoot for an average power number on a climb or for a time trial course, and if I could keep raising that number, well then, I was making progress.

Unfortunately, the 200 or so pro riders who showed up to any given race in Europe didn't care at all how my power numbers were improving. They went right to the front and smashed it. There were plenty of times when I could handle this type of violent race pace, but it was always the worst early in the season. I guess I just needed more race miles in my legs, right? Wrong. My training was fundamentally flawed for one key reason: Cycling is not a steady sport.

I'm sure you've experienced that kind of out-of-control surging that makes the peloton feel like a Class V river rapid. Up until now, you might have thought you'd always just be along for the ride, but when you reach this point of the FORM North Star of Execution, you'll be able to start utilizing Transitional Control to take control and thrive in the unpredictable, very unsteady sport of cycling.

Transitional Control ties together all of the other points on the North Star to give your legs an array of tools like a Swiss Army knife. It means changing your PTZ, varying your cadence, adjusting your Body Position, and harnessing Separation—you'll have Transitional Control at your fingertips, and it will empower you to do three critical things that will lead to success in any cycling event.

First and foremost, Transitional Control is your key to cycling's most valuable currency, momentum. You'll gain it when you need it and keep it when you have it. Executing the four other points on the star will lead to more momentum at a lower energy cost, allowing you to ride faster with less power expended and calories spent.

Second, with Transitional Control, you have the ability to control race scenarios. When you see who is with you in a breakaway or a small selection at the end of a hard race, you'll reach a point where you can evaluate their strengths and weaknesses, compare them to the cards you're holding, and hit them with a move that will put you in the best possible position to win.

Third, when you're not completely in control of the race scenario, or perhaps you're riding with a group or category that is a bit faster than you're used to, you can turn to Transitional Control to respond to race dynamics. You'll be able to follow surges and accelerations efficiently, without going beyond your capacity. You'll also be able to find the right combination of power, cadence, and body position for the terrain, even if it isn't right in your wheelhouse.

The workouts in the Appendix will teach you the basics of Transitional Control. They'll show you what it's like to shift gears with PTZ and cadence. At the same time, they'll be training your physiology to switch between fuel sources and comfortably ride at a variety of cadences. Above all, we won't be teaching you to ride a steady interval. That would be boring, and cycling is never boring.

Valverde the Executioner

When I was racing, I always struggled with accelerations on the climbs. Guys like Alberto Contador and Alejandro Valverde were always just a little too good, a little too quick. I was a skinny climber who was fixated on his weight, so I was puzzled when guys would outperform me with accelerations and changes of pace on major climbs in races like the Tour de France or the Giro d'Italia. Sure, I was a small guy, but I thought I was pretty good at punching it on a climb. But there were people who were way better than me, riders like Valverde.

I had no clue why I couldn't go with these guys on attacks. In hindsight, I can see that I wasn't practicing my Execution, and that held me back. I wasn't adding the cadence change component to my toolkit. I wasn't focused on transitioning between the power zones or body positions I needed to use for maximum speed and momentum. I was just too focused on my power-to-weight ratio and my training reflected that.

Maybe the best example of the difference between me and a rider like Valverde was the 2009 Tour of Burgos. I saw firsthand that it wasn't good enough to just have an impressive wattage number on your computer. At this race in early August, the whole peloton was gearing up for the Vuelta a España, myself included. The Tour of Burgos is in Valverde's backyard, in Spain. It's his home race. Plus, he was a Vuelta favorite and would go on to win the Spanish Grand Tour that year.

While there was a stacked lineup at Burgos—Spanish riders like Ezequiel Mosquera, Joaquim "Purito" Rodríguez, Xavier Tondo, and more—I was on great form. I won the individual time trial on stage 4 and moved into the lead on the general classification. It was a huge result for me to win this tough time trial ahead of Valverde and all of the other stars. All I had to do on the fifth and final stage was to hold onto my five-second advantage over Valverde to win the overall.

Burgos is a short race, just five stages, so after my big win, I was confident I could ride with Valverde and the other Spanish guys in the final stage. Then we reached the finish climb to Laguna de Neila and all hell broke loose.

These guys started hitting me with one-two punches, attacking, then counter-attacking, using their insane torque, Cadence Control, and Power Control to whack me over and over again. First Mosquera would go—and he was really good this particular year. I'd claw him back. Then Purito would scorch me with one of his famous attacks. He was on the same team as Valverde that year, a Spanish outfit called Caisse d'Epargne. That meant they were both completely committed to cracking me so Valverde could win the overall.

Every time they attacked, I couldn't go with them. I had more power than they did, I was light, and somehow these guys would jump and I couldn't get on their wheel. I had to claw my way back. I was perplexed. I had just beaten them all in a time trial, so I knew I was firing on all cylinders. But a time trial can't show you how good your Execution is.

Not only could Valverde call on his masterful Execution when he needed to, but he was also a smart guy. He knew he just needed a few seconds on me. So he had Purito attack me, and he would watch me try to ride him back. Then Valverde would throw a counter on me but not full on—not everything he had. Still, he could jump so well that I had to ride steady across to him, uncomfortable, burning my matches, and definitely not in control of the situation.

At 500 meters to go, Valverde whacked me with an unbelievable move. He stood up in perfect Body Position, kicked it into high cadence, moved into a Short Surge PTZ, and sprinted up this wall to the finish in the big chainring. It was perfect Execution. Responding to that move, all I had in my arsenal was standing low cadence, which was still at a pretty high power output. But he put 26 seconds into me on that short section of road, beating me in the overall.

Believe it or not, even though a rider like Valverde or Peter Sagan is a master of Execution, they probably can't put it into words and explain what they're doing. They've just spent decades racing at the sport's highest level and naturally found their way to these techniques. You watch them ride in the peloton and you see the changes in cadence. Separation, transitions between power zones, and perfect body position. They're just on a really high level, but it's not pure power like a lot of people think, like I used to think.

That's why the Execution pillar of the FORM Method is so exciting. This is the secret sauce that has made champions for decades, but as far as I can tell, it's never been put down on paper to help every rider improve and enjoy the sport. When you learn the art of Execution, you'll begin to feel like you have total control of what you're doing, how hard you're riding. You'll become a faster cyclist and you'll have way more fun doing it.

07

PLAYING TO YOUR STRENGTHS

xecution is a very exciting concept, but how does it actually work when you show up to the ride or start line? How do you know what to do and when to do it? Let's start by returning to the sports analogy I made in the Rider Types chapter. When a football team goes to play a game, the coach always draws up a plan. No matter if it's a peewee league or an NFL team that's playing in the Super Bowl, the teams all follow this same fundamental practice.

The coaches take what they know about their own team and form a strategy. What are their strengths? Maybe their offense can beat up opposing defenses to run the ball. Or they could have a gunslinger quarterback who will throw long passes all day long. Then, they consider their weaknesses. Is their defense not that good against a rush? Perhaps their field goal kicker's range is below average. Then, the strategy forms around playing to their strengths and avoiding their weaknesses.

Of course, if they have information about the other team's weaknesses and strengths, they take those into account, too. This helps them build an even more intricate and focused strategy. They're setting the team up for its best chance at success.

Play the Game of Cycling

The top pro teams that race the Tour de France and other major events are taking this same approach to cycling. Are you doing that when you head out on a group ride or line up for a weekend race? If you aren't, then you might be missing out on an opportunity to progress and truly play the game of cycling, rather than just going along for the ride. And remember, you don't have to take it as seriously as a Tour de France contender. You can start small with your own strengths and weaknesses and build a basic plan for yourself.

Ride Your Rider Type

This process begins with knowing your Rider Type. As I outlined in Chapter 3, we all have roles to play in the sport of cycling. Spend enough time on a bike, and you'll be able to quickly tell what you are good at and what is not in your wheelhouse. Some people can evolve throughout their careers to change their specialties. Even the pros do this. French rider Laurent Jalabert was once a top sprinter, winning races like Milan–Sanremo in his early years. After a bad crash, he reinvented himself as a climber, taking the Tour de France's polka dot jersey as King of the Mountains.

So, find a starting point for yourself based on our Rider Type descriptions. It's a framework that can guide you in assessing your strengths and weaknesses. Even if you don't feel you're exactly like a climber or a puncheur type, you know what you're good at, and that will guide your strategy.

Take that honest assessment of yourself and apply it to a group ride, event, or race. If you're a climber and the route includes one major climb midway through, then it's pretty clear that you'll want to find ways to get through the other parts of the route—the areas that don't suit you—and go all-in on that key climb to take your chance at winning. Someone who identifies as a classics TT rider would probably take the complete opposite approach.

Use Your PTZs Wisely

Once you have a general idea of what parts of the ride will suit your strengths, you'll use the framework of your PTZs to create a more detailed plan.

The Endurance PTZs that burn fat will be essential for the parts of this race that aren't to your liking. You want to find ways to get through those sections while burning as little glycogen as possible. Then, when you reach a point on the ride when you can really shine, where your talents as a climber or TT rider or puncheur can make a difference, launch into your higher PTZs to make a move, create a gap, or top the climb.

Follow the North Star

The final piece of the puzzle is using the five points of the FORM North Star of Execution. Riding in the right PTZ at the right time ensures you're burning the correct fuel source and it also sets you up to produce a maximal effort when the time is right. You're also using your cadence throughout the race to generate torque when you need it, build speed when you want it, and maintain momentum when you're trying to stay clear of the bunch. This all comes together with proper Body Position and Separation.

A Chameleon Demonstrates Execution for Different Rider Types

As I was writing this book, I was trying to find a great way for riders to visualize the fundamentals of Execution. I needed to give you something simple but really easy to imagine when you're in the middle of a ride. I started thinking of a few great cyclists who fall into the different Rider Types—maybe they would be a good reference point.

And then one name came to me: Peter Sagan.

This guy has to be the most influential rider in today's peloton. He's probably the most well-known cyclist and the most inspiring. I started to think about his

100+ victories, and I realized something pretty mind-blowing: Sagan is a proven winner, but, more important, he is a chameleon when it comes to Execution. He can literally do it all, and he already has before he even turned 30.

Sagan has won races, as you'd expect, playing the role as a classics sprinter. That's his bread and butter. He also has won as a puncheur. Not too surprising, right? Then we go further down the list and see he's actually won races like a classics sprinter or a classics TT rider. And finally—this one is nuts—he's even won at least one masquerading as a climber. I saw that last one firsthand, and it was incredible. So, let's all try to be a little bit like Sagan. He's savvy, he's powerful, he's got a winner's instinct, and he's versatile.

I don't expect any of you to be *that* versatile, but I think you can learn from each of these examples from his extensive list of victories. And while these examples come from the highest level of racing in the world, you can also apply these strategies in a group ride or events like a gravel grinder or gran fondo. You're going to win your ride, and that doesn't have to mean you need to win the race.

Classics Sprinter: 2016 World Championships

As soon as the 2016 World Championships were announced, I'm sure that riders like Sagan were licking their chops. The route through the Qatar desert contained none of the weakness that would usually spell trouble for a classics sprinter. There were no extended climbs. No terrain changes that might be better for a puncheur or climber. Of course, since it's a one-day race, no need to worry about the cumulative fatigue of a stage race that might be tough for a sprinter (but not Sagan, in general).

Instead, the world's course was all aces for Sagan. It was a long race, 257 km, like it always is. There was potential for crosswinds with the wind whipping off the Persian Gulf. It was great for riders who could follow explosive attacks and make moves of their own. It seemed destined to come down to a sprint finish, the ultimate explosive effort.

This race came down to two pivotal moments for Sagan. In the first, he bridged across a split in the peloton when crosswinds broke the race apart. This was a monumental effort, and the type of move that requires exceptional Execution.

As the front group pulls away in a crosswind, and you're caught on the wrong side of the action, you need to act fast. This means using your Cadence Control to switch into high cadence for a high-torque acceleration. This has to be done with a Standing Acceleration Flats body position: You're rocking the bike back and forth, resting the heels of your hands on the bars. Your core is engaged, using hip flexors to pull through the top of the stroke with your elbows in. And you are pedaling on the balls of your feet, pulling your heels up with hamstrings and glutes.

This first moment was crucial, but it happened at the race's midway point. There were still hours to go before the final sprint finish. Even if you've only done a couple of races, you probably know that there are times early on when the pace is fast, and you have to fight to avoid getting dropped. But once you make the selection, your job has only begun. After that you need to recover from the effort, and that's what Sagan did after he rode across the gap in the desert crosswinds.

It might seem tough to shift gears mentally into a more relaxed mindset and physically into a lower, Medium PTZ. You need to go from full-on attack mode to the opposite, conserving energy and recovering from the effort. Here's where you clear the lactate that accumulated in the effort by riding in the Low Threshold PTZ or ideally in your High Medium PTZ. In terms of Execution, this comes down to Power Control—holding yourself up between the floor and ceiling to avoid unnecessary drops or spikes that will kill your momentum. The Separation point on the North Star of Execution is critical to stay in the right PTZ. Even if the wind was blowing or riders were attacking the bunch, you can be sure that Sagan was riding his own pace in the field, using his cadence to ride with the ebb and flow of the pack.

How do I know he was doing all of these things? Well, he probably wouldn't explain it in the way we do with the FORM Method, but it's clear in the way he changes his cadence, shifts his Body Position, and uses the draft to maximum advantage, that he was intuitively riding his own version of the North Star of Execution.

He ended up winning the race, so you can bet that he did an exceptional job of recovering from that effort to bridge across to the group in those crosswinds. He launched an incredible sprint to beat some of the sport's modern-day legends—Mark Cavendish and Tom Boonen.

Winning a sprint finish is a perfect example of Transitional Control. Things happen so fast in the final kilometer of the race that the elements of Power Control, Cadence Control, Body Position, and Separation have to come together seamlessly. And they're being employed rapidly, on instinct. The approach to a sprint can't be too hard, or you'll be fried by the time you need to jump—that's Power Control and Separation. The cadence of a sprint varies wildly. You'll see guys in the bunch at low cadence and then a moment later, they're at 110 rpm, sprinting for the line. And, of course, that critical acceleration at the end relies heavily on the right Body Position to generate the most power.

Takeaways for Classics Sprinters

➡ Be prepared to use High Threshold PTZ and high cadence to make the selection or a split in the race.

➡ Focus on Separation and Power Control to maintain lower PTZs in the bunch as you wait for your opportunity to attack or sprint.

➡ Refine your Body Position to get the most out of your power when you're attacking or sprinting.

➡ Practice sprint finishes so you can use Transitional Control in fast, intense situations.

Puncheur: 2015 World Championships

Most riders would be happy with just one world champion rainbow jersey (I know I would), but Sagan has three. And I can't help but talk about his first world's win in this overview of his extraordinary versatility.

The 2015 World Championships course in Richmond, Virginia, was a more typical course than the one in Qatar the following year. Usually, these championship races have some hills but nothing too mountainous. That is partly because they're held on short circuits that the peloton has to ride many times before they finish after hours and hours of grueling riding.

This means that a lot of world championships are pretty ideal for puncheurs. In fact, organizers try to make things exciting for the fans, so there aren't many long, boring flat sections that are not ideal for a puncheur. As I mentioned earlier, it's an all-or-nothing one-day race, so there's no need to worry about the recovery or fatigue of a stage race. Instead, these world's courses are great for riders who like big variations in pace, thanks to the hilly terrain. They can pedal uphill with a burst of power and drop nearly everyone. And puncheurs aren't afraid to come to the line and sprint out of a small group.

This Richmond course with its cobblestone climbs was perfect for Sagan. But as is the case with any long road race, he needed to get to the critical last lap of the race with enough ammunition to launch a winning attack in the end.

He rode through lap after lap of this course in the peloton, biding his time, waiting until the race's critical moment. This is one of the hardest things about good Execution. You have to realize that there are many points in a race that are not to your advantage. Even if you're a puncheur climbing up a steep, short ascent like Richmond's Libby Hill, you have to be disciplined and know that with 150 km to go, this is not the time to spike your power into the Nuclear Zone with a high-cadence attack.

Instead, like Sagan did, you use Separation and Power Control on those undulating climbs throughout the early stages of the race. Ideally, you are in your fat-burning PTZs to conserve glycogen for the critical moments in the end. In the draft, you should also be able to use Cadence Control to smooth out your pace in the peloton as it surges and slows down.

Then, when the time is right, you put everything you have into that race-winning move. That's what Sagan did on the final lap of racing, going up the toughest climb.

As a puncheur, you know that you've got a fast acceleration and enough sustained power to drop nearly everyone on the right climb, or at least greatly reduce the group, getting rid of better sprinters who might finish you off in a flat sprint. So you wind up the cadence for maximum torque at the toughest point of the climb, out of the saddle, using a Short Surge PTZ. When you get a gap, you settle into your Seated Power Climbs body position to hold your momentum in a time trial effort. You might be on the hoods or in the drops, but either way you're resting the heels of your hands on the bar with your elbows in. Your pelvis rotates forward in the saddle to make the most out of your glutes and hip flexors. As you pedal, your heels drop with the downstroke and raise with the upstroke to use all of your leg muscles efficiently.

Sagan hit the peloton with his attack at the perfect moment, and after the last climb he got just enough of a lead to make it stick as they came into the final few hundred meters to the finish.

Takeaways for Puncheurs

- ➡ Don't get tempted to go all-in on early climbs, even if they are suited to your strengths.
- ➡ Use Power Control and Separation to manage your effort early on.
- ➡ Strike with full force when it's time to attack, engaging Cadence Control and Body Position.
- ➡ After the attack is made, use Transitional Control to maximize momentum and extend your lead as the course continues to undulate.

Classics TT Rider: 2015 Amgen Tour of California and 2018 Paris–Roubaix

Personal growth is an important part of the sport of cycling. As you develop new abilities, skills, and direction as an athlete, new opportunities will arise. This is something I want to impress upon you as it is one of the reasons we have so many layers to grow into as an athlete in the FORM Method. You never know when an opportunity for growth will arise, but you need to be ready when it does.

Sagan's overall win in the 2015 Amgen Tour of California is a perfect example of this concept of change. You don't normally see Peter Sagan chasing the overall title at the TOC. In fact, in the past he has focused his efforts solely on the sprint stages and it's worked out quite well. Sagan has won more stages than any other rider in the history of the Tour of California: 17 in total. But this edition of the eight-day race presented him with an unexpected opportunity.

Sagan's prior training opened new doors beyond winning sprint stages. He transformed into a rider with classics TT abilities, skills, and direction. This new version of Sagan could produce longer, sustained power, which came in handy for him in the time trial stage. Here, he laid down the effort needed to win the stage and take the overall stage race lead.

But that was not where this newfound opportunity for Sagan stopped. What he did next I think you will find very interesting and very applicable to your own personal cycling challenges. With a solid time advantage over the other riders, it was possible he could win the overall Tour of California title. But there was one more un-Sagan obstacle that stood in his way to winning the overall title: a mountain stage with a climb for a finish.

Sagan is not a climber rider type, so how could he possibly pull this off? He could have been stubborn and let his previous performances define him, letting the lead riders ride away on the climbs. Instead, he chose to take advantage of this new opportunity and go all-in to try and defend the race lead on the slopes of Mount Baldy.

To do this, on the brutal finishing climb up Mount Baldy, he used his new sustained high-power ability from his transformation into a classics TT rider to assist him. He would use a similar high sustained power as he did to win the time trial, but this time it would be like an uphill time trial. By doing this he had an effective strategy: maintain a hard pace that would not only keep him with the leaders, but also reduce the strength of the surges from the climbers.

Explosive riders without the ability to ride a sustained high power, like the Sagan of old, often fall into the trap laid out by the climbers. The repeated attacks a climber can put in are the greatest danger for a classics TT rider from an Execution standpoint. If you get suckered into following attacks, you'll spike your power above what you're capable of, eventually cracking with repeated efforts. Careful Power Control is the answer to this challenge. Know your Power Ceiling and be careful not to break through it. It won't be as flashy as a lot of wild attacks, but you might find yourself gradually reeling in those climbers after they get tired.

As a classics TT rider you have excellent Threshold PTZ and Endurance. In terms of Execution, this means you can keep your pace in the right PTZ (probably Low to Medium Threshold on something like Mount Baldy). You can also focus on seated power, using good Body Position to engage your core, dropping and raising your heels to efficiently engage all leg muscles. It's likely you won't vary your cadence much to follow attacks.

The key to a strong effort on a climb like this—for Sagan or us mere mortal classics TT riders—is Separation. The climb is steady, but it has its steep sections and switchbacks. It also has plenty of ambitious climbers throwing haymakers all the way to the top because it's the last chance they have to take time on Sagan in the race. None of that can impact you. You know the PTZ that will be sustainable for this length of effort. Your Cadence Control is locked in. You don't let these external factors force you into the red.

In the end, Sagan used the classics TT transformation and executed a perfect climb for a "non-climber." The impossible now becomes possible by simply changing your Rider Type execution of ability, skill, and direction.

Before we close on the Sagan classics TT rider transformation, I would like to quickly touch on another example to help you understand how to use this rider type. What if you're a classics TT rider and going for the win on flat, rolling terrain? He again is a perfect example, this time due to his Paris–Roubaix win in 2018. Sagan went on to win this major classic with a 54-kilometer breakaway. That would feel like two Mount Baldys, but on flat, extremely bumpy roads!

In Paris–Roubaix he used the classics TT rider Execution in an offense-focused plan, rather than the defense-focused plan he used on the slopes of Mount Baldy. He made many repeated short accelerations until it was one too many for the other riders. Then, finally, he was with just one other rider—Silvan Dillier—riding toward victory. Sounds like mission accomplished, right? Well, as many of you have experienced before, making the attack work is one thing, but holding it to the finish is another thing. This is where you can use the classics TT rider Execution like Sagan to bring it home.

Once you end up in that exciting (but terrifying) off-the-front situation like Sagan did in Roubaix, every detail matters. You need to hold that lead on the chasers, and Execution is one of your best ways to do it (and over a distance of 54 kilometers, it's really the only way). Power Control and Cadence Control are used strategically to gain speed out of corners and over the crests of hills. And then you shift your zones and cadence to maintain momentum once you have it. Body Position contributes to both of those phases—standing for accelerations, sitting for steady sections that carry the speed. Separation and Transitional Control are also critical to keep you from getting too excited and going into the red on a climb or in a section of the course that doesn't need to be attacked. Sagan executed all of these strategies so well, allowing him to stay off the front and ride to victory.

Takeaways for Classics TT Riders

➡ Avoid the temptation to follow attacks. Use Separation and Power Control to ride the right pace for you on climbs or in critical points of a race.

- Find your rhythm with Transitional Control to use the terrain to your advantage.
- Stick to your PTZ and the surges and slowdowns in the peloton will work themselves out.
- Be prepared for a few key accelerations that will call upon your Cadence Control, Body Position, and an effort beyond your normal PTZ.

Climber: 2011 Tour de Suisse, Stage 3

I bet when this chapter started you had doubts about whether I could actually prove to you that Sagan can race like a true climber. He's too heavy. He's meant for cobblestones and fast sprints. He could never climb with the best, right?

That may be true for a lot of riders, but Sagan is different, and I saw it in person on the third stage of the 2011 Tour de Suisse. It was cold, rainy, and wet. This is typically how it is for the Tour de Suisse. It's such a tough, mountainous race, and it has nine stages. That's long enough to really beat you up but not so long that the pace will be moderate at times and you can find your rhythm in the peloton. Honestly, it's kind of amazing that sprinters like Sagan even show up to this race.

But he didn't ride like those other sprinters on this day. The attacks were flying on the final climb of this stage. It topped the 6,500-foot Grosse Scheidegg pass before descending to the finish in Grindelwald. That's probably why Sagan put up such a fight on this stage. He knew the fast, twisting descent would favor his technical skills, and if he got over the top with the climbers, none of the skinny guys like me, Levi Leipheimer, or Tejay van Garderen would stand a chance.

What shocked me was how he rode this final pass. He didn't do it like a classics TT rider, as he did four years later at Tour of California, measuring his pace and staying in his zones. Instead, he was following all the moves. When guys like Damiano Cunego and Jakob Fuglsang attacked, he was right on their wheels.

This is a classic tactic for pure climbers, who don't prefer the steady grinding pace that a GC TT rider would use on a long climb. Instead, they love changes in pace and quick accelerations, the kind of moves that wear down the other riders who can't follow repeated jumps.

Great Execution matters for every Rider Type, but its importance cannot be overstated for climbers. These riders need that high-force acceleration to snap the elastic and drop heavier, slower riders who don't have the legs to respond on steep climbs. This means amazing Cadence Control—the best climbers can wind up high cadence at extremely high wattage to generate massive torque. They do this with all of the keys to Body Position that we've talked about previously. However, their Standing Acceleration Climbs position is their most powerful weapon. They leverage the handlebars for extra power, engage their core to drive the muscles around their hips, and they use their foot position to tap the power of their hamstrings and glutes.

Most climbers also have to rely on the Seated Power Climbs body position to maintain their speed and momentum if they ride clear of the group or are bridging a gap to another rider. As is the case with the other examples, Separation and Transitional Control are also crucial for climbers. They might use Separation in a manner opposite to what you'd expect a classics TT rider to do. Instead of separating their cadence and power from the terrain and competition to conserve energy, they might go the other direction to ride at a much faster pace when attacking with a Long Surge or a Short Surge. Most climbs also have gradient changes and switchbacks where Transitional Control can help them build momentum to hold off a chasing group.

As for how this mountain stage played out for Sagan: He won. He used climber Execution to stay with the climbers all the way up the climb, and then outsprinted flyweight climber Damiano Cunego at the line to take the victory. Even though he's an amazingly versatile chameleon of a rider, Sagan is still smart enough to know how to play to his strengths.

Takeaways for Climbers

➡ Accelerations on climbs have to be coordinated displays of Execution with Power Control, Cadence Control, and Body Position for maximal torque.

➡ Separation can mean going way above the pace of the peloton to make your attack stick.

➡ Anticipate the climb's changes in gradient and switchbacks and use Transitional Control to strategically build and maintain momentum.

➡ Get rid of the faster sprinters with repeated attacks so you don't get beat at the line!

08

STRENGTH TRAINING AND ACTIVATION

C an you race 250 kilometers? Can you climb Mont Ventoux at 5 watts/kg? Can you survive 21 days of racing? If you are reading this book, you probably don't measure up to the top WorldTour pro riders (and that's OK). But you might be surprised to know that they face a couple of the same persistent challenges that you do. And, you can address those issues with the same simple core activation and plyometric exercises that they use to improve their cycling.

Let's start with core activation. Back when I was a pro rider, I built my core routine to prevent injury as I was rehabbing from a bad crash. With a broken shoulder and a herniated disc, I was in rough shape. I tried a bunch of physical therapists and trainers. Nothing clicked until I met Allison Westfahl, an exercise physiologist and personal trainer. She helped me develop a core routine that combined strength and activation. By activation, I mean essentially switching on muscles, firing up the neuromuscular connection between your brain and your legs. These motions are purposeful but not too strenuous, just enough to wake up your system.

As I incorporated this 10-minute routine into my preparation before rides and races, I realized it could be about more than just injury prevention. It actually was helping me ride with more power, with a more efficient pedal stroke. The days when I saw the most gains were in time trials. You've probably heard the time trial called "the race of truth," and I couldn't agree more. You're out there by yourself, and you need to be ready to perform start to finish—no hiding in the peloton. As a smaller guy, I really had to have my ducks in a row to do a good time trial, but I always found myself struggling during the first half of these races. For pros, time trials are usually later in the day to sync up with prime-time TV coverage, sometimes as late as 4:00 or 5:00 p.m. I'd be sitting around all day, on the bus, maybe checking out the course in the morning, but generally sedentary.

Sound familiar? That's right, nearly everyone with a desk job faces the same problem I did on time trial days. You sit at work for hours on end and a lot of your muscle groups switch off. Then when it's time for the after-work group ride, you feel like garbage. The same thing happens when you hop out of a car to ride at the end of a road trip.

This is why activation is so important. Before I started implementing my core routine, I felt like I was treading water, lost in a huge ocean, unable to do my usual pedal stroke. I often got into a flow about halfway through the time trial, but by that point I had lost too much time. When I began incorporating activation into my pre-race routine, the difference was noticeable right away. I felt powerful through the top of my pedal stroke, using my hip flexors efficiently. At first, I thought my power meter was out of whack because I wasn't used to seeing such high readings right out of the gate in a time trial.

I think you'll notice a difference right away, too. This routine isn't a quick fix, though. The key is consistency to build your body's central nervous connection between brain and muscles. If you spend 10 minutes activating these muscles before a 90-minute ride, your body will continue to use those muscle groups the entire time, making the connection stronger, making your body stronger.

Practice and perfect these core activation exercises. Then find a way to set yourself up to easily replicate them in any place, whether that's your living room, office, a hotel room, or even in a quiet corner of an airport. You don't always have to use these activation exercises right before a ride. They are great to do when things get too busy to ride, or if you are traveling. It may not feel like you're getting in a big day of training, but if you are activating the key muscle groups, you are maintaining the mind-body connection and even making it stronger. Short-term inactivity doesn't necessarily lead to a loss of fitness, but you can lose the connection between your brain and your legs. The core activation exercises will help you avoid that, too.

OPPOSITE ARM/LEG REACH PLANK

20 reps (alternate side to side)

➡ Start in a basic plank position by coming onto your forearms and toes, making sure that your elbows are directly below your shoulders and your feet are approximately 10 to 12 inches apart.

➡ Keep your hips and shoulders parallel to the mat and lift your right foot and left hand at the same time. Extend the fingertips forward and toes backward as far as possible. Squeeze your right glute.

➡ Hold this extension for 5 seconds, then bring your hand and foot down to the mat at the same time. Repeat on the other side.

SUPERMAN

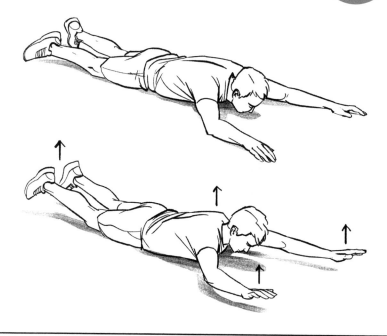

- Begin by lying facedown on the mat with arms extended above your head.
- Put space between your ears and your shoulders by dropping your shoulder blades down toward your waist. Gently squeeze your glutes and slowly raise your feet and hands off the mat.
- Do not lift more than 6 inches. Think about pulling the top of your head and your tailbone in opposite directions. Hold this position at the top for 5 seconds and gently release. Refresh your starting position each time by dropping the shoulder blades down the back before you lift. Repeat.

PRONE SNOW ANGEL

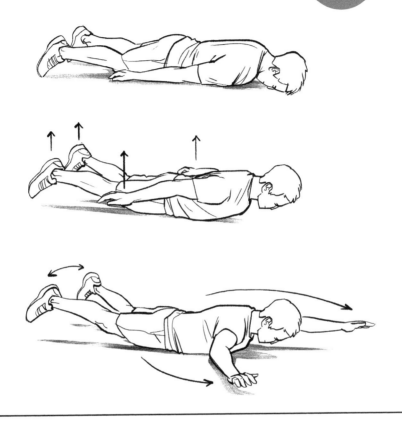

➡ Start by lying facedown with arms extended along your sides, hands at hips with palms pointed down. Keep the back of your neck long and your shoulder blades dropped down toward your waist. Gently squeeze your glutes and slowly raise your feet, chest, and hands off the mat.

➡ Do not lift more than 6 inches. Create a "snow angel" by sweeping your arms overhead and separating your feet.

➡ Without bending your arms, try to bring your hands together above your head.

➡ Return to starting position and allow your feet, chest, and hands to relax down to the mat.

➡ If your shoulders and chest muscles are tight, you will not be able to touch your hands together at first. It's better to keep your arms straight and have your hands slightly separated above your head than to bend your arms and touch your hands.

PAC-MAN

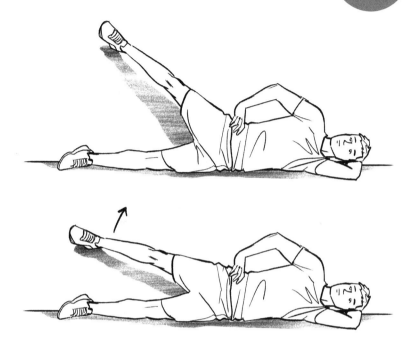

- ➡ This exercise got its name from the way Pac-Man eats up his competition. Start on your left side with your back against a wall.
- ➡ Your head should be completely relaxed; you can rest it on your extended left arm or support it with your left hand. Points of contact with the wall should be heels, glutes, shoulder blades, and back of the head. Place your right hand on your right hip and slowly begin to slide your right leg up the wall (this is abduction).
- ➡ The goal is to use the muscles of the outer hip to lift the leg instead of lifting the entire pelvis. If you feel the hip bone on your right side moving upward toward your chest, you are lifting your pelvis. Complete repetitions on one side, then switch.

SIDE PLANK

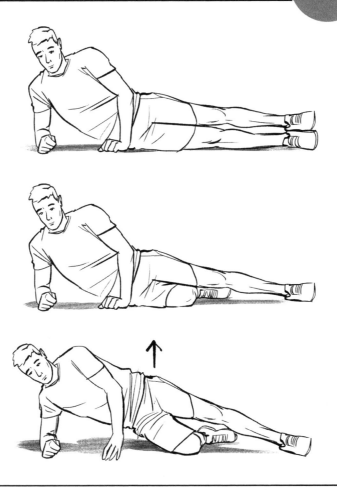

- ➡ Start on your right side with your right forearm on the mat, perpendicular to your body, keeping your right elbow directly below your right shoulder.
- ➡ Keep your left leg straight and bend the right leg to a 90-degree angle.
- ➡ Create a straight line from your left shoulder all the way down to your left ankle. Check to make sure your hips are pushed forward, tailbone is tucked, and ears are directly above your shoulders. Keeping your left hand on the mat in front of your chest for stability, push down through the right forearm and lift your hips off the mat.
- ➡ The right knee remains on the mat throughout this exercise to provide support for the low back. Lift the left hip up and down, then switch sides.

BRIDGE WITH HEEL SLIDE

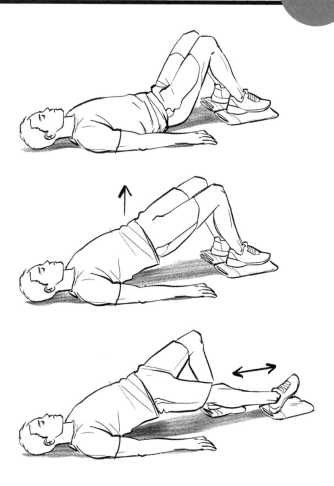

- ➡ Start on your back with your knees bent and feet on the floor approximately 6 to 8 inches from your glutes. Place a folded towel under each foot. Your arms should be relaxed at your sides.
- ➡ Squeeze your glutes, tuck your tailbone, and lift your hips off the floor.
- ➡ Keeping your hips high, slide your right foot away from your body until your leg is completely straight, then bring it back in. Repeat this sliding motion with the left foot, keeping your hips stable the entire time. Alternate feet each slide.

TIM-BERRR!

5 reps each leg

- ➡ The goal of this move is to keep the legs totally straight while they are "falling," mimicking a tree.
- ➡ Start by lying on your back and extending both legs straight up to the ceiling.
- ➡ Gently pull your toes toward your face so that the bottoms of your feet are perfectly flat. If your hamstrings are tight, you might need to bend your knees slightly. Keep your right leg straight while you lower your left leg until the right heel taps the floor.
- ➡ Try not to bend your left leg while you are lowering it. Using your lower abdominals, pull your left leg back up to the starting position, being careful to keep your upper body, neck, and head relaxed the entire time. Repeat this movement with your right leg, and continue to alternate.

SHOULDER BLADE SQUEEZE

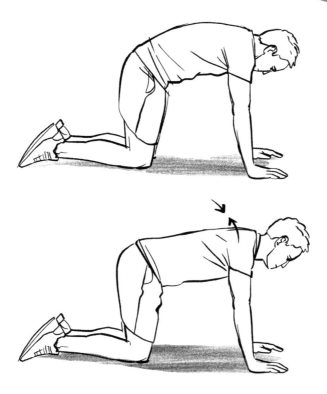

➡ Start on your hands and knees with your knees below your hips. Place your hands directly below your shoulders, as if you were going to do a push-up.

➡ Keeping your arms straight, drop your shoulder blades down toward your waist and then squeeze them together.

➡ Don't let your low back sway or your chin push forward. Hold the shoulder blade squeeze for 5 seconds and release. Repeat until you have completed the desired number of repetitions.

MUSETTE

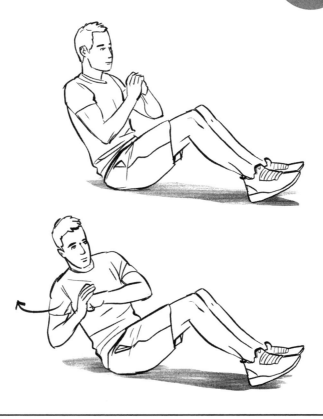

→ Start in a seated position, your knees bent and heels lightly touching the mat (for a super-advanced option, lift your heels 6 inches off the mat).

→ Lift your chest, pull your shoulder blades down and together, and keep your neck neutral. Make a fist with your left hand and push it into your right palm, keeping both hands in the center of your chest and 6 inches away from your body. With your legs held steady, twist your upper body (still pushing the left fist into the right palm) as far to the right as possible.

→ When you reach your twisting limit, push your left fist into your right hand with as much force as possible for 15 seconds. Come to center and switch sides, this time making a fist with your right hand and pushing it into your left palm.

STRENGTH TRAINING AND ACTIVATION   141

Plyometrics

The off-season is a tricky time of the year for pro cyclists. On one hand, there's opportunity to unwind, spend some time with family, eat and drink a little more than usual, and probably take a vacation to somewhere fun like the beach. That's the nice part that you probably see on riders' social media feeds. But you might not see them post about all of the sponsor obligations, meetings, and team-bonding events that fill up the fall calendar very fast. It isn't all fun and games.

While I enjoyed the off-season, I also found it presented a challenge. With this radical change in routine and the additional obligations, it was hard to train consistently. And, when I returned to racing early in the season, the intensity of the early races shocked my system.

Just like pro riders, you have an off-season, too—sometimes multiple small ones each year. They don't always coincide with the fall and winter months, either. Sometimes your off-season is a spring vacation with the family to visit grandparents. Or it could be a midsummer trip to the mountains or the beach. I imagine you also have at least a week or so of travel around the holidays that can disrupt your daily and weekly routines, especially your training.

When I joined the Discovery Channel team in the early 2000s, I was introduced to a training routine off the bike that addressed the challenges posed by a disruption in training: plyometrics. Plyometric exercises are controlled, explosive movements designed to activate fast-twitch muscles and develop your explosive strength. They don't require much gym equipment. You can do the routine in 15 to 20 minutes. And if you're like me, you'll find they are a fun break from riding a bike.

I incorporated these workouts into my off-season and quickly noticed it made a big difference in my ability to attack and surge. The transition from off- to in-season is really harsh. A lot of riders, pros and amateurs alike, struggle with it. When I kept up with my plyometrics routine well into the start of the season, I felt like integrating into the peloton was less shocking in those early races.

Just imagine how many mini off- to in-season transitions you have throughout the year. Life disrupts the consistency of regular racing and training. Plus, in some regions, race schedules aren't always booked continuously from spring to fall. It can be pretty frustrating to get dropped in the first few races after a break. You feel like everyone else has a limitless supply of brutal accelerations and you're stuck in second gear, hanging on for dear life as the peloton strings out single file.

Whether off-seasons are regular and planned, like the wintertime, or unexpected, like sudden work or family obligations, treat these times as opportunities. That's how good professional riders approach a disruption in their training or racing. With this 15- to 20-minute plyometrics routine, you can take the opportunity to make yourself a well-rounded rider by branching out beyond on-the-bike training.

When you are faced with one of these mini off-seasons, like a work trip or a family vacation, use plyometrics to develop your fast-twitch muscles and build your explosive strength. This routine is perfect for days when you don't have the time or ability to ride. Plyometrics help maintain the connection between the mind and muscles, similar to core activation exercises. Stay consistent with your routine and that first race back won't be so demoralizing.

As I hinted at earlier, plyometrics are also an important way to develop your explosive power as you train for the coming season of racing. If you're stuck on the trainer during the winter, it's difficult to really prime those fast-twitch muscle fibers. Although you might not feel particularly fast or powerful when you're logging hours upon hours of base miles in the winter, your fast-twitch muscles are still there and ready to go. Plyometrics keep the neuromuscular connection to these muscles active. When they are exercised and regularly activated, they'll be primed to perform on a bike. Plyometrics are an essential tool in your buildup to the season. You'll hop into racing already primed for the speed and intensity.

One word of caution: It's best not to do plyometrics when there are a lot of group rides, races, or events on your schedule. You'll be doing plenty to maintain your fast-twitch muscles on the bike. But when those aren't happening, always make time for plyometrics.

POSTURE STRENGTHENER

This exercise will strengthen your posterior muscle chain and stabilize the core.

➡ Stand with your feet hip-width apart, arms at your sides, with your weight on your heels. Let your knees bend, sitting back slightly, and pull your hips back as you push your chest forward.

➡ Without moving your feet, continue to lean slightly forward while activating your adductor muscles. You should feel tension in your lower back, adductors, glutes, and hamstrings; this lets you know your posterior chain is activated.

➡ Once you're in position, keep your chest high with arms back and your thumbs out to the side, shoulders pulling back and down. Hold for 20 seconds.

➡ Bring your arms out in front as you pull your hips away from your ankles. Hold for 20 seconds. Next, bring your arms all the way up, almost overhead, but reaching slightly forward, as you lift your chest a little higher. Hold for 20 seconds.

CYCLING TRIANGLE

Activate your core and stretch the hips, hamstrings, calves, shoulders, and chest.

➡ Start in triangle pose: Stand tall with a straight back, feet wider than hips, and arms in line with the shoulders (like a T), palms down.
➡ Turn your right foot out to the side and keep your left toes pointed forward. Lean to the right, reaching sideways with your right fingertips.
➡ From this outstretched position, bend at the hip, while extending your right arm toward the floor. Use your oblique and abdominal muscles to bring yourself back up to starting position. Complete all reps to one side, then switch sides. Hold the position after the reps for a deeper stretch.

HIP FLEXOR AND SIDE-BODY STRETCH

Stretch the hips, hip flexors, groin, and legs. Relieve tension in your lower body.

➡ Stand in a lunge position with your hips squared and your front knee unlocked. Your front knee should always stay behind your ankle. Your feet should be parallel and facing forward. Hold the lunge position, breathing into the movement for a deeper stretch.

➡ Next, bring your arms above your head, reaching as high as you can. Inhale as you lift your rib cage higher, then as you exhale tighten your abs to maintain this new height. Hold for at least 10 seconds.

➡ While in extension, keep your chest high and side bend away from your front leg. Hold for 15 seconds.

➡ Repeat exercise on the other leg.

HAMSTRING ACTIVATOR

This activation will strengthen the posterior of your body, especially the hamstrings and glutes.

➡ Start in a lunge. Tense your back leg muscles so the leg becomes a long straight line.
➡ Send the weight of your core forward by bending forward from the hips, keeping your back straight. Once bent forward, immediately exhale your breath and contract your glutes and hamstrings to pull yourself back to the starting position.
➡ Repeat sequence on other side.

EXPLOSIVE POWER SQUAT JUMP

Build explosive power through the legs, core, and posterior.

➡ Plant both feet on the floor slightly wider than shoulder-width apart. Point feet slightly outward.

➡ Looking straight ahead, bend at both the hips and knees, ensuring that your knees point toward your toes. Continue bending your knees until your upper legs are parallel with the floor, ensuring that your back remains between 45 and 90 degrees of your hips. This is the squat position.

➡ Once in this position, explode into a jump, propelling your body upward into the air, then land in the squat position. While landing, ensure that you land through the balls of your feet first before rolling through the flat and heel, and maintain soft knees to prevent injury.

ACCELERATION SPLIT SQUAT

Build explosive power and mobility in your quads, hips, hamstrings, and glutes. Increase bone density.

➡ Stand in a lunge position with your right leg forward and left leg back. Make sure your right knee is behind your toes. Contract your abs. Focusing on an upward movement, jump up and land with your legs together.
➡ Once your legs are together, switch legs by jumping and sending your right leg backward as your left leg goes forward. In the air, both your legs should be extended. As you land, lower your back knee as close to the mat as possible. Land softly on the midfoot, then the heels. Reset your posture in the starting position and repeat for a total of 10 jumps.

LOWER BACK/HAMSTRING
STRENGTH DEAD LIFT

Strengthen the lower back while activating the hamstrings and glutes.

➡ Start with legs hip-width apart. Feet are parallel and facing forward. Cross your arms at your chest with hands just below the shoulders. Find a micro-bend in your knees or, if you prefer, keep them straight. Begin to lean forward with a flat back, engaging and hinging from the hips.

➡ As you lower your torso, take a deep inhale and make sure your weight is on your heels.

➡ Exhale to lift with an open chest, contracting the posterior muscles in the back of your legs.

EXPLOSIVE PEDAL STROKE STEP-UP

Increase explosive power and activate the glutes, quads, and hamstrings.

➡ Firmly plant your entire right foot on a sturdy bench that is knee height, making
   sure your knee does not extend past your toes.
➡ Step up fully onto the bench, right leg straight, and ensure that you focus on
   pushing through the heel, using your glutes, quads, and hamstrings, rather
   than pushing through your toes, which places additional pressure on your shins
   and knees.
➡ As you straighten your right leg, bring your left knee up toward your chest. Release
   your left leg from your chest and lower yourself back to the floor, right foot still
   on the bench.
➡ Repeat for 10 reps, then switch legs.

KNEELING QUAD STRETCH

Increase the flexibility in your quadriceps to improve pedaling motion and prevent knee and IT band overuse injuries.

➡ Put a towel or flat cushion under your knees and kneel on it with your legs together and your back straight.
➡ Take some deep breaths, feeling your muscles slowly relax. Lean back slightly if that helps you to achieve a good stretch.

THE WHEEL POSE

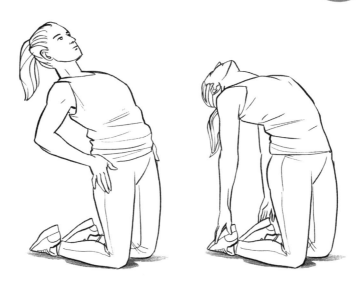

Stretch and open the front of the body, particularly the chest, abdomen, quadriceps, and hip flexors.

➡ Begin by kneeling upright with your knees hip-distance apart. Rotate your thighs inward and press your shins and the tops of your feet into the floor. Do not squeeze your buttocks. Rest your hands on the back of your pelvis, with your fingers pointing to the floor. Lengthen your tailbone down toward the floor and widen the back of your pelvis.

➡ Lean back, tucking your chin slightly toward your chest. Beginners can stay here, keeping their hands on their back pelvis.

➡ If you are able, take the pose even deeper. Reach back and hold onto each heel. Your fingers should point toward your toes and your thumbs should hold the outside of each foot. Keep your thighs perpendicular to the floor, with your hips directly over your knees. If it is difficult to grasp your heels without feeling compression in your low back, tuck your toes under your feet to raise your heels. Or rest your hands on yoga blocks placed to the outside of each foot.

➡ Lift up through your pelvis, keeping your lower spine long. To release, bring your hands back to your front hips. Inhale and lift your torso by pushing your hips down toward the floor. Your head should come up last.

PEDAL-STROKE FREEDOM
PIGEON STRETCH

1 min.
each side

Known as the pigeon pose in yoga, this move increases external range of motion of the femur in your hip socket, lengthens hip flexors, and stretches the glutes, groin, and psoas.

➡ Start on all fours and raise yourself into a downward dog position. Slide your right knee onto the floor and forward toward your right hand. Point your right knee toward the two o'clock position (near right forearm).

➡ Slide your left leg back as far as your hips will allow. Keep your hips square to the floor. If your hips are not square, there will be unnecessary force on your back, and you won't be able to open the hips to their fullest.

➡ Slide the right foot farther forward—little by little—until you feel a deep stretch. With practice, bring your shin parallel to an imaginary line between your hands. Your right thigh should have an external rotation, and your left thigh should have a slight internal rotation. This keeps pressure off the knee cap.

➡ You will be upright on your hands while sinking the hips forward and down. To deepen the pose, lower yourself to your forearms, or further, rest your chest on the floor with your arms fully extended in front of you. To get full release in the hips, breathe and release the belly.

09

FOCUS

C reak . . . creak . . . creak . . . Imagine that noise boring through your eardrums and into your head. You're on an epic climb. It's so long, so steep, and totally exposed, without an inch of shade. And all you can think about is that obnoxious creaking noise coming from your bottom bracket. That sound kicks off other thoughts in your mind, feelings of frustration, anger, fatigue, and pain.

You're pedaling a bike up that climb, but are you really riding it?

I would argue that you aren't. Your mind is off in another place. You aren't focused on the effort, and chances are, that means you're not riding to the level that you had planned. Maybe you're not staying above your Power Floor for the day's workout. Or this could be happening during a race that you'd planned and trained for over the last couple months, and instead of focusing on the effort, keeping your mind in control, that creak was the first crack that led you to a point where you aren't in control mentally . . . and you're off the back.

We are all distracted by creaking bottom brackets, both real and metaphorical, at certain points in our lives. In fact, I've consistently found that many of my clients and other cyclists I've met face similar challenges that go beyond the physiology of cycling and tap into the psychology of the sport.

These cyclists, with their raw Fitness, good Nutrition, and honed Execution skills, were missing the fourth pillar. They were building a house without a strong mental foundation. I almost wanted to start this book with the Focus pillar because it is so fundamental. It sets you up to manage the rest of the stuff that comes with being a competitive cyclist. The Focus pillar is your foundation, and if you don't have Focus, you don't have anything to stand on when a ride or race gets truly tough. That's the moment when you absolutely need to keep your head in the game. From what I've seen, the people who fall apart and give up on racing or performing at their best aren't building on the strong foundation that comes from the Focus pillar. No sport, cycling included, is solely a physical pursuit.

When those people are cycling, they're constantly asking their bodies for feedback. How do my legs feel? Am I breathing too hard? Why is my bottom bracket creaking? You're taught to look for these things. It's good to be aware, but you shouldn't actively look for that feedback in the moment and let it creep into your mental state. Ideally, you should assess it before or after the ride. In the midst of a workout or a ride, you should be just driving with your brain, using it to direct your body's effort, not the other way around.

Your mind can only think one thought at a time. In these creaky bottom bracket moments, it is wandering away from the task of driving your body on the bike. Instead of letting it get away from you like that, I'm going to teach you a mental concentration practice that will center your mind on the thoughts you need for executing an excellent bike ride. I call it Black Line Clarity (BLC), a mental process to help you check in and prime your brain for the day's effort. In this process, which I outline step-by-step below, you'll identify the necessary characteristics or attitudes to keep you motivated and performing as well as you can—keeping your Focus. I call these attitudes the Core Performance Qualities (CPQs), and they should become ingrained in you. They bring to mind what you should be thinking about on the bike—and why you're up to the challenge. These CPQs are statements, but they aren't mere words you say—they are things you should do and believe:

I See with Forward Focus

I Am the Author of My Story

I Create Grit from My Gratitude

I Possess Positive Self-Awareness

I Have the Ability to Pivot

I Am Here to Give, Not to Take

I Use Resource over Force

Personal Progress Is My Priority

I Am Fueled with CIN-ergy

My Results Guide Me—They Do Not Define Me

You'll be able to combat negative thoughts with these CPQs or even prevent them in the first place. You'll do this by repeating the mantras of a CPQ to develop your new perspective and focus.

I named this process Black Line Clarity because it reminds me of when I got glasses for the first time. Before then, everything was a little fuzzy. When I put them on, I saw perfectly crisp, fine black lines around everything with surprising depth and clarity. When you're going hard, it's tough to find that type of clarity and focus. Things blur together. You know the details are there, but you really can't see all of them. Then, on a perfect day, you feel like you've put on special glasses and can see every detail of the race. I felt that way in the 2005 Tour de Georgia on the Brasstown Bald climb.

My body felt amazing, bouncy and light. But the thing that I noticed the most was that I could just see everything—the depth in the road, the cracks in the paint, the yellow lines. I was so in the zone, so in the moment, I remember looking at the fans and seeing a guy who I raced against as a teenage mountain biker, Dustin. I hadn't seen him in years, and there he was in the crowd. I just smiled at him and I went on to win the stage. It was one of my first big victories.

Like any other training plan, consistency and repetition are key to truly getting the benefits of the Focus pillar. To a certain extent, this practice is a way to reprogram your mental approach to challenges. You probably have some established beliefs about yourself and what you can do. What I want you to get out of the Focus pillar is a new set of beliefs that are based on repeated thoughts, over and over, that put you in the state of mind to succeed at cycling and life, in general.

The Black Line Clarity Process

The Black Line Clarity process is a foundational tool that you'll use to check in and arrive at a primed or ready state before a ride, race, or anything else that requires complete focus and mental presence. I hope that it gives you the level of mental focus and awareness that I felt on that day racing up Brasstown Bald, when I saw Dustin. BLC sets you up to take on any task that you have in front of you. On the bike, this could be a workout or a race; off the bike, it could be used to prepare for a meeting or public speaking.

Make it a practice to walk through BLC before every race and some of your hardest workouts. Some of my athletes will even do this on a daily basis, right after they wake up, for instance.

Step I: Check In

1. Review your targets. Look at your personal targets for your workout and or event.
2. Review your talents. What abilities, skills, and knowledge do you possess that will help you hit your targets?
3. Review your strategy. What plan must you design and execute to use your talents to hit your targets?

Step II: Own Your Mission

Find the CPQs in the following pages that are most meaningful to you and choose a few mantras to practice. We'll go over several options for each CPQ so you can find something that is meaningful to you.

Step III: Confirm Your Commitment

Understand and believe in the meaning behind the CPQs and mantras so that the attitude truly becomes a reality. Tell yourself, "I am clear in my purpose, perspective, and desired outcome, I am now ready to go *all-in* and *win my ride*."

As you read through the explanations of the CPQs, find those that speak to you or can help you address a shortcoming you've been struggling with. You'll take those CPQs and use them to drive your performance following the BLC process. To help you identify with the CPQs, I introduce each one with a common complaint that I've heard from riders. I am sure that you've felt at least one of them at a point in your life as a cyclist.

"I'm Not Motivated" ➡ "I See with Forward Focus"

I've had a number of athletes come to me with this problem. They don't have motivation, and they think I'm the guy who's holding onto all of this magical currency like some kind of Fort Knox for motivation. Or they act like motivation is their pet dog who ran away yesterday. Can you help me find my motivation? No, I can't! You need to find it on your own, and you need to find it inside yourself.

The first CPQ, Forward Focus, helps address a lack of motivation. I find many cyclists lack motivation because they are trapped in their present state. They are fixated on the granular day-to-day challenges and can't seem to pick their heads up to look forward to see the path right in front of them. By focusing forward, a road emerges from the fog and their long-term goals become visible. This new view of the opportunity that is right in front of them now fuels the fire of motivation.

People who fall short are close-minded, stuck on only staying with the group ride or finishing in the peloton. They are not looking ahead and seeing bigger, better visions of who they can become.

When people tell me they are not motivated, I find there are usually two issues: They feel aimless because they lack a focus on their future, or they are derailed by a bad performance. And a lot of times, these things can be combined.

Often, something has come to their attention that's derailing them from their original goal, their original vision. People will make objectives like wanting to do well in a race. That could fall through and they lose the Forward Focus on the long-term objective and start making excuses for why their original goal is no longer possible. They get so focused on the past that if a workout doesn't happen or a race isn't a success, they forget the greater goal they're working toward.

This CPQ reminds you to lead with your focus on what is ahead of you, your dreams and aspirations, and to keep moving toward them, rather than get stuck in the past. I want this CPQ to push you to always move forward, no matter what you get hung up on.

Forward Focus is all about working hard on something but always looking ahead, chasing your future targets. Use this CPQ and you'll be creating all the motivation you need to accomplish your goals.

Mantras

"I flow."

"I do not force my path."

"I am unstoppable."

"No matter what."

"I Feel Burned Out" ➡ "I Am the Author of My Story"

How do you perceive your daily, monthly, and yearly commitment to cycling? Do you look at each ride like an ad in a newspaper, hoping to a yield quick sale? Or is each ride more like a chapter in the best-selling novel you are working on? If you are writing a best-selling book, then it's important to include those days of struggle. In fact, they make the story more powerful, interesting, and authentic. Just like the best seller, the good and bad days are crucial to your cycling success. Consistency trumps perfection.

I'll be the first to admit that it isn't easy to stay committed to cycling day after day, year after year. We invest so much in this sport—our time, effort, energy, emotions, money, and more. What do we get in return? A lot of days, we get our asses kicked. When you're getting dropped on the group ride, falling short of your Strava PRs, or failing to get the USA Cycling points you want to upgrade to the next category, it's natural to start questioning why you're doing it at all.

This is often when cyclists get burnt out. The riders I know who have struggled the most are on this roller coaster of burnout and motivation. They rally for two months, drill it on every workout and do OK in the races. But then they crack, and they give up for another few months.

It's easy for athletes to say they are committed, but the consistency of their training files can tell a different story. But the reality is that all days matter, and if you look at each one as a page in the best-selling story you're writing day by day, it is easy to be consistent.

Consistency in cycling is far superior to one amazing performance, one week, or even one month. With this "author of my own story" mentality, I have never seen a rider burn out in their dedication to cycling, or willingness to follow through on this personal investment. In this scenario, all days matter, and each one (good and bad) is important to making this masterpiece.

This CPQ will help remind you that the FORM Method's process takes priority over perfection. People who burn out often have unrealistic expectations and lack that self-awareness that comes with a sharp focus on your own process.

Whether you're deep in the pit of burnout or at the top of your game following the FORM Method, the same step-by-step method applies. This is all about your story. You are the author writing about your dedication, your commitment to the process, and your journey to personal progression. Use this CPQ to remain aware of this foundation for your work, to remind yourself of what your process means to you and its importance to your daily life, not perfection.

Mantras

"I own it."

"I am process-driven."

"I'm Not Tough Enough" ➡ "I Create Grit from My Gratitude"

Follow cycling for long enough and you'll see the sport's obsession with grit, pain, and suffering. Tyler Hamilton made headlines in the *New York Times* for finishing fourth in the 2003 Tour de France with a broken collarbone. Clothing company Rapha glorifies suffering in its ads and videos and on its website. From what I have seen, all of this tends to confuse a lot of cyclists.

The riders I've talked to have been indoctrinated in this crazy cult of suffering. They go out and try to harness the grit that they're told is mandatory to be a "real" cyclist, and they find out that it kind of sucks. It's hard. It's not rewarding. They get dropped in a tough race and think they're not gritty enough.

They're expecting to be able to handle an *hors catégorie* grit test before they've mastered categories 4, 3, 2, and 1 of grittiness. The Grit from Gratitude CPQ helps you understand the fundamentals of grit so that you trust that there is a purpose to the suffering.

Use this CPQ to affirm your willingness to put yourself out there, to challenge yourself. If you ask me, true suffering is what people experience when they have a terrible disease, are living in poverty, or experience trauma. When you're on a bike and you're in pain—that's optional! You knew what you signed up for. You're in charge of how hard you ride and how much it hurts. But that's what is so special about cycling. You choose to make yourself better. This is your challenge to overcome and that pain is a privilege. It has a purpose, and you need to use this CPQ to focus it in a way that makes you better.

To be a gritty person you have to be thankful, to love what you have when it comes to your ability, skill, and direction. People who are at a loss as to how to get gritty aren't embracing the privilege to challenge themselves. You have to truly love cycling and the challenge of the process. Be thankful you have this opportunity. This CPQ fuels your passion for what you're able to do on a bike (even if you're sometimes getting dropped!). Don't ever take it for granted.

When you are grateful for who you are and what you have, you can withstand anything a group ride or a race throws at you.

Mantras

"Progress is not pass/fail."

"Bad days = growth, good days = practice."

"Patience is the most critical component of my work ethic."

"When I find myself struggling, I replace my feeling
of suffering with my passion for overcoming."

"I Don't Have Any Confidence" ➡ "I Possess Positive Self-Awareness"

Trust me, I have been here before! Confidence is a precious commodity for a cyclist, and sometimes all it takes is one bad race to lose it for weeks, if not longer.

It is critical to put disappointing results or difficult days behind you. You have to pivot once a bad day is over and look ahead to the next challenge using a positive mindset to give you energy and confidence to turn that corner. Your outlook and perspective have a powerful influence on your energy level, and if you can make it a positive one, you will find yourself able to confidently move forward, and have the energy to ride another ride.

The fastest and most effective way to create this positive energy is by looking inward at yourself. The simple reflection and self-awareness of personal abilities, skills, and direction creates an energized self-confidence. You can quickly find these positive self attributes to create this energized confidence in something you have been doing well recently in training: Maybe a workout you feel strong in, a type of terrain you have been enjoying, a recent challenge you overcome, or a personal performance you have been inspired by. Whatever positive self-attributes you have, you must look inward to spark the flame of self-confidence.

Sounds easy enough, right? But it's not! Not at all. In today's world, negativity is everywhere, flooding and suffocating us before we even have a chance to look inward—at races, group rides, on Twitter. The people with negative things to say are very loud. Also, be aware of the trap of becoming negative yourself to join the others. Expressing negativity is an easy way to bond with other people because everyone has something to gripe about.

But at the end of the day, you are responsible for your success. When you consider your struggles, whether they are your fault or not, it is your choice to get stuck with insecurity, or move forward with positive confidence. At the least, I would like you to view the Positive Self-Awareness CPQ as your daily reminder to set that negativity aside, look inward, reset, and energize yourself with positive confidence.

What you will experience is that the world will look like you want it to. In every race, ride, workplace interaction, or anything else, there's always a good and a bad side. You can either see it positively or negatively. Challenge yourself to take a negative situation and flip it. Find the positive in it and feel energized with the self-confidence you pivot with.

Have you felt the low energy that comes from a negative outlook, that feeling that you can't push on? Positive Self-Awareness can turn that 180 degrees.

Mantras

"I am good enough."
"It is OK to feel the way I do."
"I have the control."
"It is my responsibility to myself, my fault or not, to move forward."

"I Can't Switch Off after a Bad Ride" ➨ "I Have the Ability to Pivot"

Imagine you are in the middle of the ocean. You are sailing along in your ship and hit an iceberg. Does this story sound familiar? As the ship starts to capsize, you have two choices: Get on the life raft or grab a bucket and start bailing water out of the ship. This CPQ is related to Positive Self-Awareness in that it pushes you to look beyond the negatives that might have come out of a recent race or ride. You have to push yourself to live with a positive mindset that thrives on problem-solving—and know when it's time to get off the boat.

Any time you have a bad race or a disappointing workout, there is something to learn. You might have made a mistake in your Execution. Perhaps it revealed a weakness in your Fitness. Even the best-prepared riders occasionally make mistakes with their Nutrition, which can also lead to a bad result. I commonly see people making the same mistake over and over. That's like the famous definition of insanity: doing the same thing over and over and expecting different results. I'm not sure if that's *Webster's* actual definition, but you get my point.

When you pivot, you consciously take the lesson learned and you use it to move in a new direction, one that works for you as a cyclist. That could mean a long hard look at your Rider Type—maybe you are trying to ride like someone you are not. It could also mean finding a new, creative approach to a ride or race that has been your kryptonite. Perhaps, on your weekly group ride, your attack on the course's one big climb hasn't worked. Why not pivot and try attacking on the descent afterward or in the rolling hills before that climb?

If you struggle with self-awareness, this CPQ is for you. People who aren't realistic with themselves are naturally inclined to put more energy into something if it's not working. If they are bad on long climbs, they constantly try to force themselves to become mountain goats. Instead they should look to this CPQ and recognize their approach isn't working. Pivot in a different direction or a different solution or process and use your abilities and skills to solve your problem in a better way.

Pivotability is the engrained ability to interpret when to change direction when facing strong adversity. When a river meets an obstacle like a rock or a tree, it can't continue to flow in the same direction, but it always finds a way around and keeps flowing downhill.

Mantras

"I feel true power when I leave the struggle behind in my wake."

"I nimbly use my mistakes as critical learning opportunities."

"I'm Not as Good as Everyone Else" ➡ "I Am Here to Give, Not to Take"

Every sport feeds our natural impulse to compare ourselves to the competition. Cycling is especially harsh that way because instead of simply winning or losing a tennis game or a round of golf, you could end up finishing 57th out of 71 riders in a race.

However, the results sheet is really one of the most disruptive things a cyclist can look at if they're trying to improve. There are so many variables that go into that one piece of paper. And the majority of those factors were totally out of your control.

Besides competition, sport can steer us toward trying to meet or beat performance expectations. PR times to hit, power to hold, and past averages can influence us to give up mid-effort because we are afraid of falling short. Riders more often than not let competition and performance expectations negatively influence their mindset, their training, and even their fundamental love of the sport.

What if you took all the competitors and performance expectations out of the equation? This CPQ is all about centering your belief on your effort that is part of your own proven process. By doing this, you immediately stop comparing yourself to others, fear of failure, and pressure to perform. Instant freedom creates the environment to give your best effort.

Master the "I Am Here to Give, Not to Take" CPQ and you'll be able to overcome the high-pressure situations, fight through the toughest of rides, and conquer the most competitive environments. The best part of this CPQ is it creates the foundation to consistently execute in the increasing number of high pressure/competitive situations you will find yourself in as you progress.

Mantras

"I am here to give, not to take."

"I do not fear failure."

"I have absolute certainty in my ability, skills, and direction from my proven process."

"I'm Not Having Fun" ➡ "I Use Resource over Force"

It breaks my heart to hear athletes say they are not having any fun riding and racing. But it also presents an exciting opportunity for me to help them rediscover what made them fall in love with cycling in the first place.

A lot of times, riders who aren't having fun have hit a plateau in their progression. For a few years, they have increased their threshold power, risen through the racing categories, and now finish at the front of group rides that used to drop them. They experienced a lot of progress, but now they are stuck. Or so they think.

Progress is addictive, and when you lose that high, cycling quickly becomes far less fun. The FORM Method is designed to teach you a new way of cycling, a dynamic form of the sport that is tuned specifically for the rhythm of a race or a group ride. With this all-encompassing approach, you can rely on more than just brute force to create progression. Now new concepts are entered into the performance arena, concepts like application, technique, timing, strategy, and style. With all of these tools and strategies, a.k.a. your resources, the execution of these skills allows you to perform at a higher level, and oftentimes use less energy.

The Resource over Force CPQ is designed to focus your attention on the execution of the total sport of cycling—not the simple power-meter contest that a lot of people get obsessed with.

This CPQ means you'll proactively create a strategy, then efficiently execute it with your particular tools. It's your reminder to be resourceful on the roads, on the trails, and in the peloton. Most of the other riders on your rides or races probably expect to do what everyone else does and hope they have it in the end. Instead, the Resource over Force CPQ reminds you to look at your skills and abilities and use those tools to proactively and resourcefully be your best for a given course or event.

If you bring this CPQ into your cycling, the sport becomes more fun as you skillfully execute a strategic use of your strengths while exercising absolute resourcefulness.

Mantras

"I am driven to do more with less."

"My focus is to deliver precise power over maximum power."

"I execute proper timing instead of forcing speed."

"Why Am I Trying So Hard? This Isn't My Day Job" ➡ "Personal Progress Is My Priority"

This excuse is such a cop-out. Think of all your riding buddies, the ones who live and breathe cycling. I'm sure a lot of them put in as much effort on the bike as they do at their job . . . maybe more in some cases! Just because you aren't getting paid to do something doesn't make it less worthy of your time, effort, and devotion.

What separates the best athletes from the rest is their devotion to their personal progression, not the support they have doing it or the level of reward they get from it. This hunger for progression feeds them as cyclists, and a lot of times, this same mentality translates into the rest of their lives—yes, even their day jobs.

I want you to challenge yourself to truly buy into the state of constant personal progression that comes with following the FORM Method. Make improvement a habit—own it, and go into your life with that commitment.

Be prepared to challenge yourself with this CPQ, though. Know that you'll have failures and setbacks as you prioritize personal progress. That's the nature of what we are doing. You're not repeating something you've done before. If you broke a physical barrier last year, it's time to level up this year. This puts you in a scary zone of the unknown. Make a habit of going to that uncomfortable place by embracing uncertainty. Get comfortable with being uncomfortable.

This CPQ helps you cope with the increasing challenge presented by bettering your best. Constant improvement is fulfilling, and I find it motivates most cyclists. But as you get better, it becomes harder and harder to get better. When you get to that point you have to check yourself and return to the "Personal Progress Is My Priority" CPQ. You pushed yourself to this point and got to this level—that is amazing. Now what?

Make progression your habit. It's what you do. Wake up motivated because every day is an opportunity to better yourself. Use this CPQ to give yourself clarity of focus. You are here to improve and progress. That is a privilege. You're doing it for yourself, not for other people, not to prove anything. You're doing it because it's part of your daily, process-driven habit. As you evolve, the process gets harder and harder, and that is OK.

Eventually, this becomes a routine process that is driven by the opportunity of constant progression. You won't have that opportunity if you don't embrace the risk of failure.

Mantras

"I am process-driven instead of results-focused."

"I know I must train consistently using my tools and processes
to be able to use them when I need them the most."

"I Don't Feel Like I'm Accomplishing Anything on My Rides" ➡
"I Am Fueled with CIN-ergy"

We cyclists are obsessive. By this point in this book, you've read my thoughts on things like FTP, TSS, and weight loss. Hopefully I can eventually convince you that you shouldn't fixate on these single factors that always trip up competitive cyclists. There is a bigger picture here, and if you're finishing a ride and feeling lost or unproductive, this CIN-ergy (that is, CINCH Cycling's version of synergy) CPQ is your reminder that we are working on a much greater project than just a single workout or power number. The whole of your own journey through the FORM Method is worth much more than the sum of its parts. A lot of people just look at one thing and think it will solve all of their problems as cyclists. They get dropped on a flat, fast group ride, so of course they just need to dial up more power. They are dropped in a hilly road race, so obviously it means they should get skinnier.

These granular obsessions are irresistible to us cyclists. But a truly extraordinary result occurs when you put your ability, skill, and devotion together to work hard and achieve something much greater than the sum of those elements added together. That's synergy.

This is why I've designed the FORM Method around the Four Pillars. It is meant to spread the load around so you can still win your ride even if you can't match up to the competition on raw fitness alone.

If you find yourself losing sight of the bigger picture, this CPQ is for you. It reinforces the fact that your process has to be multifaceted to get you to the place that you really want to go, to chase your ultimate goals. Doing one climb fast doesn't make you a perfect climber. You could do it every week for a month and you still wouldn't be there. However, when it is combined with all the other parts of FORM, it can add up to truly making you a better climber.

Remind yourself that you have to have all of the pillars of FORM together to truly get to a higher level. In fact, it's a lot more fun to bring it all together like that rather than to just beat your head against the wall on the same climb every week. Even if you get dropped in a ride or a race, when you focus on CIN-ergy, you have the opportunity to succeed in a variety of ways and feel more fulfilled because you're improving yourself for the long-term.

Mantras

"The journey over the destination."

"The Results I Get Don't Match My Expectations" ➡ "My Results Guide Me—They Do Not Define Me"

I bet that practically every time you finish a group ride or race, you come to the finish and mill around with your fellow competitors, and someone there is griping about their race or making excuses for why it didn't work out the way they wanted.

It's natural to have expectations of the results you are targeting. Sometimes you beat them; sometimes you match them; and sometimes you fall short. However, no matter the outcome, there is always something positive and critical to your growth you can pull from them.

Most people look at results from a very unhealthy and unproductive perspective. They look at them as if they are a confirmation that they need to justify their effort. Or they look at results as proof that they are what they think they should be. But using results to define who you are in this manner will leave you stuck in your tracks. If you succeed, you are at a standstill, complacent as you are overly content and using your past to define your future success. If you fall short, then you are also at a standstill, paralyzed with shame and disappointment, reluctant to try because you think your future will be like your past, a failure.

But what if you change your view of results from a need of confirmation to a guide of direction? Suddenly a result goes from a pot of gold to a road map. The frantic sense of need you had shifts now to a confident sense of direction.

We are in this for the long game, for the constant personal progress and continuous fulfillment. With this CPQ, now you can perform the FORM way. Free yourself from the pressure of using results to define you, and instead use results as guides on your continuous path forward. No matter what is on paper, now you will always win.

Mantras

"I win my ride."

"I create my own path; I don't compete by taking the path of others."

Putting My Brain Back in Charge

You might not believe this, but at one point in my professional career, a staff member on my team suggested that "maybe you aren't a climber." They were so disappointed with my performances throughout 2008 that they were grasping at straws to answer why I'd been riding so poorly. I was, too.

Of course, only I could truly know what was leading to this underwhelming season. A lot of it came down to anxiety. The root of the problem was pretty strange. When I had success—winning a race or finishing well in the overall—I had problems in my personal life at the same time. And of course when I raced poorly, that also set off a cycle of anxiety because I wasn't performing up to the team's standards or my own expectations.

I started to develop this really weird fear of success because that feeling of anxiety was closely associated with days when I performed well. I basically crossed back and forth between fear of failure and fear of success. I had no way of succeeding because I was panicking now matter how well I rode.

Plus, that 2008 season was one of turmoil. I was dealing with a shattered shoulder and a herniated disc. I had switched to a new team, which is often stressful, and I was coping with depression. It was a struggle.

Then, I watched a movie that set me on a path to create what would eventually become the Focus pillar of the FORM Method. The movie was *What the Bleep Do We Know*, a documentary-style film about the spiritual connection between quantum physics and consciousness. Some of it was pretty crazy and pretty weird. But there was one guy in the film who made sense to me. He was talking about how the brain is totally in control of your body. He said that every thought influences your body either positively or negatively. He explained experiments where he'd look at people with cancer or other diseases. In some cases, he said, their brain power cured them. In the case of others, their negative thinking led to disease.

This person was Dr. Joe Dispenza, and I'd soon realize that he was my key to getting back on track as a pro cyclist.

Let me also add that in college I was a psychology major, and I'd always wanted to be a sports psychologist, so this sort of thing was right up my alley. All fired up after watching that movie, I did what I usually do: I made up my mind that I was going to talk to this guy and found a way to get in touch. He wrote me back, and I eventually hired him and worked with him to be my best.

I think I might have gotten his attention because I was a pro cyclist. He was also a cyclist. Back in 1986, he was hit by a car while racing a triathlon in Palm Springs, California. The crash broke six of his vertebrae. Doctors said he'd be paralyzed. They offered to put a rod in his back that would at least allow him to walk again.

He wasn't happy with that prognosis and talked to everyone he could, especially brain experts, and learned all that he could, trying to cure himself of paralysis. As crazy as it sounds, that's exactly what happened. Nine and a half weeks after the crash, he was walking again. He was back to normal activity 12 months after he was hit by that car. And today he says he never suffers back pain. Needless to say, that story grabbed my attention.

He took me through all the basic mental exercises that gave me this concept of driving with your brain, the core of the Focus pillar. The FORM Method's concept of the CPQ comes from the way he coached me to lead with my thoughts, sending messages through my body.

You have a belief system—we all do. But it can get out of whack, and that is when we need to correct it and reset the foundation for ourselves as cyclists or simply as human beings. A thought can become a belief after it is repeated over and over again, as a sprout can become a giant trunk of tree.

First, you have to break the old foundation. The rotten foundation I was trying to build on in 2008 was made up of that anxiety, those negative thoughts and feelings. By thinking the right thoughts, my own mantras, over and over again, I overcame my anxiety. It wasn't easy or quick. I'd say it took about four months, and I was talking to Dr. Dispenza every week. Even at times in that process I would have panic attacks because I was still messed up. Fortunately, I turned it around by the end of 2008. Dr. Dispenza helped me reprogram everything.

Before I started working with him and building my Focus foundation, I'd have moments in a race when I would pull myself out of the final, give up and drop myself, and have a panic attack. It seemed like my legs were just seizing up, but it was really all in my head. ➡

I hated positioning. Going into the climbs, I'd always fall back when it got really sketchy, having to do a big effort at the bottom. A lot of times it cost me results. Instead of coming up with a different way to approach these situations, I'd train to get better at the surge to the front. Instead of pivoting, I tried to improve my already shitty way of reacting to positioning.

Looking back, one of the best CPQs I could have used would have been "I Have the Ability to Pivot." Instead of wishing my anxiety didn't come up or stubbornly doing my surge strategy, I should have pivoted to a better plan. I needed to regroup and find something that worked for my own abilities, skills, and direction.

The "My Results Guide Me" CPQ would also have helped. I could have acknowledged the anxiety, and chosen a strategy based on my abilities, skills, and direction. I would own my approach, focus on my personal process, and take away all the pressure and fear. That way, I could climb in a race the way I knew I could in training, without letting my expectations get in the way.

And yes, I was still a climber, despite that unwelcome advice I got in that time of struggle and depression.

The last thing I want to make clear is that what I'm teaching you here is a process, and that is different than therapy. I know when I say I was talking weekly with Dr. Dispenza it sounds like therapy, but I don't want to scare you away. You don't have to invest time and money like that. What you do need to do is invest yourself in the process, in the CPQs and BLC.

The FORM Method is a program that helps you build your own tools that actually fix your own problems, habits you keep for your life. I'm just a coach: I teach, help, support, and make it fun. You don't have to rely on me or anyone else at the start of a big race to say "You can do it." Instead, you'll be telling yourself "I know I can do it."

10

THE PERFORMANCE CHAIN: MATCH YOUR MINDSET TO THE EFFORT

When I was falling in love with mountain bike racing as a teenager, I would be really nervous in the final minutes before the start whistle. That countdown was charged with energy as we all stressed about the all-out sprint to get into the narrow singletrack trails. This was a crucial part of the race. You have to clip into your pedals right away, put in a maximal effort, and manage to handle your bike through a pack of riders all trying to get the same line as you. We were a bunch of amped-up juniors, all hoping to make it as pros, trying to prove ourselves on tough, rocky, rooty, muddy courses throughout New England and around the country.

As I matured, I started to notice that my best starts happened when I didn't let the nervous energy of this pressure cooker affect me. Things went well when I wasn't bothered by the intense techno music the announcer was playing, and on days that I didn't look at the other riders who were quivering like racehorses in the gate. Instead, I was cool, calm, and relaxed, and got the holeshot. And the days when I missed my pedal off the line or got too fired up and overcooked the first corner? Usually those were the days when I sat on the start line with a head of steam, burning with energy and anticipation.

The Performance Chain: A Process

As I began to develop the Focus pillar of the FORM Method, I remembered my days as a junior mountain bike racer. I started to connect the dots between my state of mind and my performances. Sometimes they lined up perfectly, other times they were totally at odds with each other. And as I began coaching cyclists, I saw how some riders could mentally check in when they needed to and relax when the opportunity presented itself. They were extremely efficient with their mental energy, which impacts their overall physical performance.

I realized that the fundamental difference was whether the mind was in control of the body's actions or if it was simply reacting to stressors like the sensations of a hard paceline effort, a steep climb, or start-line nerves. To help riders (myself included) put their minds in control of their bodies' efforts, I developed the Performance Chain System. This aspect of the Focus pillar is more advanced than the Core Performance Qualities, or Black Line Clarity. I think of those elements as the foundation of your house. When it is time to start building, the foundation should be complete, solid, ready to anchor everything that comes after. And that next step is the Performance Chain, which is your house's framing.

The chain starts with a trigger, like an attack by one of your rivals, or a climb that rears up in front of you with 10 kilometers to go to the finish. When you are presented with a trigger, the Performance Chain allows you to respond to it with a cue that you have ready to go, something familiar that you've practiced. Initiating the cue then brings you to the right kind of mindset for the situation—both the circumstances on the road and in your body and mind.

By practicing Performance Chains, you are building a tool through memorization so that on command you can change your mental and emotional state in an instant. I've found in coaching and my own personal experiences that without a clear strategy it can be very challenging to change your mental state when you are already in a heightened state of anxiety. The cue is the imagery or the word that serves as a bridge between the trigger and the optimal mindset states. When you match the cue to the trigger, your mind drives your body to arrive at the right state for a situation. That could be a super-intense state, like sprinting to the finish. Or it could be a mellow, smooth state that helps you relax and recover to save yourself for when it really counts. This is an advanced skill, but when you get it dialed in, the Performance Chain empowers you to look at what is happening in a race or ride and respond to it appropriately.

Here's how it works. You'll be paying attention to your surroundings, the pace, the terrain, your body. Something changes—that's the trigger. You decide to respond mentally to that trigger. Pick a cue to help guide you to the state of mind that aligns with the PTZ and tactic you need to be in to best respond to that trigger. Cues can be mental imagery, a phrase you repeat to yourself, or a physical change you make on the bike.

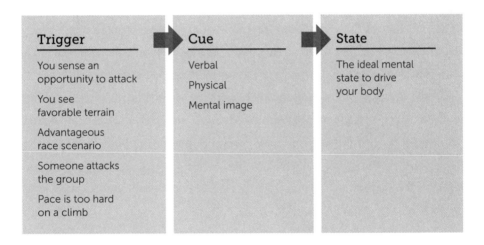

Trigger	Cue	State
You sense an opportunity to attack	Verbal	The ideal mental state to drive your body
You see favorable terrain	Physical	
Advantageous race scenario	Mental image	
Someone attacks the group		
Pace is too hard on a climb		

On one hand, the triggers for this chain can vary wildly. They can also be debatable—usually in your own mind. How should you respond—or should you even respond? For instance, the kamikaze that attacks your group ride isn't usually worth worrying about. The cues that you will use to respond to any given trigger are more specific. You'll need to be disciplined to internalize the cues so you can fully use them to your advantage and arrive at the right state, but trust me, it is worth the effort.

Get into the Right Mental State

I have framed the states as four fundamental mindsets. I relate them to natural elements, things that everyone can visualize so that it's easy to tap into them when you're caught up in the pandemonium of a bike race or tough ride. The four mindsets are:

Cloud / Water / Fire / Lightning

The goal of the Performance Chain System is to train your mind to shift between these four mindsets, depending on what is happening in the ride. I'll explain each mindset in more detail, but as you can tell, when you progress from Cloud all the way to Lightning, your mental intensity increases with each new mindset. The key is to only use Fire and Lightning when absolutely necessary. This allows you to save mental energy with Cloud or Water when the race situation is more relaxed.

As I hinted at in the beginning of this chapter, your mindset has to match what your body is doing, your exertion, your effort. However, the key to this system is that it is a one-way conversation. You are not letting your body tell your mind how to feel or think. You are using your mind to drive your body's performance by establishing these mindsets, working off of cues, and communicating that to the rest of your systems to perform.

Each mindset is directly linked to the PowerTrain Zones. People run into trouble when they're in the wrong mindset for a given PTZ. They could be too wound up and intense when they're recovering on a downhill. Or, they could be too laid-back and relaxed when they need to deliver a race-winning attack. Here's how the mindsets line up with the zones:

Cloud	Water	Fire	Lightning
Base zone	Low Medium, Medium, and High Medium zones	Threshold zones	Explosive zones

I know that this might seem a little bit too mystical to some of you. We're just riding bikes, right? Shouldn't it always be intense? Shouldn't we always have our game faces on, burning with fire and throwing lightning-bolt attacks like Zeus? This is a common mistake I see many beginner and intermediate cyclists make. Like my example of teenage Tom, flying off the mountain bike start line with raw intensity, there are times when it pays to be relaxed and calm, to float like a cloud or flow like water. To prove that to you, I'm going to provide examples for each of the four mindsets from one race, a criterium. That's right, even in one of the most intense, chaotic road race disciplines, there are appropriate times for each of the four mindsets.

Let's get into the specifics of how each of these mindsets works, how you can use cues to arrive at the right mindset, and how it can drive your body's performance on the bike.

Cloud

The Cloud mindset is the most relaxed. It uses the least amount of energy. You are floating along with carefree ease. A cloud is practically effortless, not in a rush to get somewhere, supported by thin air: It's soft, fluffy, and light.

Don't underestimate the Cloud, however. This is a critical mindset for recovery, to set you up for what will come next. In some cases that means it is a recovery mindset between hard intervals on a climb. If you fail to switch into Cloud mindset after your Garmin beeps at you, your interval didn't really stop. You need to shift gears mentally to make the most of that recovery, to avoid the unnecessary mental stress that will drain your energy.

Cloud mindset is also important to employ in long, low-intensity rides. As I mentioned in the 10 Keys to Success, you need to go low before you can go high. That means that a Base-intensity ride is driven by a Cloud mindset. Don't think you can ride at that PTZ when you're burning up inside with a Fire mindset. That's why group rides are often a bad option for true Base rides. Things get too intense and hard, pulling you away from the PTZs you need to ride in and influencing your mindset by introducing unproductive stress.

The Cloud mindset is so relaxed and soft that it seems wrong for a criterium, doesn't it? Of course, you wouldn't want to drive your body with the Cloud mindset in the final sprint—that would be misaligned with the PTZ you need to produce. However, there are brief moments when a Cloud mindset provides a crucial opportunity to recover from a stressful moment.

If you're racing a hilly crit course, that could mean that you shift into Cloud on the downhill section where you can coast. Cloud mindset is also great for cornering. You enter the corner, stop pedaling, allow yourself a second or two of easy respite, and then you shift back into a mindset that matches the race intensity. In fact, some of the riders who have difficulty cornering well—whether in a crit or on a long mountain descent—aren't shifting into a more relaxed mindset. More than just recovery, Cloud can help you ride technical roads smoother and faster because it helps you relax mentally, and that translates to more relaxed body movement.

Cloud Cues

Mental Imagery: Imagine lying in a grassy park and looking up at a pure, white, fluffy cloud floating through the sky.

Verbal: "I am feeling free. I am feeling light."

Physical: Deep inhalation through the nostrils

PTZ: Base

Water

Some of the most enjoyable parts of a ride often come when you are in the Water mindset. You are flowing. Things are smooth. Effort is low, but not quite as low as in the Cloud mindset. That means you get to go a bit faster, but not to the point of it becoming painful or stressful.

Cycling thrives on this flow. Imagine how the peloton smoothly pinches through narrow roads and around corners or builds speed on descents and carries it into flats. When you're riding in a group you should be in this Water mindset.

This state uses enough energy to keep you well positioned, in the flow, and avoiding trouble. But it doesn't unnecessarily stress your nervous system, and it keeps you in a lower PTZ to help you conserve energy. You remain in the fat-burning PTZs. Here, you set a fast pace in the medium zones, sustainable for hours on end. You can also shift into the Water mindset to recover from a hard, sustained effort. Like the Cloud mindset, Water is also great for long descents. It is great for those that have more corners, requiring flowing, smooth bike handling.

When it comes to our criterium example, Water mindset is ideal. Unless you're one of those riders who attacks from the gun and tries to lap the field, you'll probably spend a lot of time sitting in the wheels during a criterium. It's a lot easier to maintain your position and avoid wasteful braking when you are flowing with the bunch. This also lets you save energy for the race's key moment, when you'll need to shift to another mindset and attack or sprint to win.

Water Cues

Mental Imagery: A swift, smooth river cutting through a valley, easily flowing around rocks, hills, and other obstacles

Verbal: "I do not force my path."

Physical: Relaxed hands

PTZs: Low Medium, Medium, and High Medium

Fire

As we shift from Water to the Fire mindset, there is a big difference. Fire is always a destructive state, and the more you use it, the more you burn down. Be careful because you cannot undo that damage. The intensity of this mindset demands more mental energy than the Cloud or Water mindsets. Fire mindset brings the heat. It can pay off, but it also commands a hefty price.

This intense, destructive mindset is key if you want a chance at winning. This mindset compels your body to dig into its Threshold PTZs, pushing at intensities that aren't sustainable for more than an hour or so. When you're on the attack, riding a time trial, or part of a breakaway move, Fire mindset is the tool you'll use to drive your effort.

Experienced riders can shift between Fire and Water mindsets frequently throughout the course of a race, sometimes even during a paceline. They pull through with a Fire mindset, then shift to a Water mindset to get a moment of rest before pulling through again. Beginners, or those who lack control of their mindsets, are often stuck in a Fire state for an entire race, which is really exhausting. You can be sure that when the key moment of a race comes along, they won't have as many matches to burn if they've been stuck in Fire mindset for hours on end.

Fire Cues

Mental Imagery: A hot, roaring fire burning through a forest, an unstoppable force that goes over any terrain

Verbal: "I am invincible."

Physical: Forceful exhalations

PTZs: Low Threshold, Threshold, and High Threshold

Lightning

Lightning is one of the most awe-inspiring forces of nature. It is fast, unexpected, and before you know it, it's gone. Similarly, there aren't that many occasions in most rides and races to switch into Lightning mindset and use your Explosive PTZs. You only harness this type of effort for key, brief moments when you absolutely have to bridge a gap to a breakaway or launch a sprint.

Like the Fire mindset, Lightning is all about intensity, and it drains your mental energy quickly. I have seen inexperienced riders use Lightning mindset and the corresponding effort repeatedly while they ride in the peloton. They panic, try to move up as quickly as possible, and find themselves mentally exhausted after an hour of riding. You can only draw on the Lightning mindset so many times before those efforts are blunted. If you are sprinting and attacking just to sit in the bunch, you'll lose the crucial, shocking high intensity that can win races.

As you'd expect, the Lightning mindset is one of the key weapons used in our criterium example. It can fit into a variety of strategies, depending on how you want the race to play out. If you're a pure sprinter, you'll save the Lightning mindset for the line in the last 200 meters. If you need a breakaway for a chance at victory, you're probably shifting into this state to attack the bunch on a short climb or as you exit a sharp, technical corner that forces everyone to brake and slow up. You could also cover attacks with an effort that is driven by a Lightning mindset.

Lightning Cues

Mental Imagery: With a flash of light, the lightning bolt streaks across the sky, destroying anything it touches and disappearing in an instant.

Verbal: "My intensity is explosive."

Physical: Lightning snap at the bottom of the pedal stroke with hip flexors pulling the foot back up

PTZs: Nuclear, Long Surge, Short Surge, Maximum Explosive Strength

Proactive and Reactive Riders

Generally speaking, I have found that there are two types of cyclists in terms of their mentalities: Some people are proactive and others are reactive. One isn't necessarily better than the other. They are just different and, fortunately, the Performance Chain works in both cases.

The proactive riders I have worked with are usually very good at structured training. They thrive on a calendar that schedules out every interval to the minute. They enjoy the progression of following workouts step-by-step through the weeks and months of a season. Sometimes they can be a bit too rigid, and if a plan doesn't pan out in an unpredictable race, they might not be as flexible when it comes time to pivot and follow a new plan.

On the other hand, reactive riders love the surprises that come up in any given day of bike riding. They prefer to fill their schedules with races and group rides. They are motivated to chase after their rivals' attacks, follow their instincts to make the breakaways, or roll the dice in a field sprint. As you might guess, they are less motivated by structured training plans that keep them away from the races and group rides that they love.

Rider Types: Proactive or Reactive

Your proactive or reactive nature often aligns with your Rider Type. We often see this kind of correlation:

Proactive: Climber, classics TT rider

Reactive: Classics sprinter, puncheur

Again, don't assume one of these types is better than the other. Instead, take a critical look at your own motivations and understand who you are as a rider. This self-awareness will help you work through your strengths and weaknesses to adapt the Performance Chain to your needs. I don't want you to get stuck in the same pattern or habit that you always use for every race or ride. Ideally, you reach a point where you can use this mental tool in both a proactive and reactive way, no matter what your normal tendencies are. Whatever the trigger is on any given day, you are equipped with a tool that can handle the situation.

Going back to our criterium example, the best rider will have a proactive approach planned out, but will also be prepared to shift into a reactive Performance Chain if needed. Their initial plan could be to launch an attack after the first prime to initiate a breakaway. They shift between Water and Cloud mindsets during the early stages of the race to save mental energy and ride smoothly in the peloton. As the pace heats up in the prime lap, they shift into the Fire mindset to hold position and keep up with the bunch as the race gets strung out. Finally, after the prime sprint, they shift into Lightning mindset to drive a Short Surge effort, followed by Fire mindset in the High Threshold PTZ.

But wait—there's a problem. No one else followed that attack. Now they are alone off the front, burning up in Fire mindset without any support to make the move stick. The peloton chases them down, and in a couple laps, the attack is over. Now it's time to shift into reactive mode.

So, our rider returns to the peloton and uses the Cloud and Water mindsets for recovery and efficiency. Now they are on the lookout for promising attacks that they could follow. There are a few big teams in the race. Maybe a rider from one of those squads will make a move and their teammates will help block the chase in the bunch.

Sure enough, an attack goes away a few laps later, and our rider is well-positioned to seize the opportunity. They again use the Lightning mindset, this time for a Long Surge effort to bridge up to the breakaway over the course of the next lap of racing. After the catch, they might sit in the Water mindset for a minute to regroup and then it is full-on Fire mindset in Threshold zones to help make the breakaway stick.

And when it does stick, the sprint finish will again demand that Lightning mindset to out-sprint the other breakaway riders and win the day.

The Will to Win

When you reach the final week of a Grand Tour stage race—the Giro d'Italia, the Tour de France, or the Vuelta a España—your body is basically shutting down. It's a struggle to get up in the morning and have breakfast. Your body is telling your mind to go back to bed. The best riders in the world can tell their bodies to shut up and keep going. But even some of the best end up dropping out of these races as the fatigue accumulates.

I found myself at this turning point on stage 17 of the 2006 Vuelta. I had a rough start to the race and was struggling with anxiety. When you feel this way, cycling can be such a demoralizing sport. You look around the peloton and see other riders who look good on a bike. They are pedaling smoothly at high cadence. Some of them are even talking or joking. But you feel horrible, and your body is telling you to stop, feeding that doubt and anxiety.

This was decision time. The mind has to tell the body to do it, to keep pushing, even if it means limping up the climb. You make a commitment and keep working the pedal stroke until the fatigue and pain start to fade. That's the choice I made on stage 17 because I was fed up with the self-doubt, anxiety, and personal baggage.

All race, I kept hearing the same Jay-Z song in the mornings before the race began, "Dirt Off Your Shoulder." Maybe you know it. This hip-hop song has a lot of lyrics that I won't repeat here. But the one that stuck with me was repeated throughout the song and in my mind: "Go and brush your shoulders off." To me that meant brushing off all the bad feedback from my body and the anxiety it fueled. I decided to go out and lead with my brain on stage 17.

I remember going on the attack on the last of two climbs that day, Alto de Monachil, which is near Granada. All day long I had followed the GC guys up the climbs. Before this point, I had second-guessed myself and never rode at this level. Going into the stage I was 10th overall and eight minutes behind on GC. I just took a chance on this stage and led with my mind instead of listening to my body. I brushed all that crap off my shoulders and went for it.

Eventually, I was off the front alone on this last climb. Behind, there was a massive battle between race leader Alejandro

Valverde and Alexandre "Vino" Vinokurov for the overall lead. I heard on the radio that they were attacking each other on this last climb, with about 20 km to go. My body was saying, "I don't know if I can do it," but I just didn't listen to it. I told myself I was going to throw this baggage away and go for it. I was going to climb the way I wanted to climb, and I just got into the pain. I knew I loved to burn, to light up these climbs. I forgot about the race and forgot about the guys behind.

I got over the top solo, went down the descent, and I remember the helicopters coming in, and more TV motos . . . *Wow,* I thought to myself, *something is happening.* Vino bridged up to me after taking a lot of risks on the downhill. He had dropped Valverde. He came across to me, and I just thought, *Holy shit.*

He attacked me straightaway, but I brushed off my shoulder and said I was going to get on his wheel, in full Fire mindset. I felt that power and technique. I didn't get absorbed in the moment and I didn't ask my body what to do. I just told it, *We're fucking doing this.* I went pull for pull with him, easily one of the baddest guys in the peloton.

When we got to the last kilometer, I had so much clarity that I knew exactly what to do. I stopped pulling. I told myself, *OK, to do the sprint I need to do to win this stage, I need to sit here and recover.* I needed to get out of my Fire mindset that I had used to drive my breakaway and shift into the Water mindset. I was not going to be able to shift into Lightning after more than an hour of Fire, especially against a rider like Vino. I got super relaxed, even though I knew I had never won anything like this before, and I was sitting on this guy who at the time was a two-time Tour de France stage winner, twice a Paris–Nice champion, and a winner in other huge one-day races like Liège–Bastogne–Liège. You don't mess with Vino!

I just sat there. He knew he was racing for the overall win in the Vuelta, so he kept pulling all the way to the finish. I saw the clock reading :00, the finish banner, the whole scene—but it didn't change my mindset. I forgot all the baggage I had, all the work I had struggled through, and sat there in a Cloud or Water mindset. I was so clear, so relaxed, and then I just went. He started to sprint and I didn't care. I was full Lightning, and I won.

It was hard but, at that point it didn't feel that way. It was an amazing experience. Previously, when I was having two-way conversations with my body it was not doable, but when I led with my brain, made decisions, and changed it to a one-way conversation, it worked. I was able to tell my body what to do and pull off the impossible. Nothing in my body told me I could do that—go off the front, hold them off, go pull for pull with Vino, and beat him in a sprint—no way. But my mind was in a state where I'd brushed off all the doubts and negative dialogue from my body, and I was able to drive with my mind.

PUTTING IT ALL TOGETHER

11

GETTING STARTED

Now it's time to put everything you've learned into action. You have an understanding of the Four Pillars and what makes this program different. Hopefully you're inspired and ready to get started. Taking this first step can be challenging and maybe even a little scary. If you have been riding bikes seriously for a few years, you're probably accustomed to the rhythm of your typical schedule, workouts, and races. It can be hard to leave that familiar terrain behind. But if you've read this far, I bet you're looking for something more out of your cycling. I promise you that the reward you'll earn as a FORM athlete is completely worth the risk you're taking by setting off on a new training system.

In this chapter, I'll break down the ways you can get started into digestible pieces. Mastery of all Four Pillars can take some time, but don't get discouraged. Your daily, weekly, monthly, and yearlong practice of this system will continuously pay off in your cycling, regardless of how much longer your journey lasts.

I will begin by explaining the four things you should do in your first month with the FORM Method. Then, I'll get into detail on how to plan out your season, building your calendar around goals, designing workouts, and more. Finally, I'll help you address three common concerns that might come up.

Your First Month

Don't be afraid to dive right into the FORM Method. Even if you are reading this in the heat of your summer racing season, you can start your transformation. A lot of the preliminary work I do to bring athletes on in my coaching program isn't too intrusive and it doesn't radically alter the riding that they are already doing.

Three of the most important steps are centered on figuring out who you are as a cyclist in terms of your psychology (Focus pillar), Rider Type, and what your PowerTrain Zones (PTZs) should be. Also, in this first month, you'll incorporate weekly training sessions that help you learn and internalize the Four Pillars. I'll explain these in a moment. They'll mesh with your normal riding schedule, and they will be progressive, so you'll have a new challenge each week to build your way into the system.

Identify Your Vision

There are a few core reasons why you are a cyclist. You spend money on the gear, travel to events, ride for hours on end, and you've even picked up this book and read it (nearly cover to cover!). But why do you ride? Maybe you've given this some thought, but a lot of the cyclists that I know have never taken the time to look inward.

To get started with the FORM Method, you need to find your vision, your "why." Take the time to write that down, so it is real, right in front of you in black and white. This process can be a little scary for some people.

On the next page, you'll find the Vision Questionnaire. Spend some time thinking about it and filling it out. Sometimes it works well to read the questions, go for a ride, and then fill in your answers. You could also fill it out, sleep on it, and return to the questionnaire the next morning and make any revisions that came to you overnight. Above all, do not skip this step in the process. I can assure you that the people who avoid this step or do not take it seriously are the cyclists who need it the most.

Find Your Vision

The vision is your line of sight: It's where you want to go in your transformation through cycling. Without your vision, you risk becoming lost during your journey. We are chasing progress, but we must accept that failure and adversity are truly the foundation of success.

There are three components to the vision: purpose, perspective, and outcome. Your vision, focusing on these three elements, will guide you as you find your way through successes and struggles to becoming the best possible you.

Purpose
- Why did you start cycling?
- What specifically about the sport of cycling hooked you?
- What sensations do you remember from your first rides?

Perspective
- What are your physical strengths?
- What are your mental strengths?
- What are your physical weaknesses?
- What are your mental weaknesses?
- Who are you in your life? (age, personal interests, job, location where you live)
- Who is in your life? (family, friends, coworkers)

Outcome
- List three words that describe what progress means to you (can be within or beyond cycling).
- How do you personally measure progress in your life?
- What are the top skills or qualities that you would like to develop in your cycling (and in your life)?

Sometimes people get their own motivations confused with those of their friends or peers. They take the questionnaire and realize that their "why" is out of sync with how they've been riding and training for years. Similarly, a lot of people overemphasize racing and results. Can they remember who won the masters 45+ state points series last season? Does it actually matter to their daily practice of cycling?

The process of clarifying your vision will free you from these extrinsic motivations. Once you take stock of your personal relationship with cycling and see what truly drives you to spend all that money and ride all of those miles, you'll feel a deeper, more genuine motivation that is intrinsic.

Don't think you can take this questionnaire and simply file it away in your sock drawer and transform into the world's best cyclist. This vision needs to be out in the open for you to see daily. When I write training plans for athletes, I often put their vision in the notes, so they are reminded of why they are out there doing hard intervals. When you write it down, remind yourself of it regularly, and act on it, you take control of your vision to start your transformation. Trust me: That is exciting, empowering, fulfilling, and completely worth it.

Finally, know that your vision might evolve over time, and that is OK. Just like the 21-year-old version of yourself might never have imagined having three kids and a mortgage, your cycling self can evolve. I know that I have.

Determine Your Rider Type

As I explained in Chapter 3, we all have physiological and psychological tendencies that define who we are as cyclists. I bet that you read that chapter and quickly decided which Rider Type suits you. You might be correct. I have also found that people have a tendency to define themselves in unrealistic ways.

Unlike the Vision Questionnaire, I don't want you to spend hours or days thinking through your Rider Type. If you haven't already, go take the Rider Type quiz (p. 42) or if you did take it, revisit your findings. Go with your gut on these questions. Be honest with yourself because in the long run, that will help you become the best version of yourself as a cyclist. Even if you do end up with a Rider Type that isn't exactly right for you, you'll learn something in the process.

Sometimes it helps to remember a ride or a race that was particularly successful or fun for you. What parts went well? When did you feel amazing? A lot of times that can guide your decision on a Rider Type as you think back to how the terrain or tactics played into your success on that particular day.

Lead with your Rider Type when it comes to your thinking and your strategy. A classics sprinter rider shouldn't just say, "Climbs are bad for me." They should say, "I know who I am as a rider, so I'm planning to climb in a way that suits my own strengths." You don't have to hate climbing to be a classics sprinter! And for that matter, you don't have to love climbing to be a climber.

When you go through the quiz and determine your Rider Type, don't let it hold you back. You should never look at a ride or event and say, "Well I shouldn't do that because I'm a climber (or classics sprinter or any other type)." Instead, knowing your Rider Type empowers you. Most riders who have a bad time on a ride are unaware of their Rider Types and how to use their talents strategically. Well, now you know yours, so use it to set yourself up for success.

Just imagine Julian Alaphilippe in the 2019 Tour de France. When he found himself in the yellow jersey, racing a route that was billed as the highest ever with the most climbing, he didn't cry onto his baguette and give up because he is a puncheur. Instead, he owned his Rider Type and he used it to his advantage well into the final week, wearing yellow for as long as possible before finally losing the overall to a pure climber, Egan Bernal.

Knowing your Rider Type won't always win the race for you, but I promise you'll finish each day knowing that you made the most of your own talents.

Calculate Your PTZs

OK, at last we can get you out on the bike! The PTZ test is very effective at determining a rider's zones, and it doesn't require a lot of time or a monumental effort to get a baseline established.

If you are an experienced rider, you've probably done some form of testing before to determine metrics like your FTP or your threshold. I've found that some experienced riders like to game the system and pace themselves in a way that alters the results. That is great, but make sure you're giving it an honest effort.

I have found that inexperienced riders don't have a good sense of the distinctions between the different gradations of a "hard" effort. They go out hard, they finish hard, and while it might have all felt the same to them, you can see by the power graph that they completely blew up after a minute and were crawling through the final minute at a far lower output than if they had ridden steady.

The test is not about beating a particular number you might have in your head from a previous coaching program or a friend's power files. It is also not about burying yourself deep in the pain cave. You should feel like you are control because when we take this data and use it for your PTZs, your workouts should also feel controlled. It's not realistic to absolutely bury yourself anytime you are in a workout or racing. I've seen it myself—the best pro riders are always within themselves, in control, when they're in the middle of a workout.

As you might remember, key 2 of the 10 Keys to Success (Chapter 2) is "You have to go low before you can go high." Initially, your PTZs might seem low. The efforts might not seem that hard. That means you are on the right track. We are taking the first step toward building your engine. Once you have mastered all 11 PTZs, then we can consider raising the zones.

Above all, the goal is consistency. When you can perform in each zone with control, then you'll be shifting gears in your body's engine and using your efforts strategically in everything from your average lunch ride to the biggest race of the season.

Using RPE in Lieu of Power Meters

You've probably realized that a power meter is an essential tool for training. The FORM Method's PTZs rely on precision. One of the keys to improving as a cyclist is Power Control—staying in those zones, above the floor and below the ceiling.

If this book can help you refine your zones, use them purposefully, and become a better rider, then I'll consider that a success.

However, cycling is an expensive sport, considering the bike, components, and extra gear needed just to get started. Plus, a lot of the gear wears out, like tires, chains, and cleats, so you're faced with the cost of upkeep. Power meters have become more affordable and easier to come by in the last 10 years. But a good one will still cost you at least $500. So, I can understand your reluctance to run out and buy one if you're just trying to see if serious training is right for you.

The good news is that you can train with the FORM Method using the rating of perceived exertion (RPE) scale. This is a common system that's been around for decades. Simply put, your own senses will serve as your power meter. What does the burn feel like in your legs? How hard are you breathing? What is your cadence like? How much pressure do you feel yourself applying to the pedals? These sensations are all quite subtle and subjective. You'll need to be really in tune with your body to tell what is happening. If you are new to the sport, you might consider taking notes after rides to think critically about your RPE for a given workout.

When applying the PTZs to RPE, you should do two things to be as precise and consistent as possible. First, we'll group some RPE and PTZ values into pairs, essentially ending up with seven levels of effort. I find that the differences between some of the zones are too subtle to perceive without a power meter to delineate them. However, we can still speak of RPE in 11 points, giving us more of a range with upper and lower limits of those two-point efforts (Table 11.1 shows how RPEs and PTZs line up). This will also help you find the desired RPE when I prescribe a specific PTZ in a workout (see Appendix). Rank each ride based on that scale so you can look back at your training and track RPE over time.

Second, be conservative when you are determining the RPE of an effort. It should be your RPE for an average workout, not your best-ever effort. Don't get greedy and think that the harder you push, the faster you will progress. Even though you aren't riding with a power meter, the goal is the same. I want you to

TABLE 11.1. RPE and Corresponding PTZs

RPE	Effort	PTZs
RPE 1	Base, all-day	1
RPE 2–4	Medium, 2–4-hour efforts	2–4
RPE 5–6	Low Threshold: 40–60-minute efforts	5–6
RPE 7–8	High Threshold: 8–15-minute efforts	7–8
RPE 9	Long Surge: 3–6-minute efforts	9
RPE 10	Short Surge: 1–3-minute efforts	10
RPE 11	Maximum Explosive Strength	11

develop each zone and control your effort for each of them. Strive for mastery of every zone, not an all-time personal record of your maximal one-minute surge.

Often, when using RPE, it is best to lead with your workout duration to achieve the correct intensity. If you are planning a 15-minute Threshold effort, consider what pacing is realistic and repeatable, based on your ability on an average day.

Create Your Training Calendar

Your training calendar should reflect what is happening in the real world. There's no reason to be going against the grain and riding easy base miles in the middle of the race season. Similarly, it's hard to focus on high-intensity explosive efforts mid-winter when you're stuck indoors on the trainer. When you're planning your training, strive to avoid friction, matching your work to what's going on around you.

Let me offer an example. In 2005, I dropped out of the Giro d'Italia about halfway through the race. I had a bad knee injury and needed to take two or three weeks off the bike entirely. As the Giro happens in May, this was pretty much the worst possible time to be away from training.

When I had recovered and got back on the bike, I didn't try to force myself to rebuild my base. That sort of training would have been out of sync with all the racing happening in late June and early July. Instead, I hopped right in, stimulating

TABLE 11.2. A General Training Schedule for 12 Months

Month	Priority PTZs
November–December	Medium
January–February	Low Threshold
March	High Threshold
April	Explosive; first races and group rides begin
May–August	Race/event season: Train all zones
September–October	Go by feel, mixing in Medium, Threshold, and Explosive PTZs

all of my PTZs, which is typically what you are doing in the heart of the season. I went to the Tour of Austria in July and I ended up finishing fifth overall—not bad.

The point is, no matter your starting point, jump into the FORM Method at any time in the season. Eventually, when you become experienced with FORM and use it for an entire season, you'll enjoy the full benefits that come with it.

Each month is devoted to a specific PTZ. This periodization system is designed to build your body's engine step-by-step. As you'll remember in the 10 Keys to Success, "You have to go low before you can go high." Following this program, you'll progressively master each PTZ, starting with your Medium zones (Table 11.2).

The rule of thumb for training your PTZs according to the calendar says that 20 percent of your time should be spent in that given PTZ. For instance, in March, about 20 percent of your ride time should be spent doing intervals in the High Threshold zone. The rest of your riding should primarily be in the Base and Medium zones. This is a critical rule that I can't emphasize enough. Lots of riders who suffer overuse injuries are riding too hard when they should simply be in their Base zone. If you are integrating every pillar of the FORM Method into your training, you'll remember that one of the points on the North Star of Execution is Separation. Find clear separation between your PTZs when you shift in and out of your intervals to purposefully train the zones that are on the plan.

TABLE 11.3. Example Training Schedule for January–March

Month	Week	Focus
January	1	Low Threshold PTZ training week
	2	Low Threshold PTZ training week
	3	Low Threshold PTZ training week
	4	*Rest week*
February	1	Low Threshold PTZ training week
	2	Low Threshold PTZ training week
	3	Low Threshold PTZ training week
	4	*Rest week*
March	1	Low and High Threshold PTZ training week
	2	Low and High Threshold PTZ training week
	3	Low and High Threshold PTZ training week
	4	*Rest week*

It is OK to mix in other zones here and there. Don't lose your focus, though. Your PTZs, Nutrition, and Focus mindsets should all be aligned with your objective for each phase of the periodization system.

As you build out your schedule, you can organize training into roughly one-month blocks (Table 11.3). Do three weeks of focused training, and then the fourth week should involve lighter efforts, lower volume, and a focus on recovery.

Throughout the course of any given three-week training block I would like you to prioritize the consistency and details of the workouts over increasing the time you spend in the PTZs. Better control leads to progression, and you don't necessarily need to increase duration to do that. Eventually, when all of your PTZs are dialed and you can comfortably execute in any of them at will, then it's time to increase, but don't rush to get to that point. You are always going to have a weakness in one of your PTZs. You'll see that in your Power Control when you analyze your workout data. Once you are confident and in control of every zone, perform another PTZ test to reevaluate your zones.

TABLE 11.4. Example Weekly Schedule

Day	Training
Monday	*Off*
Tuesday	1.5 hours, PTZ intervals
Wednesday	1.5 hours, Base PTZ
Thursday	1.5 hours, PTZ intervals
Friday	*Off*
Saturday	2–3 hours, PTZ intervals
Sunday	2–3 hours, Base PTZ

To build out your weekly schedule, focus on the work you need to do, and build it into days that have low friction (Table 11.4). Don't feel obligated to ride a certain number of hours each week. Your weekly, monthly, or yearly training hours tally isn't an input. It is just an output, one tiny measurement of the work you are doing. Sure, the pros go out and ride all day, every day. And science will tell you that more training volume will yield more fitness. But we're operating in the real world, building your training around your life. The good news is that the FORM Method will make you better without demanding 20 hours per week.

When you're planning your weekly training, start with a workload that you can handle. Challenge yourself, but don't go too deep into a hole. I always recommend following the 80 percent rule—don't go 100 percent. On the bad days, when you're feeling a bit tired or stressed, you'll need to use that extra 20 percent that you saved to get your workout done. Each workout should feel challenging, but you shouldn't come home on your hands and knees.

If you have an event on your schedule, build in a rest week two weeks beforehand to allow yourself to recover and regroup. Then, the week before the event, do a mix of efforts in all of your PTZs. You don't want to stress your system too much. Instead, look at it as a way of tuning up your system. After the event, take one or two days off, but not much more than that unless you've planned a vacation or a work trip, or it's the end of the season. Even if it was a big goal event for you, it's best to avoid disruption in your training flow. I want you to remain focused on the bigger picture. Maintain your momentum and growth. If you take too much time off after a big race and relax for a few weeks, you risk losing fitness and wasting time that could be spent on improvements. I do not recommend this unless you need to take time for a work trip or family vacation, or if you need the time off to rediscover your mojo, improve your mindset, or figure out your nutrition.

Along with low friction, another key to the periodization system is constant progression. I have always noticed a lot of similarities between planning a cycling season and how good businesses operate. The world's most successful corporations are hell-bent on progressing and improving day after day, month after month, and year after year.

Instead of riding through peaks and valleys throughout the course of a year, this system puts you on a track of steady progression. Some pro riders can get away with extended breaks from training and riding, but they can also go to some quaint Mediterranean island for a two-week training camp to rebuild fitness. Those of us in the real world don't have that luxury. Stay on the steady growth track, just like a business, and you'll earn record profits.

Common Concerns and How to Resolve Them

Cyclists are generally motivated self-starters who have an eye for details and a desire to improve. Cyclists who take the time to read a book like this one to guide their own training are even more driven, focused, and analytical. Although we are a rare breed, every once in a while we need help. That's why there are so many cycling coaches out there.

Although I can't address each and every individual concern, setback, or question you might have, I can hit on three very big issues that always seem to come up. Use this final section of the chapter to diagnose and remedy some common problems that you might face after a few months of using the FORM Method.

"My Power Numbers Haven't Improved."

Before we dive into details, repeat after me: "I am not my FTP!" This is the first of my 10 Keys to Success for a reason. Remind yourself that the number on your computer is just a kind of language that explains what you're doing on a bike. It's an output, not an input.

Now, with that out of the way, the biggest thing you need to ask yourself is, "Am I being consistent?" Usually this is the number-one reason people do not improve when they train with the FORM Method.

Training needs to be a regular part of your weekly regimen. Whatever your schedule ends up being, you need to fit in a minimum of four rides per week. Ideally, you train five times per week. Some weeks, you'll fall short and only fit in two or three. That's OK, but the majority of your weeks should have that consistent training rhythm. Consistency wins every time, even when compared to monster five-hour weekend rides followed by days of recovery. It's better to do a 20-minute ride with two intervals to activate your key PTZs than to miss a ride.

There are a few factors that always seem to disrupt peoples' consistency. The first might surprise you: riding too much, too hard. If you crush a big ride on the weekend (one that's beyond your current fitness) or fit too many intervals into a midweek workout, you overdo it. Then you need more rest and miss the next couple of rides. You might even lose mental focus and burn out. Less is more. Remember the 80 percent rule.

Another factor that ruins consistency is when people rely on other riders to get in their training. Sometimes that comes down to motivation. If you depend on your buddy to get you out the door on a ride, it's time to reevaluate your vision in the Focus pillar. In other cases, people rely on group rides to dial up the intensity. In that situation, you have zero control. Seasons change, schedules change, other peoples' fitness changes, and you never know who will show up any given week. For instance, on the local Denver rides, I've noticed what I call "The Greg Daniel Factor." The former US national champion occasionally shows up, making the ride insanely hard. Or, if he's off at a real race instead, the rides are too easy for most riders. This is the pinnacle of inconsistency. Don't completely swear off group rides, but treat them as a reward, a time to socialize, or a chance to practice skills. Remember key 4: "Group rides do not count as training."

Last, your daily schedule can impact consistency. I see it time and time again—people who plan their workouts late in the day often skip them. Schedule your rides earlier in the day, and you're more likely to get them done. Wake up extra early if you have to.

Similarly, plan your nutrition ahead of time to make sure you are fueled right for a consistent workout. If you follow the 3-Sigma System, especially the Timing sigma, your nutrition will give you what you need to perform. Bring in a Tupperware with food to work if you have to. Don't rely on the cafeteria or lunches out with coworkers. This ties into another key, "Planning is part of your workout."

If you feel your consistency is good, then it's likely that your Power Control needs to improve. Remember that this is all about efficiency in your PTZs. If the zones are not getting easier and your power numbers aren't improving, that means you're drifting too much between zones. You need to revisit the concept of Separation in the Execution pillar, purposefully shifting between PTZs and not allowing them to smear together.

Often, riders who struggle with Power Control need to improve their pedal stroke, which is part of the Execution pillar as well. Take an honest look at your position on the bike to see if you're falling short with the Three Points of Power—hands, core, and feet.

Usually, pedal stroke issues come down to bad execution of the upstroke. The hands could be too extended. When you are riding with straight arms, you are not stabilizing your upper body to hold the upstroke. Instead, you're balancing your upper body on handlebars, unable to get stability for the upstroke.

Moving on to the core, the pelvis could be too far behind the bottom bracket. This is often directly related to the arms and might be improved by adjusting bike fit. When the pelvis is too far back, you end up pedaling down and out, resulting in a pedal stroke that is all downstroke. This happens a lot with bigger riders who are quad-dominant. They have tons of power at their disposal, but with poor pedal stroke, they are missing a lot of power from their upstroke, power that would be coming from the hip flexor. With your pelvis too far back, you are unable to use the hip flexor to pull up.

Finally, at the feet, riders are generally not raising their heels at the bottom of the pedal stroke. This means they don't engage the calves, hamstrings, glutes, and hip flexor in the upstroke. It is almost like playing the hammer bell carnival game with a sledgehammer: One quad smashes down and shoots the other leg up to smash it down, over and over again.

Power Control can also be compromised by a reactive approach to terrain or even what you're seeing on your bike's computer. On undulating terrain, riders with good Power Control change gears over the crest of a hill and surf the downhill to remain in the zone with good Power Control. They are consistently focused on the torque applied to the pedals, not fixated on their cadence.

Some riders get too fixated on their power meter, which counterintuitively makes for bad Power Control. They are too reactive. They see a number that's too high and quickly ease off the cranks. Or, they accelerate if power goes below the floor for just a moment. Instead, just quickly check in on your power meter once in a while and go off leg feel—the tension and strain you perceive. Remember the fifth key: "Focusing on averages makes you average." Power Control is about precision. Stay in the PTZs you plan to ride. If you're bouncing up and down to reach an average power written on your training plan, you aren't getting better.

If You Aren't Seeing Improvement in Your Power Numbers

1. Remember: "You are not your FTP."
2. Commit yourself to consistency—minimum four rides per week.
3. Focus on Power Control. Improve your pedal stroke with body control, and avoid a reactive approach to terrain or your power numbers.

"I Haven't Lost Any Weight Yet."

First of all, this concern applies to riders who need or want to shed a few pounds. You may not be in this group. But if you are, the solution might surprise you. If you feel like you aren't losing weight like you should, there is a good chance you aren't eating enough. Yes, that's not a typo. I see it time and time again, especially with average-size people who get the cycling bug and settle on this incorrect notion that they need to starve themselves like a pro cyclist. What they are doing is sabotaging their body's natural system instead of giving it the fuel necessary to perform and evolve. It's a vicious cycle. They don't eat anything, so they can't do the power, and then they keep skipping food because they aren't seeing the results.

A lot of cyclists are walking around with beautiful engines—giant muscles, big heart and lungs—and they are not using them because they aren't giving them the right fuel. If you're a 200-pound person, you need a lot of carbs and protein to fuel your body for the work you're asking it to do. When your engine doesn't get that fuel, it works poorly, or it doesn't work at all. When this happens, your metabolism drops. You don't have to be a nutrition expert to know that fast metabolism burns more fuel, leading to weight loss.

Eat enough macronutrients based on the 3-Sigma System. Fuel the zones you're using in training and do it with the correct Timing. I promise this will raise your body's metabolism. Everyone I've coached or ridden with who follows all the FORM pillars looks the part.

Fuel correctly, train hard, and your body will morph into what it needs to be for optimal performance. Weight loss is something that follows as a result of your hard work. It comes from dedication to the FORM Method.

Now before you think this is a license to pig out and eat anything you want, remember the Purpose sigma of the 3-Sigma System. Why are you eating? What will this give you in terms of fuel? Some people will grab a handful of candy, order an extra glass of wine, or snack mindlessly, and before they know it, they are off track. Rice and beer are both carbs but only one translates to fitness and great workouts.

It is common for people to be impulse driven. Many will self-medicate with food, even if that's not the purpose of food. Be conscious of these impulses. Be kind to yourself and remember the 80:20 rule—once in a while you can let loose and splurge. Just do it in a way that won't leave you regretting it the next day, especially if you're supposed to get out for a training ride. This relates again to the Timing sigma of the Nutrition pillar.

If you're confident that you're fueling correctly and you aren't losing weight, you might not be riding in the correct PTZs. A lot of people who start using this system find themselves riding in zones that are lower than they're used to. (Yes, here is another Key to Success: "You have to go low before you can go high.") Some of these cyclists that are starting the FORM Method are experienced, and they are always riding in their threshold zones that use sugar, reinforcing their body's inclination to use glycogen for fuel. They are not efficient at burning fat because they don't do it that often.

Don't neglect your Medium PTZs. This is how your body burns that fat, leading to weight loss. It is important to train your body to go back and forth between fueling systems during the ride, from sugar to fat and back. Riders that are used to pushing hard to hit unrealistic power numbers are always burning sugar. They have trouble losing weight because they aren't burning fat. They train too hard all the time and are not respecting the importance of Base and Medium zones. The Medium zones are your bread and butter. They really put pressure on your metabolism and will turn your body into an efficient, fat-burning machine.

Occasionally, I'll also encounter riders with the opposite issue. They ride almost exclusively in the Base zone. Yes, that burns a little fat, but the Medium zones are far more effective at doing that, and they are going to contribute more to your overall fitness.

One final reason why people often struggle with weight loss is consistency. I go into that issue in detail in the previous section on power.

If You Aren't Losing Weight

1. You aren't eating enough to fuel the training you need to boost metabolism.
2. Train in the correct PTZs with a focus on Medium zones, which almost exclusively use fat as fuel.
3. Commit yourself to consistency—minimum four rides per week.

"I Keep Getting Dropped at Events and Group Rides."

I see it all the time. People get dropped from a ride or event, they get frustrated, and they say something like, "I don't belong here in this group/category/event/ sport." But the answer is YES, you do belong here! Instead of leaving, you need to change your way of thinking, your strategy, what you expect to get out of a day on the bike.

This starts with your vision. Why are you riding, and what do you want to get out of it? People look to events to give them clarity on who they are and what they are doing as cyclists. That's not going to get you anywhere, because it's too dependent on what other riders are doing. Your motivation needs to come from within. Take control over your performance in events and stop being influenced by what is happening with other people in the peloton. This relates to key 9: "Chasing after other someone else's level pulls you further away from improving your own."

Cyclists of all experience levels often make the mistake of participating in group rides and events with people who are much better than they are. The idea is that if they ride with people who are better than them, it will force their body and brain to match theirs.

Well, you'll definitely get in a hard effort, but you'll be pushing yourself in the wrong direction. Pain does not always lead to gain. If you are outside of your zones, you have no footing for a strong performance. You are building a roof with no foundation. And I'm sure that you're not in a situation where you can consciously use the Focus pillar to drive your performance. Instead, you're just hanging on by your fingernails.

To shift your mindset in group rides and events, you have to devote yourself to Focus. When people take on races that are above their level, all they have to go on is a reactive mindset. That's OK, but you have to recognize that from the beginning and have the self-awareness to hold back a suicidal attack that will torpedo your chances. Come up with a plan to drive and control your day with your brain, your mindsets. This is related to your Rider Type, what your PTZs are, and how you can control those zones with your mindsets. The goal is to win your ride, to compete on your own terms.

Sometimes that might actually mean getting dropped. If you make a conscious decision to let go of someone's wheel because they are surging or you know you're out of the PTZs you planned to use, that's OK. If you're in control and driving that all with your mindsets, you are succeeding.

One of the biggest things you can do to prepare yourself for group rides or events is to use the Focus pillar consistently throughout your training. This means finding a CPQ that is meaningful to you. It means using Black Line Clarity as a regular priming process for any ordinary workout. And, of course, you should strive to reach the point where you can shift between mindsets—Cloud, Water, Fire, Lightning—to drive your PTZs.

Train like you race, right? Everyone knows that simple rule for the physical side of cycling, but it is essential to apply it to the mental side of the sport as well. Too often, people show up to rides or events and are shocked by the unexpected, by the group dynamics, by the chaos. Unless you exclusively race time trials, you can't expect to show up and not have to deal with other competitors.

Use the Focus pillar to drive your training and you'll be able to do the same when it's time to race. Take control and win your ride.

If You're Still Getting Dropped at Rides and Events

1. Review and solidify your vision—the "why" behind your commitment to cycling.
2. Take control with your CPQ and prime yourself with Black Line Clarity.
3. Train like you race. Use the Focus pillar daily and you'll naturally use it in group rides and events.

12

TRANSFORMATION

With all the planning you can set into place and adhere to as strictly as possible, there's still no guarantee that you'll always, only, be on the up, always winning, never facing challenges. In fact, the point of the FORM Method is to address weak spots in your cycling and build them up. It feels fantastic to celebrate a big win or a new PR, but we need to be prepared when we miss the mark or have a bad day. As crazy as this might sound, I believe you'll get far more from your failures than you will from your successes.

It is natural to have a fear of failure. I definitely did throughout my years as a pro cyclist. I found myself holding back in races, not performing to my full capacity because I was afraid of what might happen if my race-winning move imploded or was caught or countered by an even better move. Unfortunately, I was really missing out. In cycling, and in real life, failures, challenges, and struggles are your greatest opportunities. They are a chance to reinvent yourself, to become the next best version of who you are.

I didn't always see failure that way. Over the years, I often resisted it. I'd make excuses. I'm sure you have heard all of these from fellow cyclists: The other riders were on better form, I wasn't feeling very good that day, the course wasn't right for me. Making excuses is the worst possible response to failure. Excuses only hold you back, leaving you stuck and unable to progress. They prevent you from transforming.

Transformation is the only option to move forward after you fail. It's not easy to do. It can be a painful struggle. To do it right, you have to confront your failure head-on. This might be intimidating at first. After all, you're just riding bikes for fun. Why worry about a heavy topic like transformation—making tangible changes to your attitude and behavior?

Cycling might not be your livelihood like it was for me, but no matter what level you're at, the lessons you take from this sport will enrich your life. And transformation is one of the biggest lessons. I'm going to take you through my method to transform after a failure and become a better, stronger version of yourself. And I think you'll find that this method is just as useful in real life, when your bike is put away and you're facing challenges or failures at the office or at home.

To guide myself and my athletes through a transformation, I created the ASCEND Process; I did it with a little inspiration from my love of climbing. (By this point in the book, that shouldn't be a big surprise.) When I am faced with a challenge or a failure, I view it as a big mountain. I'm at the bottom. The road only goes in two directions: up and over the top or back where I came from, and you can be sure I'm not going backward. Let's walk through the six steps of the ASCEND Process to help you climb your own mountains and transform.

ASCEND

A: Assess the Need

S: Set the Foundation

C: Create the Opportunity

E: Evolve with Growth

N: Next-Level Arrival

D: Demonstrate the Transformation Daily

Assess the Need

Here we are at the bottom of the mountain, the beginning of your transformation. By now you should have confronted the fact that you had a bad race, struggles in training, challenges with keeping a consistent riding schedule, or a lack of improvement, to name a few examples. This is the step in the ASCEND Process when you take an honest look at what is going on and what you need to do in order to transform.

Positive self-awareness is the fundamental trait needed to Assess the Need. Take a step back and see things in perspective, referring to your vision from the Focus pillar. Be honest and realistic. Think about your ability, skills, and direction, then ask yourself how they can offer you an opportunity to transform. Don't retreat or make excuses.

However, at the same time, don't be too hard on yourself. It is key to frame self-awareness in a positive light. What do you have in your arsenal? How can this transformation help you grow that arsenal so you're even better at the end? Transformation starts when you hit a low point. It's going to be challenging, and negativity will only make it harder. Most people hit an obstacle, give up, and move on to something else. So, by tackling your challenge head-on, you are already outstanding. Channel that positive inner strength.

With that positive self-awareness, begin to diagnose the problem. The great news is that, since you're working with the FORM Method, you have every tool you need to start your transformation in a purposeful way. Look at your problem in the context of the Four Pillars. Your area of need should become clear pretty quickly. This will also help you simplify your solution and focus on a single area so you aren't overwhelmed.

For example, you might be struggling on long climbs. Is the problem rooted in your Fitness pillar? Your PTZs might be incorrect, or you might be underdeveloped in a key PTZ, like Low Threshold. Or perhaps your Execution pillar is the issue. Body Position, Power Control, Cadence Control—any of these or the other points on the North Star of Execution could be the culprit. Nutrition may also be holding you back on those long climbs. If you aren't fueling with the right amount of macros, your body simply won't have what it needs to ride the way you're asking it to. And finally, your Focus pillar could be the source of the problem. I've seen great climbers pedaling squares because they were in the wrong mindset, or they simply didn't do their homework with Core Performance Qualities and Black Line Clarity.

Once you pin down the area of need, the thing you must alter to transform and improve, then you can move on to the next step of the ASCEND Process.

Assess the Need

Be honest with yourself

Stay positive

Find the pillar to improve

Keep it simple

Go beyond your comfort zone

Set the Foundation

This step is a research and planning stage to develop the instruction manual for transformation. Depending on what need you found and chose to work on, you must find the "how," or the program that you will follow to improve it. This program could be as simple as following a simple premade training plan or as involved as hiring a coach to work with you personally.

You're about to undertake a difficult, potentially long process. Everything has to be in place before you begin so that your work is productive, pushing you to the top of that mountain.

Putting the right program in place and planning how it will fit in your schedule sounds obvious, but it's not. In fact, a lot of people skip it, and that's a bad idea. Think about all those people—you may be one of them—who just focused on improving by doing more, or by copying other people. While you might have seen improvement, there likely was no foundational fitness and repeatable program to fall back on to keep performing the transformation month after month, year after year. This second step will ensure that the work in your transformation is the right course, a strong foundation to hold the new level, and easy to repeat in the future.

Let me take you through an example of how you could set the foundation for a common need: improved climbing. Many people struggle on climbs because their Threshold PTZs are too low or they've only developed one Threshold PTZ. I would begin by testing to find their High Threshold and then look at their efficiency in PTZs 2, 3, 4, and 5. This is the research part of the "set the foundation" step. If this testing confirms that they do need to establish and then increase their Threshold PTZs, we continue on to the second part of this step, planning. We'd create the best training program for the Threshold PTZ growth they need. Then, I would teach them the new exercises they will be performing and the concepts behind the purpose. For example, I might first teach them the concept of Power Floors and why they are essential to growth. Last, I'd customize their training schedule.

No matter what your specific need as identified in the first step of the ASCEND Process, don't just jump right to the solution. Instead, create this foundation for your process. Your work has to be repeatable. We want you to be able to establish new habits that will drive your transformation.

This is a challenging step. You'll be adding something different to your routine, establishing a new mental pathway, or introducing an uncomfortable change to your daily life. A lot of people quit when they see the work ahead of them, so again return to that positive mindset and know that you're already above average by committing yourself to transformation. You don't have to be perfect. You just have to be open to the process, to learn and absorb the new methodology.

Set the Foundation

What did you learn from the first step—how does it practically apply?

Return to the key parts of the pillar you're working on

Outline a process for improvement

Make sure your process is repeatable

Establish a new habit with consistency

Create the Opportunity

Now we reach the uncomfortable step of the transformation process. It's time to start putting things into place and doing the hard work to climb your mountain. I hope you were thorough in the first two steps, because you need that clear focus on your need and a foundation for a repeatable, habit-forming process to make this work pay off.

You have your plan, so now you'll need to give yourself room—or time—to execute it, fitting it into your already established training or day-to-day life. Depending on which pillar you are taking on, this step could be a time to map out how to build out your aerobic system or spend time refining your Threshold zones. Or you might be setting a core strength or plyometrics routine to improve your Execution. For some people, the work might happen off the bike. It might be all about shifting the way you shop for groceries and plan your weekly meals. The work could be entirely mental—no physical effort is required if your goal is to establish the right practices with Black Line Clarity or the Performance Chains.

One of the keys to this step is to give yourself room to grow. Many people do not grow because they're stuck doing the same kind of workout day after day, week after week. Or they eat the same diet for years and wonder why their performance suffers or even why they are gaining weight. Install this new process into your day-to-day life, based on the first two steps of this process, and avoid falling back into your previous patterns. Be open to something truly different and new.

Create the Opportunity

Attack the barrier that has held you back

Make changes that give you room to grow and push your limits

Be ambitious

Don't fall back into your old habits or routines

Evolve with Growth

The grind: Some people love it, but a lot of people can't handle the regular, daily work needed to transform into something better.

Growth is not a linear process. In fact, this part of a transformation is often two steps forward, one step back—and that's a best-case scenario. So while you make progress then maybe fall back a little, always remember that struggle is growth. Success is practice. It may not feel like it, but if you're sticking to your proven process, working off of a good foundation, you will be adapting and growing.

People also find this step challenging because it is the longest of the six parts of the ASCEND Process. Your growth might take months or even a year. Why is this step so long and difficult? If you're truly setting yourself up to transform, you pushed your limits in the previous step of the process, setting ambitious goals. Those will require time and effort as you adapt to the new workload, or as you establish new habits. It may be intimidating to see months of work ahead of you, but you can tackle that challenge with confidence because you were careful in the first two steps of this process. You charted the right course by assessing your need and setting your foundation. Now we climb.

Evolve with Growth
Growth is not linear
Expect setbacks
You're in it for the long haul
Take time to adapt to the workload and establish new habits

Next-Level Arrival

This is a milestone, the point where you achieve mastery of the skill or quality you've been working on for months. It is a little hard to pin down exactly when you reach this point.

For instance, over the last few years, I've given a lot of speeches. They're usually on topics like transformation, so I know the subject well and I am passionate about it. I have practiced my talks a lot, and I've figured out the best way to express these concepts. But this skill is still not truly ingrained in me. I can't quite do it over and over again on command.

On the other hand, if we were riding up a steep, tough climb together and you attacked me, I'd cover your move instantly. Maybe I'd even counterattack with a standing acceleration. It would be pure instinct. That's a skill I've mastered thanks to years of practice.

That's the difference between simply being good at something and Next-Level Arrival. When you actually get to the next level—the goal for your transformation—all of that habit-forming growth and repetition becomes part of who you are.

You can't predict when you'll achieve this mastery. You can't force it, either. But there should be no question at all when you hit this milestone. The habit will become so ingrained in your practice that you'll be able to do it on command in an event or on a group ride. You'll be surfing terrain without even thinking about it. Or your meal preparation will be a seamless, automatic part of your daily life.

This is a really exciting feeling. It's why I value transformation so much, both on the bike and in real life. All of your effort, struggle, and time will feel completely worthwhile.

Next-Level Arrival

Performing the skill on command

Ingrained habit is automatic

You have become the change you were working toward

Don't predict it

Don't force it

Demonstrate the Transformation Daily

So that's it, right? Why would we need a sixth step in the ASCEND Process if we have just arrived at the next level? We need another step because transformation isn't about achieving a result and putting it on your mantle. It is about becoming a better version of yourself and owning that new way of being.

You might know someone who has finished an Ironman® triathlon. It is a popular goal to chase after, and it is a pretty big challenge for most people. However, those friends of yours who did an Ironman—are they still living that lifestyle, and continuing the practice that got them to the finish line of that grueling test? A lot of the Ironman finishers I see have let it slide because for them it wasn't a full transformation. They rose up to achieve that goal but they didn't stay up there after the race finished. To put this in different terms, you can't call yourself a pilot if you aren't flying regularly and practicing your trade to keep your license. Same goes for doctors or musicians.

Define the new version of yourself with your actions. Be that person all the time by your consistent daily actions that reinforce who you have become through this long and difficult transformation. Here is some good news: Once you've gotten to the final step in this process, your habits will be so ingrained and frictionless that it will feel natural to continue as your new self. You'll have adapted to the training load—you'll probably even crave it. You'll feel the thrill of great execution and have no reason to regress. A better nutrition plan will give you a feeling of well-being and energy that powers you through the day. Who would give that up? Or your new mindset will make you happier through life's ups and downs.

Don't just do it. Be it. And enjoy this new, better self.

Demonstrate the Transformation Daily
Define the new version of yourself with actions
Focus on intrinsic motivation to stay at this new level
Sustainability is key
Don't just do it. Be it.

The process of transformation is as rewarding as it is challenging. I know it seems intimidating at first, but I encourage you to embrace it. When a failure or a setback comes your way, address it head-on, right away. It is tempting to procrastinate, but this process is even more difficult if multiple problems pile up before you start.

Also, be prepared to restart the process after you've worked through a problem or a challenge. Just like riding an epic mountain stage, you'll face one climb after another. The great thing about the ASCEND Process is that it gives you a chance to have moments of success, achievements when you work through a problem and make a transformation, no matter how small it might actually be.

My Ultimate Transformation

I want cycling to transform your life. My entire coaching philosophy is based on my confidence that transformation—real change—is entirely possible. And so it only makes sense that everything from my coaching company to this FORM Performance Method started with a huge transformation: my own.

This was a transformation that I never saw coming. It sprung out of a major event that I had no control over, one that I thought was actually pretty unfair. In fact, it ended my pro cycling career. At first that might seem like a terrible thing. At the time, it was extremely hard to handle in every way. But it forged me into an even better version of myself.

It all began at the worst possible moment, the night before the 2015 Tour of Utah. I came into that race as the odds-on favorite, as I had won the past two editions of the six-day race. Plus, I absolutely loved the high-altitude climbing that defined the route and was highly motivated to go for the win again.

At dinner with my teammates, the start of the race less than 24 hours away, I got a phone call. It was the US Anti-Doping Agency (USADA). For nearly any other rider, this would be a reason to panic. However, I had a history with these guys. Back in 2012, I voluntarily gave USADA testimony to help them pin down Lance Armstrong in one of cycling's biggest doping cases. I didn't have to do it, and I didn't expect my testimony would ever be publicly linked to me, but I decided it was the right thing to do. I confessed to doping during my time with Armstrong's Discovery Channel team. I hate what doping has done to pro cycling. That's why I left Discovery Channel with a year left on my contract to go to Garmin-Chipotle, a little upstart team sponsored by a burrito chain that was committed to riding clean. I wanted to put that dirty side of cycling behind me.

I had been riding clean for years at that point. So, when I got that call, I assumed it was just some follow-up to ongoing testimony related to the Discovery Channel doping case. It wasn't.

Instead, the voice on the other end of the line told me that I had failed a doping test. I freaked out. I told my teammates at the dinner table. I was shaking, crying. I tweeted the news immediately because I knew I ⇒

was innocent. It seems naïve now, but I just put that news out into the universe, hoping someone would come to my rescue. Out of the race, I left Utah and headed back to Colorado with my then girlfriend, Kourtney.

That was early August 2015. The next five months would prove to be the most frustrating and challenging time I'd ever faced. I hired experts, endured interviews that were more like interrogations, spent most of my savings on the uphill battle to prove I hadn't deserved these charges. Working with an expert scientist in the supplement industry, I discovered that a contamination of a common supplement I'd taken for years was to blame for the positive test result. With my resources dwindling, I knew I had to change direction. First, I needed a job. I thought of getting into marketing, as I had graduated college with degrees in marketing and psychology. I ended up having coffee one day with a successful marketer who founded his own company and had worked for many major ad agencies and marketing companies.

His advice shocked me. "You don't want to get a job. You need to start a business," he said. "Start with those cycling camps you've been doing and see where it goes."

"But everyone hates me in cycling. No one will come to my camps," I said.

"You are one of the best cyclists in the world. You are an expert in your field. You are a nice person who is good at communicating. You are a patient person who loves to teach. People will come to your camp," he assured me.

Finally, someone had gotten through to me and woken up the positive self-awareness I needed to Assess the Need in my situation. I was good at running these camps. This was something I could focus my energy on to move forward. Kourtney and I put all of our eggs in the camp basket.

Before I knew it, we had scheduled nine weeks of winter cycling camps in Tucson, Arizona. Things started slow, with only a couple of people in our first few camps. We made it work, but barely. A friend helped me design a logo and a website, and another, renowned cycling chef Sean Fowler, worked as our cook basically for free. But eventually word spread. Cyclists started to show up, and they were really getting a lot out of what I was teaching them.

At the start of this book, I described that Mount Lemmon time trial we did on the final day of a camp in January 2016. I already kind of spoiled the ending: This 4,600-foot climb out of the desert changed my life. But it was even more of a crossroads than I let on in the beginning: It was truly a life-changing experience. All the emotions of my struggle fueled what turned out to be my best climbing performance ever, with perfect Execution and great power numbers. Then I descended and followed each person up, giving them pointers and encouragement along the way. The energy was electric.

As I mentioned in the introduction, at the end of the day, when we debriefed with our athletes and discussed the day's event, they couldn't stop talking about how much it meant for them to have my encouragement and coaching. I helped them ride better than they could have done alone. It wasn't about my own power numbers or my own result. It was about how I had positively influenced their day and their bigger journey through cycling.

That's when it hit me. My purpose in cycling—my "why"—was to inspire other riders. Back when I was a pro racer, I loved being able to inspire people with my riding. In fact, I didn't actually like beating people. That wasn't why I did it. That January in Arizona, I saw clearly that I'd found a new motivation: to guide people through the world of cycling, inspiring and teaching them along the way.

At this crossroads, I finally realized how I could pivot and do something I loved, something positive. I left the case and the damage it would have caused behind. Now, my direction was 100 percent focused on inspiring people through coaching.

The business grew. I was seeing results in the athletes and in the business. We were able to pay off our debt. Things turned around.

My transformation was so difficult. At the time it felt like the worst possible luck, but it ended up being an amazing experience. Kourtney and I created our own business, and in doing so we fulfilled our "whys," our purpose. It was a magical experience, and it's why I'm so adamant about overcoming adversity with transformation. It saved our lives. We survived because we were willing to transform. I feel like I have an obligation to show other people the way with this process.

I'll tell you one last thing: You're not alone. Kourtney and I went through this ordeal, and my coaching clients overcome their own obstacles every year. You'll have your own setbacks and challenges along the way, too. But you can do it.

We're all one big community. We're going to face these struggles together and use the strength of cycling to bring us all up to another level, to an even better version of ourselves. It will be a long climb, but the view at the top is amazing.

APPENDIX

SAMPLE TRAINING PLAN AND WORKOUTS

What follows is not merely a list of workouts. It's a Four-Pillar training plan to develop your PTZs and the other skills that I've explained are crucial to well-rounded improvement on the bike. After a few weeks focusing on physical work, I introduce the other pillars in a methodical way to add to but not disrupt your physical training. So be sure to infuse your workouts with smart fueling, matching effort to mindset, and the five points of the North Star of Execution: Power Control, Cadence Control, Body Position, Separation, and Transitional Control. You'll see efforts on the following pages that require seated and standing positions at prescribed cadence, for example, or reminders to check in on your vision, Black Line Clarity, and the CPQs explained in Chapter 9. Practice everything. When there are high-intensity efforts paired with lower ones (those not identified as recovery times), really focus on showing excellent separation when you change the PTZs, cadences, and body positions. Just nailing the Execution technique alone will help you create much more speed from your power. But as you will see, this requires more strength than just the force stomped on the pedals.

By the end of this training period, you will have established 11 well-defined PTZs and gained the knowledge and habits to continue your development. In this timeframe, I've often seen a 5–10 percent boost in overall power, including Threshold PTZs.

Reading the Plan

Remember key 3 from Chapter 2: Planning for your workout is part of your workout. This means you'll review the workouts across a week, fit them into your daily schedule, and also plan the workouts' terrain and nutrition. Know what you're aiming for and stay focused when you execute the day's ride. As a workout's components become more varied and robust, I'll leave more notes to help you understand what the day's goal and focus are, or what the expected result should be.

You'll see total ride times at the top of the workout, but you'll soon see that the workouts don't add up to that total. Use the remaining time in that ride to warm up and cool down, or get to the part of your route if terrain, like a climb, is key to the workout.

PTZ Testing: Day 2 and Day 57

I intentionally begin this plan with a rest day to start you off on the right foot for the Day 2 test (see Chapter 4 for more details on this test and PTZs). You'll need to be well rested for it. In this test, we'll determine how your body responds to a sustained climbing or time trial-like threshold effort. You'll then identify your PTZs to use during the remaining weeks. I won't give you any hints on how to pace yourself or suggest what power level or wattage to hold. How you interpret the effort, and how your body reacts to your pacing guidance, is part of the test. This can be done indoors or outdoors.

During the 12-minute effort, you have to try to keep a steady (and high) pace for the whole 12 minutes. If you start easy and then massively ramp up the last 4 minutes, you will need to retest. When done correctly, the last 4 minutes is just +/-10 watts within the average of the whole 12-minute effort. After the test, use the average power of the last 4 minutes of the test to calculate your PowerTrain Zones according to the table on p. 68.

A FOUR-PILLAR
TRAINING PLAN

DAY 1	DAY 2	DAY 3	DAY 4

DAY 2 — PTZ TEST
1 hour

Now that you're rested, find a good test course, warm up, and crush the time-trial effort in the PTZ test; you'll find the complete instructions on p. 68.

---

20 min. warm-up, PTZs 1 and 2

1 × 12 min. at the highest power you can hold for this duration

30 min. cooldown and recovery

Calculate your PTZs according to the table on p. 68, using the average power from the last 4 minutes.

DAY 1
Rest

DAY 3 — MEDIUM PTZS
1.5 hours

It's a fairly easy ride today, but what's most important now that you have your PTZs identified is to stay true to them for the duration of the effort.

---

15 min. warm-up PTZ 1 (Base)

1 × 10 min. PTZ 2 (Low Medium)

5 min. recovery

1 × 10 min. PTZ 3 (Medium)

5 min. recovery

1 × 10 min. PTZ 4 (High Medium)

10 min. cooldown

DAY 4 — THRESHOLD PTZS
1.5 hours

No matter what your training looked like before you started this plan, you're going to get into hard efforts right away. Again, focus on staying at your new PTZs throughout the effort.

---

20 min. warm-up, PTZ 1 (Base)

2 × 5 min. PTZ 5 (Low Threshold)

5 min. recovery after each set

2 × 4 min. PTZ 6 (Threshold)

5 min. recovery after each set

2 × 3 min. PTZ 7 (High Threshold)

5 min. recovery after each set

Rest

EXPLOSIVE PTZS

1.5 hours

You're going to blast into some high-intensity efforts today, so be sure the recovery time is at a low PTZ, allowing you to be ready for the next high-PTZ interval.

---

15 min. warm-up

3 × 2 min. PTZ 8

5 min. recovery after each set

2 × 4 min.:
2 min. PTZ 5
1 min. PTZ 9
1 min. PTZ 5

5 min. recovery after each set

Here, you're practicing the correct use of your Long Surge, PTZ 9. You attack to it from PTZ 5 and then return to PTZ 5, where you can hold a fast pace and clear lactate.

2 × 4 min., alternate between:
30 sec. Power Floor of PTZ 10
30 sec. Power Floor of PTZ 2

5 min. recovery after each set

This is how you would use your Short Surge to launch repeatable controlled attacks. Most people can't attack for a full 30 seconds, so it is effective for eventually dropping people or covering their attacks in a very calculated way.

1 × 10 sec. full-on sprint

This is the maximum strength effort you would use to sprint.

PTZ MIX

2 hours

Today you'll combine work in the Medium, Threshold, and Explosive PTZs to get used to working different energy systems in one workout.

---

15 min. warm-up

1 × 10 min. PTZ 3 (Medium)

5 min. recovery

1 × 8 min. PTZ 4 (High Medium)

5 min. recovery

**TRANSITION BETWEEN
HIGH AND LOW MEDIUM PTZS**
1 × 6 min., alternate between:
1 min. PTZ 4
2 min. PTZ 2

5 min. recovery

**LOW THRESHOLD TO
HIGH THRESHOLD PTZ BUILD**
2 × 3 min.:
1 min. PTZ 5
1 min. PTZ 6
1 min. PTZ 7

5 min. recovery after each set

REPEATED SHORT SURGE
1 × 5 min., alternate between:
30 sec. attack in PTZ 10
30 sec. PTZ 2

Rest	**LOW THRESHOLD BUILDER**	**THRESHOLD ATTACKS**	**THRESHOLD POWER DEVELOPMENT**
	1.5 hours	1.5 hours	1.5 hours

LOW THRESHOLD BUILDER

1.5 hours

Low Threshold is your most important zone for climbing and time trialing. It's the foundation from which all high-intensity efforts flow. Improving this PTZ will help you clear lactate and surf the terrain better during time trials.

15 min. warm-up

1 × 12 min. PTZ 3, 90 rpm

10 min. recovery

3 × 6 min.,
alternate between:
2 min. PTZ 5
1 min. PTZ 6

*5 min. recovery
after each set*

THRESHOLD ATTACKS

1.5 hours

This workout will develop the area between your Low and High Threshold zones. It's useful for time trials or when you break free on a final climb. It is below your threshold, so you can still clear lactate.

15 min. warm-up

1 × 10 min. PTZ 3, 90 rpm

5 min. recovery

3 × 5 min. PTZ 5, 80 rpm

Each minute do a
10 sec. attack, PTZ 7

*5 min. recovery
after each set*

The key to recovering from attacks at high intensity is to take deep exhalations to get your breathing back in rhythm.

1 × 10 min. PTZ 2, 90 rpm

THRESHOLD POWER DEVELOPMENT

1.5 hours

With shorter intervals, we can focus on holding the right power while knowing the finish line is in sight. Be careful: This workout is deceptively hard, as it's Day 3 of a very hard training block. Glycogen levels will be less than ideal.

15 min. warm-up

2 × 8 min. PTZ 3, 100 rpm

*5 min. recovery
after each set*

1 × 5 min. build:
Start in PTZ 3 and increase intensity by about 25 watts each minute, until the last minute is PTZ 6

5 min. recovery

3 × 5 min. PTZ 6 to PTZ 7

*5 min. recovery
after each set*

DAY 12   **DAY 13**

DAY 14

Rest

BODY POSITION & LOW THRESHOLD

2 hours

Work on your efficiency in and out of the saddle. This will teach you to adapt out-of-saddle riding to the changes in terrain, while becoming more efficient.

15 min. warm-up

2 × 10 min. PTZ 3, 90 rpm

At least 5 min. recovery after each set

STANDING/SITTING INTERVALS
2 × 9 min. PTZ 5:
1 min. standing
1 min. sitting
2 min. standing
2 min. sitting
3 min. standing

At least 5 min. recovery after each set

1 × 20 min. PTZ 2, 90 rpm

SURF THE TERRAIN & THRESHOLD

1.5 hours

Practice building and maintaining momentum through changes in terrain, as you would in a time trial. You will do a 10-second surge to build momentum and then 50 seconds at Low Threshold to maintain it. While in a race you will probably TT closer to your threshold, with Low Threshold you can stay in control and focus on the 10-second surges.

20 min. warm-up

2 × 8 min. PTZ 3, 90 rpm

5 min. recovery after each set

1 × 5 min. build:
Start in PTZ 3 and increase the intensity about 25 watts each minute until the last minute is PTZ 6

5 min. recovery

TT SURF INTERVALS
3 × 5 min., alternate between:
10 sec. PTZ 8
50 sec. PTZ 5

5 min. recovery after each set

Rest

BODY POSITION & CADENCE CHANGES

1.5 hours

Today you'll work on the critical Low Threshold PTZ while developing power and pedaling efficiency with the low-cadence intervals. Switching between sitting and standing will test how well you hold yourself out of the saddle and teach you how to accelerate better out of the saddle.

---

15 min. warm-up

1 × 10 min. PTZ 3, 90 rpm

5 min. recovery

3 × 6 min. PTZ 5, alternate between:
1 min. at 50 rpm, seated
1 min. at 70 rpm, standing

At least 5 min. recovery after each set

1 × 10 min. PTZ 3, 90 rpm

LONG SURGES FROM LOW THRESHOLD

1.5 hours

Today you will build your efficiency at flooding and clearing lactate near your threshold. This exercise also practices changes in tempo, which can be used to drop other riders on climbs or build momentum in time trials and steady, hard efforts.

---

15 min. warm-up

1 × 10 min. PTZ 2, 90 rpm

At least 5 min. recovery

3 × 6 min., alternate between:
2 min. PTZ 5
1 min. PTZ 9

At least 5 min. recovery after each set

1 × 10 min. PTZ 2, 90 rpm

DAY 18

NUCLEAR PTZ

1.5 hours

Let's raise the roof! Today you'll push the limits of your cardiovascular system in PTZ 8. This calculated effort will rely on the maximum output you can hold for a prolonged period. In these moments, your body has to use every bit of oxygen available.

---

15 min. warm-up

1 × 12 min. PTZ 3, 90 rpm

10 min. recovery

3 × 3 min. PTZ 8, 80–90 rpm

5 min. recovery after each set

1 × 12 min. PTZ 2, 100 rpm

DAY 19

Rest

DAY 20

LACTATE-CLEARING EFFICIENCY

2 hours

This workout is all about raising your sustained lactate-threshold efficiency in PTZ 7, which is used for climbing, breakaways, and time trialing. What's unique here is alternating between the Low Threshold PTZ 5 and the High Threshold PTZ 7. This will flood and then clear lactate while still producing high power.

---

15 min. warm-up

1 × 12 min.:
4 min. PTZ 4
4 min. PTZ 2
4 min. PTZ 4

5 min. recovery

3 × 6 min., alternate between:
2 min. PTZ 5
1 min. PTZ 7

5 min. full recovery after each set

1 × 12 min. PTZ 3, 80 rpm

DAY 21

Rest

DAY 22

STANDING BODY POSITION

1 hour

We are allowing your body to recover but still be challenged, keeping your zones in check. The focus is on executing the standing positions, where you should activate the glutes and core during the pedal stroke.

---

15 min. warm-up

2 × 4 min. PTZ 2, 50–70 rpm:
1 min. standing,
1 min. seated,
1 min. standing,
1 min. seated

4 min. recovery after each set

STANDING HIGH MEDIUM INTERVAL
5 × 2 min. PTZ 4, 50–70 rpm

3 min. recovery after each set

DAY 23

THRESHOLD FORCE

1 hour

The first interval is all about effectively using the Low Medium and High Medium PTZs. For the second interval, we are gently building your ability to produce higher force with the Threshold PTZs, as you'll use them more in the next block of training.

---

15 min. warm-up

1 × 9 min., alternate between:
2 min. PTZ 2
1 min. PTZ 4

5 min. recovery

2 × 6 min., alternate between:
25 sec. PTZ 7, 50–60 rpm, standing
35 sec. PTZ 4, 80 rpm, seated

5 min. recovery after each set

DAY 24

LOW THRESHOLD PEDAL STROKE

1 hour

While you get some needed recovery, we will be keeping your Low Threshold zone in place. Using a lower cadence will improve your pedaling technique.

---

15 min. warm-up

1 × 9 min.:
3 min. PTZ 4
3 min. PTZ 2
3 min. PTZ 4

5 min. recovery

3 × 3 min. PTZ 5, 50–70 rpm

5 min. recovery after each set

1 × 9 min.:
3 min. PTZ 4
3 min. PTZ 2
3 min. PTZ 4

DAY 25

Rest

DAY 26

MEDIUM CADENCE BUILDS

1.5 hours

The Medium and High Medium PTZs (3 and 4) will connect the input from the mind to the body. The cadence builds to give the central nervous system stimulation to stay sharp. This effort shows you how to use cadence to increase speed/momentum without increasing the power.

---

15 min. warm-up

1 × 12 min. PTZ 3, 90 rpm

5 min. recovery

3 × 3 min. PTZ 4:
1 min., 50 rpm
1 min., 80 rpm
1 min., 110 rpm

3 min. recovery after each set

1 × 12 min. PTZ 2, 100 rpm

10 min. cooldown

DAY 27

LOW THRESHOLD & SURF THE TERRAIN

1.5 hours

The early PTZ 2 interval will stimulate your fat-burning metabolism. Then, you'll do some alternating Low Threshold work with cadence changes to build and maintain power at different rpms.

---

15 min. warm-up

1 × 12 min. PTZ 2, 90 rpm

5 min. recovery

3 × 2 min. PTZ 4,
50–60 rpm, standing

2 min. recovery after each set

2 × 6 min., alternate between:
20 sec. PTZ 5, 100 rpm
40 sec. PTZ 4, 80 rpm

5 min. recovery after each set

DAY 28

SURF THE TERRAIN

1.5 hours

Today we focus on the concept of surfing the terrain. This means reading changes in terrain to find places to build speed and then use Transitional Control with PTZs, cadences, and Body Positions to make small accelerations to further gain speed. Then, you'll use a lower PTZ Power Floor and lower cadence to maintain speed.

---

15 min. warm-up

FAT-BURNING PTZ
1 × 12 min. Power Floor of PTZ 2, 80 rpm

5 min. recovery

SURF THE TERRAIN
3 × 5 min., alternate between:
20 sec. Power Floor of PTZ 6, 100 rpm, seated
40 sec. Power Floor of PTZ 5, 80 rpm, seated

5 min. recovery after each set

We use 20-second accelerations, but in the real world this might be as brief as 5 seconds.

FAT-BURNING PTZ
1 × 8 min. Power Floor of PTZ 2, 80 rpm

5 min. recovery

EXPLOSIVE STRENGTH
5 × 30 sec. PTZ 10 standing accelerations

30 sec. rest after each set

10 min. cooldown

EXECUTION

Now we incorporate the Execution components of Power Control, Cadence Control, Body Position, Separation, and Transitional Control.

DAY 29

PROACTIVE ACCELERATION

1.5 hours

Today we are going to work on an offense-oriented acceleration on flat or rolling terrain to drop other riders right off your wheel. Dropping someone on this type of terrain requires a unique type of acceleration.

15 min. warm-up

FAT-BURNING PTZ
1 × 10 min. Power Floor of PTZ 3, 90 rpm

5 min. recovery

30/30 THRESHOLDS
2 × 6 min.,
alternate between:
30 sec. Power Floor of PTZ 7, 50 rpm, standing
30 sec. Power Floor of PTZ 5, 70 rpm, seated

*5 min. recovery
after each set*

OFFENSE ACCELERATION
1 × 5 min.:
3 min. Power Floor of PTZ 5, 80 rpm, seated
2 min. Power Floor of PTZ 7, 100 rpm, seated

5 min. recovery

FAT-BURNING ENDURANCE WORK
1 × 10 min. Power Floor of PTZ 2, 100 rpm

10 min. cooldown

DAY 30

THE LONG ATTACK

1.5 hours

The key to the initial acceleration in a long attack is gear selection. Choose a gear that you can turn over immediately, in a high cadence. Then, make sure you shift gears perfectly, not letting the tension you have on your chain drop as the momentum from the acceleration drops the resistance.

15 min. warm-up

FAT-BURNING PTZ & STRENGTH CONTROL
3 × 3 min. Power Floor of PTZ 4, 50–70 rpm

*3 min. recovery
after each set*

THE LONG ATTACK
6 × 2 min.:
1 min. Power Floor of PTZ 9, 80 rpm, standing
1 min. Power Floor of PTZ 7, 100 rpm, seated

*3 min. recovery
after each set*

Focus on the transition to the seated position and use your high cadence to keep the speed you created despite backing off the power.

FAT-BURNING PTZ MEDIUM POWER FLOOR
1 × 12 min. at Power Floor of PTZ 2, 100 rpm

DAY 31

Rest

DAY 32

STRENGTH ON FLAT TERRAIN

2 hours

Focus on remaining between Power Floors and Ceilings to hold speed on the flats. I've thrown in some curve-balls to work on your technique, so focus on the Three Points of Power (hands, core, and feet) to execute this one well.

15 min. warm-up

FAT-BURNING PTZS
2 × 10 min. PTZ 2–4, 80–90 rpm

*5 min. recovery
after each set*

FLAT TERRAIN STRENGTH
3 × 6 min.,
alternate between:
2 min. Power Floor of PTZ 5, 70 rpm, seated
1 min. Power Floor of PTZ 4, 80 rpm, standing

*5 min. recovery
between each interval*

FAT-BURNING PTZS
1 × 12 min. Power Floor of PTZ 2, 100 rpm

5 min. recovery

LONG ATTACK SURGES
5 × 1 min.:
30 sec. Power Ceiling of PTZ 10, 80 rpm, standing
30 sec. Power Ceiling of PTZ 7, 70 rpm, standing

1 min. recovery after each set

DAY 33

ENDURANCE WITH ACCELERATION/DECELERATION

3 hours

We will be working on one of the components of executing a good acceleration or attack: your ability to decelerate before it (the "Stall") and then launch. This platform of the deceleration is really where the speed comes from, and it's more important than the output across the duration of the attack.

Ride in PTZ 1 to PTZ 3 for 3 hours

Every 30 min.:
1 × 10 min. PTZ 5, 80–90 rpm

5 min. recovery

1 × 5 min., alternate between:
20 sec. Power Floor of PTZ 10, high rpm, standing
40 sec. Stall in PTZ 4, decreasing cadence from high to 60 rpm, standing

Recovery: PTZ 1

MINDSETS

Now we bring in some Focus practice to the workout. We add in priming with the Black Line Clarity process and matching the mental states with the PTZs.

DAY 34

Rest

DAY 35

STRENGTH FOR MID-CLIMB PACE CHANGES

1.5 hours

Today we are working on using transitions in Body Position and cadence to change the pace on a climb to create an unpredictable and hard-to-follow effort for others. This is best done in key areas such as switchbacks or changes from steep to shallow gradients. You need to use powerful Transitional Control where you simultaneously change power and cadence.

---

15 min. warm-up (Cloud mindset)

FAT-BURNING HIGH CADENCE (WATER MINDSET)
1 × 12 min. PTZ 2, 90 rpm

CLIMBING STANDING PACE CHANGES (FIRE MINDSET)
4 × 5 min.:
2 min. Power Floor of PTZ 5, 50 rpm or lower, seated
1 min. Power Floor of PTZ 6, 70 rpm, standing
2 min. Power Floor of PTZ 5, 50 rpm or lower, seated

4 min. recovery after each set (Cloud mindset)

FAT-BURNING HIGH CADENCE (WATER MINDSET)
1 × 10 min. PTZ 3, 90 rpm

MAXIMUM EXPLOSIVE STRENGTH SPRINT (LIGHTNING MINDSET)
5 × 10 sec. PTZ 11 in a standing sprint

Full recovery between each sprint

Rest

SHORT SURGE & THRESHOLD COMBO

1.5 hours

This workout strings together Explosive and Threshold PTZs with good timing and Execution to make an effort that others will doubt they can follow. This effort is best done on a climb or in a tailwind or crosswind. It can be done at any point during the climb or ride to create a gap.

15 min. warm-up (Cloud mindset)

FAT-BURNING HIGH CADENCE (WATER MINDSET)
1 × 10 min. PTZ 3, 90 rpm

SHORT SURGE AND THRESHOLD COMBO (FIRE AND LIGHTNING MINDSETS)
3 × 3 min.:
1 min. Power Floor of PTZ 10, 80 rpm, standing
1 min. PTZ 6, 90 rpm, seated
1 min. Power Floor of PTZ 10, 80 rpm, standing

5 min. recovery after each set (Cloud mindset)

FAT-BURNING HIGH CADENCE (WATER MINDSET)
1 × 10 min. PTZ 2, 90 rpm

STANDING STRENGTH (FIRE MINDSET)
3 × 2 min. Power Floor of PTZ 5, 50–70 rpm, standing

Full recovery after each set

LIGHTNING CLIMBING SURGES

1.5 hours

We are developing your Nuclear Zone with short, 40-second efforts in a controlled situation and your standing climbing surge. You'll use your Standing Acceleration Climbs body position. While in a normal climbing surge you would use the Short or Long Surge zone, today we are using a slightly lower PTZ to really work on that standing technique. Make sure you bring in the Lighting mindset for the 40 seconds!

15 min. warm-up (Cloud Mindset)

FAT-BURNING HIGH CADENCE (WATER MINDSET)
3 × 4 min. PTZ 4, 100 rpm

2 min. recovery after each set (Cloud mindset)

STANDING CLIMBING SURGES (LIGHTNING MINDSET)
3 × 5 min., alternate between:
40 sec. Power Floor of PTZ 8, 80 rpm, standing (Lightning mindset)
20 sec. PTZ 2, seated (Water mindset)

5 min. recovery after each set (Cloud mindset)

FAT-BURNING HIGH CADENCE (WATER MINDSET)
1 × 10 min. PTZ 2, 90 rpm

5 min. recovery (Cloud mindset)

STANDING STRENGTH (LIGHTNING MINDSET)
5 × 30 sec. Power Floor of PTZ 10, 50–70 rpm, standing

Full recovery after each 30 sec. effort

Rest

SEATED STRENGTH

2 hours

Today we develop your seated power by working on your Body Position and pedaling technique to control high power on difficult terrain, all while holding a low cadence. This is a high-level Power Control exercise. Focus on the details like terrain, speed, and shifting to keep control over your Power Ceilings and Power Floors.

15 min. warm-up (Cloud mindset)

FAT-BURNING HIGH CADENCE (WATER MINDSET)
1 × 15 min. PTZ 2, 90 rpm

SEATED STRENGTH (FIRE AND WATER MINDSETS)
3 × 6 min., alternate between:
1 min. Power Floor of PTZ 4, 90 rpm, seated (Water mindset)
1 min. Power Floor of PTZ 7, 70 rpm, seated (Fire mindset)

5 min. recovery after each set (Cloud mindset)

FAT-BURNING HIGH CADENCE (WATER MINDSET)
1 × 10 min. PTZ 3, 90 rpm

MAXIMUM EXPLOSIVE STRENGTH SPRINT (LIGHTNING MINDSET)
6 × 10 sec. PTZ 11, sprint from a slow roll or stop

Full recovery after each sprint

ENDURANCE & PTZ/TERRAIN MATCH

2.5 hours

The first objective is to get some volume in and work on your fat-burning Endurance Zones. The second objective is to practice planning your ride. This means you'll choose a route and, based on the terrain, plan which PTZs you are going to use to master it. If you would like, take it one step further by matching the mindsets with the PTZs.

15 min. warm-up

When cruising, stay below PTZ 2.

On flats and when you want to set a faster, sustained tempo, use PTZ 2 to PTZ 4.

On climbs, use the Low Threshold PTZ 5 as a Power Floor and use standing low cadence for the steep sections and seated higher cadence for the shallower sections to keep the power steady but overall climbing speed higher.

When you are 1.5 minutes from the top of a climb (1 every 45 min.), use PTZ 7 at a higher cadence, standing.

Rest

DAY 43

STRENGTH FOR THE COUNTERATTACK

1.5 hours

This workout simulates what it would feel like to cover attacks, recover between them, and then look for the right moment to counterattack.

15 min. warm-up (Cloud mindset)

FAT-BURNING HIGH CADENCE (WATER MINDSET)
1 × 10 min. PTZ 2, 90 rpm

COUNTERATTACK (FIRE AND LIGHTNING MINDSETS)
3 × 5 min.:
30 sec. PTZ 10, 50 rpm, standing
1 min. PTZ 5, 70 rpm, seated
30 sec. PTZ 10, 50 rpm, standing
1 min. PTZ 5, 70 rpm, seated
30 sec. PTZ 10, 50 rpm, standing
30 sec. PTZ 5, 70 rpm, seated
Counterattack: 1 min. PTZ 9, 70 rpm, standing

5 min. recovery after each set (Cloud mindset)

FAT-BURNING HIGH CADENCE (WATER MINDSET)
1 × 10 min. PTZ 3, 90 rpm

MAXIMUM EXPLOSIVE STRENGTH SPRINT (LIGHTNING MINDSET)
5 × 10 sec. sprint, PTZ 11, standing

Full recovery after each sprint

DAY 44

SURF THE THRESHOLD

1.5 hours

Today's workout is all about raising the Threshold PTZ. We'll go a little bit above it with the 20-second accelerations and then a little bit below it with the 40 seconds clearing at the Low Threshold Floor.

15 min. warm-up (Cloud mindset)

FAT-BURNING HIGH CADENCE (WATER MINDSET)
1 × 12 min. PTZ 2, 90 rpm

HIGH THRESHOLD (FIRE MINDSET)
3 × 5 min.,
alternate between:
20 sec. PTZ 7, 80 rpm, standing
40 sec. PTZ 5, 80 rpm, seated

5 min. recovery after each set (Cloud mindset)

FAT-BURNING HIGH CADENCE (WATER MINDSET)
1 × 10 min. PTZ 3, 90 rpm

STANDING STRENGTH (FIRE MINDSET)
3 × 2 min. Power Floor of PTZ 5, 50–70 rpm, standing

Full recovery after each set

DAY 45

TIME TRIAL FIRE

1.5 hours

Today I want you to light it on fire as if you are doing a TT, so you'll work on your Threshold PTZ and your Fire mindset. This is going to be uncomfortable, but throw in a 30-second rest to both clear some lactate and give yourself a mental rest.

15 min. warm-up (Cloud mindset)

FAT-BURNING HIGH CADENCE (WATER MINDSET)
3 × 4 min. PTZ 4, 100 rpm

2 min. recovery after each set (Cloud Mindset)

TT THRESHOLD (FIRE MINDSET)
2 × 5.5 min.:
3 min. PTZ 6, 80 rpm, seated
30 sec. lactate clear, PTZ 3
2 min. PTZ 6, 80 rpm, seated

5 min. recovery after each set (Cloud mindset)

FAT-BURNING HIGH CADENCE (WATER MINDSET)
1 × 10 min. PTZ 3, 90 rpm

5 min. recovery (Cloud mindset)

SEATED STRENGTH (LIGHTNING MINDSET)
3 × 1 min. Power Floor of PTZ 8, 50–70 rpm, seated

Full recovery between each

DAY 46

Rest

STRENGTH FOR SURGES IN THE PELOTON

2 hours

Corners, the accordion effect, super pulls . . . you name it, they are all reasons why being able to have the snap to quickly increase your speed is important. We are going to practice your surge, but seated and Lightning quick. Use a Low Threshold Power Floor.

15 min. warm-up (Cloud mindset)

FAT-BURNING HIGH CADENCE (WATER MINDSET)
1 × 12 min. PTZ 3, 90 rpm

PELOTON SURGE (FIRE AND LIGHTNING MINDSETS)
3 × 6 min.:
Hold Power Floor of PTZ 5, 70 rpm, seated (Fire mindset)
Every 25 sec. do 5 sec. PTZ 10, 100 rpm, seated (Lightning mindset)

5 min. recovery after each set (Cloud mindset)

FAT-BURNING HIGH CADENCE (WATER MINDSET)
1 × 10 min. PTZ 2, 90 rpm

MAXIMUM EXPLOSIVE STRENGTH SPRINT (LIGHTNING MINDSET)
5 × 10 sec. sprint, PTZ 11, standing

Full recovery after each sprint

ENDURANCE & PTZ/TERRAIN MATCH

3.5 hours

Today's workout is a free ride with some simple objectives. First, get some volume in and work on your fat-burning Endurance Zones. Second, plan your ride's terrain and add some Fire (Threshold) and Lightning (Explosive) mindsets and efforts to it. Check in using the BLC priming process, too.

30 min. warm-up

MATCH THESE ZONES WITH THE TERRAIN:
When you are just cruising, stay below PTZ 2.

On flats and to set a solid sustained tempo, use your Medium Zones, PTZ 2–PTZ 4.

On climbs, use Low Threshold PTZ 5 as a Power Floor and use standing low cadence for the steep sections but on transitions from slow to fast use seated higher cadence in PTZ 7 to increase your climbing speed.

When you get to 1.5 minutes from the top of the climbs you choose (1 every 45 min.) use your Nuclear Zone PTZ 8, standing, at a higher cadence.

Rest

REST WEEK

STANDING BODY POSITION

1 hour

You will get some needed recovery time but also keep your zones in place. The focus is on executing excellent standing position and efficiency. This should activate the glutes and core, delivering power and control to the pedal stroke.

---

15 min. warm-up

3 × 4 min. PTZ 2, 50–70 rpm, alternate between:
1 min. standing
1 min. seated

4 min. recovery after each set

STANDING HIGH MEDIUM
6 × 2 min. PTZ 4, 50–70 rpm

3 min. recovery after each set

THRESHOLD FORCE

1 hour

We're nearing the end of this training program, although it's not at all the end point in your progression. Show how well you can hold the PTZs at work today, now that you've had plenty of practice in them. Stay focused. You'll need that concentration in Threshold on Day 57, Test Day.

---

15 min. warm-up

1 × 9 min.,
alternate between:
2 min. PTZ 2
1 min. PTZ 4

5 min. recovery

2 × 6 min.,
alternate between:
25 sec. PTZ 7, 50–60 rpm, standing
35 sec. PTZ 4 seated, 80 rpm

5 min. recovery after each set

LOW THRESHOLD PEDAL STROKE

1 hour

While you get some needed recovery, we will keep your Low Threshold zone in place. You'll use a lower cadence to spend some needed time working on your pedaling technique.

15 min. warm-up

1 × 9 min.:
3 min. PTZ 4
3 min. PTZ 2
3 min. PTZ 4

5 min. recovery

3 × 3 min. PTZ 5, 50–70 rpm

5 min. recovery after each set

1 × 9 min.:
3 min. PTZ 4
3 min. PTZ 2
3 min. PTZ 4

Rest

DAY 54

MEDIUM CADENCE BUILDS

1.5 hours

We are using the Medium and High Medium PTZs to connect the input from the mind to the body as the cadence builds, stimulating the central nervous system. This effort demonstrates how you use cadence to increase speed and momentum without increasing power.

---

15 min. warm-up

1 × 12 min. PTZ 3, 90 rpm

5 min. recovery

3 × 3 min. PTZ 4:
1 min., 50 rpm
1 min., 80 rpm
1 min., 110 rpm

3 min. recovery after each set

1 × 12 min. PTZ 2, 100 rpm

DAY 55

LOW THRESHOLD SURF THE TERRAIN

1.5 hours

This day is designed to provide you with a proper workout but leave you feeling fresh afterward. The early Medium PTZs stimulate your high power/fat-burning metabolism. Then, do some Low Threshold 20/40s with cadence changes to simulate how you would build and maintain speed by changing the cadence and PTZs.

---

15 min. warm-up

1 × 12 min. PTZ 2, 90 rpm

5 min. recovery

3 × 2 min. PTZ 4, 50–60 rpm, standing

2 min. recovery after each set

2 × 6 min., alternate between:
20 sec. PTZ 5, 100 rpm
40 sec. PTZ 4, 80 rpm

5 min. recovery after each set

DAY 56

Rest

PTZ RETEST
See p. 244

DAY 57

PTZ RETEST

1 hour

After about two months of concentrated training across all Four Pillars, how have your Fitness, Execution, Nutrition, and Focus changed? Look back at your performance and take stock. Revisit the Vision Questionnaire and check in with Black Line Clarity to refine your focus; you're not the same rider as you were two months ago, so make adjustments to continue your growth. Perform the same test as you did on Day 2 and find your new PTZs.

---

20 min. warm-up PTZs 1 and 2

1 × 12 min. at the highest power you can hold for this duration

30 min. cooldown and recovery

Calculate your PTZs according to the table on p. 68, using the average power from the last 4 minutes.

ACKNOWLEDGMENTS

To my wife, Kourtney: This book is an extension of how we live our lives, authentically us. Writing a book about the concepts, ideas, and stories that we created and experienced together was the most incredible adventure for me. You have always been a strong leader in our family and our business, but you rose to a new level with this book. It was you who took the lead on this project and kept the fire burning strongly throughout the entire process. When I felt overwhelmed, you were there to calm me. In the moments when I was uninspired, you found a way to ignite a new passion in me. You helped to bring my complicated concepts, 20-step processes, and crazy ideas to life, rather than reject them because they didn't make sense at first. I have always believed you are capable of so much, and the way you took charge, dug deep, and brought this book to life, from the beginning to the end, was incredible. I owe this whole book to you.

To all the athletes I have been fortunate to work with: As a coach, I believe it is my job to guide people in accomplishing the goals they have set for themselves by teaching them the essential tools and processes. It is also my job to inspire and motivate, and, more importantly, show people how to find and unlock their true potential. Through that viewpoint, I've realized that this book would not be possible without the insights, challenges, and lessons every athlete that I have coached has shared with me. I have had the luxury of working with professional athletes both as a coach and in my professional racing career, along with the sport's best and brightest coaches and trainers. However, the bulk of the concepts in this book have evolved from my coaching clients. I work with athletes who, just like anyone reading this book, have busy lives, stressful jobs, families, and limited amounts of time—and many are coming back from serious injuries or setbacks in life. While these athletes might be ordinary people, their mindsets are far from ordinary. It is your passion and attitudes that inspire me to wake up before sunrise every day, filled with gratitude and enthusiasm for the day ahead. It is your journeys that inspired me to write this book, and I look forward to all that lies ahead.

To my team of coaches and the OG fab four—Holly Mathews, Travis Lecher, Sophie Johnson, and Stephen Strayer—who took a blind leap of faith and helped us start CINCH, I am grateful for the support and unwavering dedication to bettering your athletes through our program.

This book quite literally would not be possible without the people who helped me frame, edit, and distill my complex ideas into the very best presentation. A special thanks to Andy Read, Spencer Powlison, and the whole team at VeloPress for gently nudging me along and believing this book is what the sport needed!

To Ike Dana, who I like to refer to as "client one": You were the first person to attend my cycling camp all those years ago and you then became the first person to ask me to personally coach them. A special thanks is also due for willingly and sometimes unknowingly being my human guinea pig when I was creating and testing new training methods. It was your belief in me that started this whole thing. Thank you.

To the reader: Thank you for taking the time out of your busy life to read this book. It is my hope that you will throw out any preconceived notions on age, gender, or experience and replace them with the concepts in this book to unleash a new level of cycling performance.

INDEX

ABOUT THE AUTHORS

TOM DANIELSON is a former Tour de France cyclist, author, entrepreneur, cycling coach, and the founder and CEO of CINCH Cycling, Inc. After racing his bike professionally for 15 years, Tom wanted to take the knowledge he garnered racing at cycling's highest level and bring it to working professionals.

Known for his incredible climbing ability and his large lung capacity, Tom currently holds the record for the fastest ascent of Mount Washington in New Hampshire and the Mount Evans Hill Climb in Colorado. His racing accolades include an eighth-place general classification finish and a stage win in the Tour De France, two wins at the Tour of Utah, a win at the Tour of Georgia, a stage win in the Vuelta a España, and multiple top-10 general classification finishes in Grand Tours.

Tom grew up in East Lyme, Connecticut, where he rode dirt and mountain bikes, eventually finding his stride in MTB racing. He holds a BA in marketing and business from Fort Lewis College, Colorado, where he helped create the Fort Lewis College Cycling Scholarship fund to assist young collegiate cyclists.

KOURTNEY DANIELSON is an avid cyclist who travels the world in search of the best experiences on two wheels. Her cycling journey began when she learned to ride on the beautiful roads of Girona, Spain, with her husband, Tom. She now resides in Colorado, and you can find her on the podium of road, gravel, and mountain bike races around the world.

Kourtney's passion for cycling led her to start CINCH Cycling with Tom. At CINCH she is the head of the 3-Sigma Nutrition program as well as head of operations. She holds a BA in journalism and mass communication from the University of Utah as well as a sports nutrition coaching certification from Precision Nutrition.

VISIT
VELOPRESS.COM

for more on running, cycling, triathlon,
swimming, ultrarunning,
yoga, recovery, mental training,
health and fitness, nutrition, and diet.

SAVE $10
ON YOUR FIRST ORDER

Shop with us and use coupon code
VPFIRST during checkout.